PENGUIN BOOKS

NORTH OF SOUTH

Shiva Naipaul was born in 1945 in Port of Spain, Trinidad. He was educated at Queen's Royal College and St. Mary's College in Trinidad and at University College, Oxford. He makes his home in London with his wife and son but at present is living in the United States, where he is writing a new book. Mr. Naipaul is the author of two widely acclaimed novels: *Fireflies* (1971) and *The Chip-Chip Gatherers* (1973).

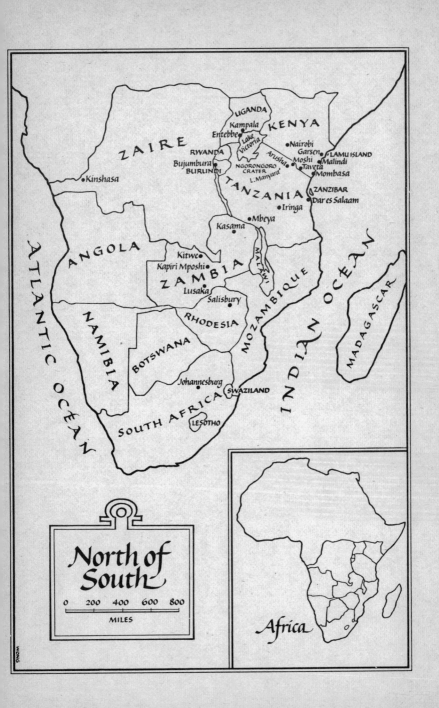

North of South

0 200 400 600 800
MILES

Africa

NORTH OF SOUTH

AN AFRICAN JOURNEY

Shiva Naipaul

PENGUIN BOOKS

Penguin Books Ltd, Harmondsworth,
Middlesex, England
Penguin Books, 625 Madison Avenue,
New York, New York 10022, U.S.A.
Penguin Books Australia Ltd, Ringwood,
Victoria, Australia
Penguin Books Canada Limited, 2801 John Street,
Markham, Ontario, Canada L3R 1B4
Penguin Books (N.Z.) Ltd, 182–190 Wairau Road,
Auckland 10, New Zealand

First published in Great Britain by
André Deutsch Ltd 1978
First published in the United States of America by
Simon and Schuster 1979
Published in Penguin Books 1980

LIBRARY OF CONGRESS CATALOGING IN PUBLICATION DATA
Naipaul, Shiva, 1945–
North of south.
1. Kenya—Description and travel. 2. Tanzania—
Description and travel. 3. Zambia—Description and
travel. 4. Naipaul, Shiva, 1945–   I. Title.
DT433.52.N34   1980   916.7   80-10408
ISBN 0 14 00.4894 4

Printed in the United States of America by
Offset Paperback Mfrs., Inc., Dallas, Pennsylvania
Set in Janson

The author wishes to acknowledge the help he received from the
Phoenix Trust while writing this book.

Permission to excerpt from the following is gratefully acknowledged: "White
Christmas" by Irving Berlin; copyright 1940, 1942 by Irving Berlin; copyright ©
Irving Berlin, 1968, 1969; reprinted by permission of Irving Berlin Music Cor-
poration. *Out of Africa* by Isak Dinesen; copyright 1937 by Random House,
Inc.; copyright © Rungstedlundfonden, 1965. *Which Tribe Do You Belong To?*
by Alberto Moravia; translated from the Italian by Angus Davidson; English
translation copyright © Martin Secker & Warburg Ltd, 1974; reprinted by permission of Farrar, Straus & Giroux, Inc.

FOR TARUN

Contents

NORTH OF SOUTH

Introduction

An introduction is a temptation: it can turn so easily into a self-justifying exercise, a kind of special pleading in behalf of a book whose nature and purpose might so easily be misunderstood. Especially a book about "Africa"—a subject that, in the ex-imperial West, is labeled "fragile," "handle with care," "this side up." In order to avoid temptation, I will repeat here the letter I wrote to my English publisher when the idea of my undertaking an African journey was first discussed.

"Of course [I wrote] it is impossible to be precise about the end product; and, in any case, I don't think it would be wise to overcommit myself—if for no other reason than that the kind of book one eventually writes will be determined by the kind of experiences one has actually had. And I wouldn't care to anticipate what those experiences might be. Still, I shall try to give you some idea of what I have in mind.

"The idea is that I shall travel in East Africa for a period of (say) five or six months, visiting Kenya, Tanzania and Zambia. But it is not my intention to write a straightforward travel book; nor do I intend to write a 'current affairs' type of book. I won't be setting out to compete with the journalists.

"The book will arise, I hope, out of my own concerns—or, if you prefer, obsessions. What do terms like 'liberation,' 'revolution,' 'socialism,' actually mean to the people—*i.e.*, the masses—who experience them? For example, in Tanzania,

Julius Nyerere has evolved a paternal socialism that he believes reflects—or recreates—all the virtues of traditional African culture. The theory requires that people be moved into villages organized on a cooperative basis. It all looks good on paper, and Nyerere has been much praised. All the same, the attempts to achieve this ideal have involved the burning of crops and homesteads to encourage the reluctant, those who doubt the virtues of *ujamaa*—familyhood. Certain questions arise. How wide is the gap between the rhetoric of liberation and its day-to-day manifestations? How much cynicism is there? How much apathy? How much sheer incomprehension? How much fantasy? What kind of Marxism is possible in Africa? The answers to such questions cannot, I believe, be found in the abstract speculations of theorists and professional revolutionaries—who often simply don't *see* the world in which they live. The answers, I feel, can be found only by experiencing the heat and dust, so to speak, of the countries themselves. Do the people actually care? What are they like as individuals? What is their level of knowledge? Should we despair? Or should we continue to hope?

"Beyond all this—but not entirely unconnected with it—is the relationship of black and white and brown. Very interesting. I would like, for instance, to have a look at the surviving expatriate community in Kenya: the role of white men in independent Black Africa is, to say the least, intriguing. What kind of shadow does the colonial-settler past continue to throw?

"It is possible to go on and on. But I think I have said enough to give you some idea of the kind of book I would like to write—not (to repeat myself) a straightforward travel book or a current affairs book or (God forbid!) a sociological treatise but (almost) a kind of novel, a montage of people, of places, of encounters seen and interpreted in the light of the questions I have outlined above. I would like to believe that it might be read by people who are not interested in Africa, as such; or in politics, as such."

Since finishing *North of South* nothing has occurred in Africa that would prompt me to change any of the opinions uttered in it. There has been one event of note—the death of Jomo Kenyatta, the founding father of Kenya. However, the tense of a few passages excepted, his death does not affect anything I have written. Africa goes on.

Shiva Naipaul
November 1978

Prelude

ODDLY ENOUGH, one of the cheapest ways of getting from London to Nairobi is to travel from Brussels via Kinshasa on Air Zaïre.

"There's no need to worry," the travel agent had said when I expressed anxiety at the news that he had booked me a flight on the Congolese national airline. "They have good planes—Boeings—flown by white pilots."

So Africa began with Air Zaïre. To be more precise, it began in one of the transit lounges at Brussels airport.

*

"You from Kenya?"

A middle-aged Sikh in a blue turban sat down beside me, his gray-bearded face creased into an ingratiating smile. He had, I knew, been eyeing me with intent for some time. Nervous, unable to stay still for more than a few seconds, he took his British passport out of his pocket and looked at it; he leafed through his yellow-paged booklet of vaccination certificates; he examined his air ticket. I did not want to be infected by his alarm.

"No. I'm not from Kenya."

"Tanzania?"

I shook my head.

"Uganda?"

I shook my head.

"Mauritius?"

"I come from Trinidad," I said at last, tiring of the depressing litany of place bred by our Indian diaspora.

"Trinidad . . . in the West Indies?"

"Yes."

"Going to Nairobi on business?"

"No."

"On holiday?"

"Yes. On holiday." I watched a plane climbing into the sky.

He was silent for a while. Then: "What is it like for Asians where you come from?"

It was one of the questions to which I was to become accustomed.

"Fine."

"I come from Tanzania. For our people it's no good." He spoke in a whisper and, while he spoke, he looked anxiously about him, as if fearing the presence of eavesdropping enemies.

The public-address system crackled into life.

He grasped my arm. "What is it? What are they saying?" He seemed terrified.

"The flight will be delayed an hour."

He relaxed his grip. He was returning to Tanzania, he said, in the hope of bringing his mother out. But there were problems. There were too many problems. Exit visas, entry visas, foreign-exchange restrictions. It was all too difficult, too complicated. He did not have much hope of success. Still, his mother was his mother. A son always had to try to do his best for his mother. Asians were having a hard time everywhere. Why was that? Why did nobody like Asians? What crimes had they committed? He had heard that even in

Canada they were beginning to have a hard time. Soon there would be nowhere to go. The British were making a fuss about giving his mother an entry permit. What harm could an old woman do? To survive these days you had to be either black or white. It was no good being brown. No good at all.

I wanted to get away, put distance between us. Rising abruptly, I walked away from him.

The flight was not going to be crowded. Not that that mattered—the flight from Brussels to Kinshasa was Air Zaïre's "prestige" run. Cancellation would come about only if President or Madame Mobutu suddenly decided he or she needed a plane. Then anything could happen. But neither the President nor his wife was in Europe at that moment. So there was no danger of the aircraft's suddenly being commandeered for reasons of state.

Two English girls came and sat down beside me. One—the older—was stocky and buxom and blond. The other was schoolgirlish in appearance and speech. From their conversation I gathered that the former was going out to Nairobi to visit her boyfriend who was in the safari business. Being something of a Kenya expert, she was giving much useful advice to her younger friend. "Africans will go out of their way to help you because you are English," she said. "In fact, the more English you are, the more they'll respect you. At least, that's been my experience. If you're firm, you'll be quite safe." Her disciple listened intently. She was a quick learner—that I could see.

Most of the European passengers were Belgians: expatriates, mainly teachers, heading back to their ex-colony on one-, two- or three-year contracts. I could sense that the mood of Africa, of expatriate existence, was already upon them. A peculiar, self-absorbed remoteness seemed to envelop them the moment they stepped into the neither-nor world of the transit lounge. They shed their individuality, assuming the collective, abstract identity of a people set apart, a people under siege. The women, locked away behind dark glasses, read magazines or fussed with their children; the men smoked and guarded their gaily colored plastic bags packed with duty-free goods. They were not sahibs and memsahibs. They were their withdrawn successors, neutral and untouchable. Africa held no risks for them. They were supremely disinterested, supremely irresponsible. Africa would help to pay the mortgage. That was all.

*

The man tapped the camera that was hung around his neck.
"You like?"
He was elegantly dressed in a gray suit, part of a contingent of equally well-attired blacks, all equipped with technological trophies—transistor radios, portable television sets, cassette tape recorders and the like—acquired in the duty-free shops. They had appeared in the lounge about fifteen minutes before, talking noisily and excitedly comparing their buys. The irruption had provoked muted, sardonic comment among the expatriates.
"I like," I replied.
"A very good camera. Very expensive. Japanese." He rested a finger on the trademark. It was a Nikon.
But it was not the camera that drew my attention: it was the metal badge, pinned to his lapel, showing the benign, bespectacled countenance of President Mobutu. The rest of the contingent, I noticed, were similarly adorned.
He saw me looking at the badge.
"That is our President. You like?"

"I like."

He fondled the badge. "A very historical man. A great leader not only of Zaïre but of Africa. A liberator of humanity."

(Some weeks later I was told a joke by a German adventurer resident in Mombasa. In downtown Kinshasa there is a traffic circle. In the middle of the traffic circle is displayed a gigantic photograph of Mobutu. Question: What is the difference between the photograph and the man himself? Answer: The photograph has been *developed*.)

"You would like me to take a picture of you?"

"Of me? No . . . no. . . ." My gaze strayed toward the other members of the contingent. "Have you been touring Europe?"

"We have been in Washington. We are a financial delegation."

I examined him more closely. He was extremely young: barely, I thought, into his twenties. His face was smooth and shapely, full of eager, coltish curiosity.

"Please let me take a picture of you."

Again I declined the offer. "Tell me about Washington."

"Washington?" He was absorbed in his exploration of the camera. "We were discussing finance. It was a conference. In Washington there were many good things to buy. I liked it."

"What aspects of finance were you discussing? Foreign aid? Loans?"

He looked at me assessingly. "That I cannot tell you. That is a secret." He was apologetic; he wanted to please.

"Are you by chance the Minister of Finance?"

He smiled. "I am a financial adviser. We are *all* financial advisers." His arms swept out embracingly toward his friends.

"You seem very young."

"Our President believes in youth. Please let me take a picture of you. . . ."

I continued to refuse. Losing interest, he wandered away from me. The other financial advisers were busy with their toys. They had been "discussing finance" in Washington! I studied the expatriates. They were more remote, more self-contained than ever. They accepted no responsibility for the charade being enacted around them. None of our business, they seemed to be saying. None of our business.

The public-address system crackled. Someone grabbed my arm. It was the Sikh.

"What is it saying?"

"It is saying we must board the aircraft now."

*

The NO SMOKING, FASTEN SEAT BELT signs were ignored by the financial advisers, who, as the plane taxied along the runway, strolled with proprietorial ease up and down the aisle. Out of the mouth of one, strange to say, protruded an electric toothbrush. They took off their jackets, loosened their ties. There was a great deal of loud laughter. Music played. The plump, steatopygous stewardesses distributed hard candies. (Earlier, they had given a most unconvincing demonstration of emergency procedures.) They too displayed Mobutu badges, pinned to their sarong-style uniforms. The atmosphere was so like that of a country bus that I half-expected to see goats and chickens tethered to the seats.

We were in the air, Brussels slanting away beneath us. A heavily bearded expatriate was sitting across the aisle from me. Our eyes met; he shrugged.

"It is always like this," he said. "But soon they will be

quiet. Soon they will drink whisky and fall asleep." He rested his head on his palm and closed his eyes.

"You fly Air Zaïre often?"

"It is cheap."

He taught French in a primary school in Lubumbashi. He was on his third contract.

"You must like it there," I said.

"I have no complaints. Since Independence it is very good for us."

I tried to look surprised.

"It is true," he said warmly. "Where would they be without us? They need us. We are *indispensable*." He pronounced "indispensable" French style. "Without us they would still be swinging from the trees."

Far below us, like a quilt spread over the body of the earth, lay the ordered fields of Europe, safe, serene, blessed.

*

In the early dawn I felt ill. We were flying low over feature-less bush country, still indistinct in the pink-washed half-light. My ears were blocked, muting the whine of the engines to such a degree that, for the most part, we seemed to be floating in eerie silence over the gray desolation that was my first sight of Africa. We should have touched down in Kinshasa some hours before, but the flight had been delayed first in Rome, then in Beirut.

My head swam. I rang for the stewardess. Nothing happened. I rang again. Some minutes later she came, bad-temperedly rubbing the sleep from her eyes. I asked for some coffee. She went away without a word of acknowledgment. The financial advisers were awake, walking up and down the aisle, occupying the lavatories. No coffee came. We floated lower, falling toward the violet-colored land whose inconsequential detail was now beginning to stand out with greater clarity. Rectangles of wan blue light appeared below us; the engines whined suddenly louder as we dropped sharply and the ground rushed up to meet us. Long before the aircraft had come to a halt the financial advisers were thronging the approaches to the exit.

At the foot of the stairs, the teacher bound for Lubumbashi tapped me on the shoulder. We shook hands and wished each other the best of luck. He turned and strode quickly away from me across the tarmac. The Sikh sidled up beside me. He looked more alarmed than ever.

"This is a bad place," he whispered. "A very, very bad place."

"How do you know that?"

"I *know*. I have heard many stories about this place." He gazed at me with dilated eyes. "Here they rob you and cheat you without mercy. Here they do not have law. They will take the clothes from off your back. They are very, very bad men."

At this hour of the morning there was no food or drink of any kind to be had. Only a down-at-heel stall selling beads, basketry and crudely carved animal and human figures was open for business. Having nothing better to do, I went over to have a look. My presence galvanized the dozing attendant. He reached under the counter and brought out two ponderous human figures. One was of a warrior in a loincloth holding a spear; the other was an amply proportioned steatopygous girl.

"You want man?"

"No."

Without more ado, he returned the warrior under the counter.

"How about girl? You want girl?"

"No."

With inane lasciviousness, he began to caress the pear-shaped wooden breasts. He adopted the wheedling tone of the professional pimp. "You don't like African girl? Very nice. Very cheap. Only one hundred dollars American."

"I don't have one hundred dollars American."

"I give you for fifty dollars American. Bargain price." He giggled, continuing to stroke and caress the wooden breasts. "No?"

"No."

He returned the girl under the counter and brought out an elephant. "Only twenty-five dollars American," he said. "Look." He turned it upside down and pointed to its genital region—or what I assumed would be the genital region of an elephant. "*Girl* elephant." He giggled.

Was he drunk? Drugged? Mad? I shook my head. He returned the elephant to its place under the counter and moved morosely away to the farther end of the stall, refusing to have anything more to do with me. I saw the Sikh heading toward me, wringing his hands. He was moving with difficulty; he seemed to be in great pain.

"This is terrible! Terrible!"

"What is terrible?"

"I cannot go to the toilet without a visa." He was crumpled with despair.

"Who told you that?"

He pointed to the two armed sentries who were guarding the exit leading to the nontransit zone. "*They* told me. When I begged them to let me through to go to the toilet they asked

me if I had a visa to enter Zaïre. What is the world coming
to? They give us Asians a hard time everywhere. They said
they would only let me through if I deposited money with
them. It is terrible. I'm not a young man anymore. I can't
hold my water as I used to."

"But there is a toilet in here. You don't have to go out
anywhere."

He stared at me incredulously. I showed him the sign. He
clutched my arm—and was gone.

A number of new passengers—perhaps a dozen—had made
their appearance. The two English girls sat side by side on
one of the wooden benches scattered about the hall. The
younger—the disciple—was reading Robert Ruark's novel
Uhuru. A leather traveling case lay open on the lap of her
buxom companion. She was grooming herself, grimacing into
the mirror attached to its lid. A public rather than a private
performance, it invited voyeurism. The two sentries—they
who had demanded a visa of the Sikh—watched with sullen
interest.

The morning was dismal, promising rain. At the entrance
to the building stood an African girl in traditional dress, a
baby strapped to her back. She stood there, perfectly immobile, looking out across the tarmac toward the bush country.
Her hair, plaited into tiny pigtails, projected stiffly from her
scalp—like antennae. Her spectral anonymity was faintly disturbing. When next I looked, she had disappeared.

A soft drizzle was falling when the connecting flight to
Nairobi was called.

*

Central Africa was, for the most part, hidden under cloud.
Occasionally, though, the cloud cover frayed to reveal, far

below, unremarkable olive-green plains crisscrossed by wind-ing tracks; or ranges of hills—at this height mere corrugations of light and shadow; or the brown loop of a nameless river. Then the clouds would close in again.

It was nearly midday when we landed at Bujumbura, in Burundi. We would, in normal circumstances, have flown to Entebbe, but not many planes went there nowadays. We were ordered off the aircraft and herded onto the veranda of the wooden bungalow that served as the air terminal. The equatorial sunshine was dazzling. Insects hummed among the beds of bright flowers. The terminal had the tranquil air of a rural railway station rarely patronized. In the little bar be-yond the veranda I bought a beer. Soldiers lounged in door-ways. The room was graced by a photograph of the local dictator, Micombero, in military uniform. His handsome face was unsmiling. The caption below the photograph proclaimed this frightening individual the Savior and Father of his people. Those, however, were the halcyon days: Micombero has since been overthrown and the people of Burundi blessed with a new Savior and a new Father. I do not know who he is.

"This place gives me the creeps," the buxom English girl said in a low voice.

"There have been massacres and things here, haven't there?" Her disciple, sipping a yellow drink, stared at the photograph. "Or am I thinking of Ruanda?" She frowned thoughtfully.

"Both Ruanda and Burundi have had their massacres," her guru said.

The disciple shuddered.

"Mind you," her guru added, "they only kill each other as a rule. They never touch Europeans—or hardly ever."

"In Burundi do the tall ones kill the short ones or the short ones kill the tall ones? I know Burundi does one thing and Ruanda the other."

"I'm never sure myself," her guru said.

Her disciple sighed. "I find African politics so very confusing." She smiled charmingly at the barman. He did not return the courtesy. She nudged the guru. "Is he a tall one or a short one?"

"I'm not sure, to be honest."

Her disciple sighed again. "I wished we'd stopped at Entebbe instead. That would have been so much more exciting. . . ."

Panic-stricken fingers tightened around my arm. "Did I hear her say we are going to Entebbe?"

I had not realized the Sikh was lurking behind me.

"Yes," I said cruelly.

*

Through a break in the clouds Lake Victoria flashed blue. Then—magically—we were out of the clouds and sailing in sunshine, the uplands of East Africa spread out below us. We crossed the Rift Valley, a hallucinatory fusion of earth and light and space. Our journey was almost over.

*

The Sikh did not know that "British citizens of Asian origin" needed a visa to enter Kenya.

"Always visa. Wherever I go it's visa this and visa that. What is a man to do?" He wrung his hands. "What is wrong with my passport? A British citizen is a British citizen."

The Immigration Officer remained unmoved. "Stand aside, bwana. You're holding up the queue."

The two English girls were next in line. He glanced cursorily at their passports. They were stamped and returned with a smile. "Enjoy your stay and welcome to Kenya."

Beaming, the buxom girl swept through the barrier, chased by an approving leer.

"Please tell me why I need a visa, bwana." The Sikh was back again. "My passport is British like theirs—is it not?"

"Do as I told you, bwana. Stand aside." He looked vaguely threatening. "Don't make even more trouble for yourself."

It was my turn. I did not need a visa, being a citizen not of the United Kingdom but of Trinidad and Tobago. He worked through my passport carefully, page by page. "Where's your visa?"

I said the Kenya High Commission in London had told me that I would not need one.

"They told you that, did they?" He squinted at me. "Is Trinidad and Tobago a member of the Commonwealth?"

"It is."

Again he squinted at me. He consulted a booklet. "You're right," he said, as if surprised to confirm the truth of what I had told him. He studied me. "You were born there?"

"I was."

He stamped my passport. "Now, *bwana*, let's discuss your little problem." He beckoned over the Sikh.

I lingered, wanting to see what would happen. The officer shooed me away. I went through to collect my luggage.

Ten minutes later the Sikh joined me.

"You made it!"

We watched the baggage belt rotate. The Sikh muttered under his breath.

"You must have been very persuasive," I said.

"He's a Kikuyu. I knew what I had to do. They will sell their grandmothers to you if you give them a chance."

"Well," I said cheerfully, "he let you in—that's the main thing."

The belt ceased its clattering rotation. My luggage had not come off the plane. Nor had the Sikh's. The Sikh groaned and put his hands to his head.

The Customs Officer looked at his gold watch.

"Our baggage hasn't come off the plane," I said.

The officer called over a khaki-clad official. "They say their luggage hasn't come off the plane."

"That is not our responsibility," the khaki-clad man said.

"Whose responsibility is it?"

"It is the airline's responsibility," the khaki-clad official said. "What airline did you come by?"

"Air Zaïre."

He looked at me pityingly. "That is bad," he said, "very bad."

The Sikh groaned louder.

"Very bad," the first official confirmed. "You may as well forget all about it."

"How can I forget about it?" The Sikh waved his arms about. "Am I to walk the streets naked?"

"You can buy new clothes," the khaki-clad man said. "You Asians are rich people." However, he went away and returned with two forms. "You can fill these in if you want to," he said. "But it won't guarantee you anything. It is important to remember that it is not an admission of liability."

"Guarantees you nothing," the first official emphasized, gazing fondly at his watch. It must have been a *very* recent acquisition.

I filled in my form and helped the Sikh to fill in his. It took
a long time—the Sikh went into meticulous descriptive detail.
The khaki-clad man signed both forms with a happy flourish.

"Remember, it is not an admission of liability. It's just for
the record."

The Sikh and I shared the cost of a taxi into Nairobi. I got
off at one of the downtown hotels.

"You know," he said, clasping my hands in his, "I just
remembered something."

"What?"

"I think I had eight pairs of underpants. Not seven."

*

A week later my suitcase (it had been left behind in Kinshasa)
did—miraculously—turn up, minus my transistor radio and a
number of lesser items.

PART
ONE

CHAPTER 1

Bright Lights

IT WAS midmorning, and the open-air pavement terrace attached to the New Stanley Hotel was crowded with tourists dressed for Africa. Bush shirts and sun hats banded with leopard skin of synthetic garishness were everywhere in evidence. Cameras and binoculars dangled from sun-tanned necks. German, French and American voices rang in the air. Out on the street was parked a convoy of zebra-striped Volkswagen vans. The smell of safari—of tented bush, of elephant, of hippopotamus, of lion—suffused the bright morning. Noisy traffic choked the broad expanse of Kenyatta Avenue. Fashionably dressed blacks streamed along the pavements, the men carrying briefcases, the women swinging handbags. Nairobi vibrated with cosmopolitan splendor. A crippled beggar, his knees padded with foam rubber, his hands encased in sandals, crawled nimbly on the periphery of the terrace. "Jambo . . . jambo . . ." The waiters, smartly dressed in white-and-green tunics, kept him at bay. A thorn tree, rising centrally from the terrace, threw a dappled green shade across the metal tables.

Without asking if they could, two Americans came over and sat down at my table. They were an oddly contrasting pair. One was well over six feet tall, slope-shouldered and concave-stomached. His hair, frizzled and teased out in

"Afro" style, formed a dark, woolly halo; his skin, bronzed and toughened by exposure to the sun, was leathery in appearance. The other was at least six inches shorter and anemically white. He had lank, shoulder-length hair. His pale blue eyes, unfocused and restless, hinted at a kind of semi-idiocy. The tall one produced a roll of cigarette paper and a packet of loose tobacco.

"Got any stuff on you, Stan?" The idiot boy drummed his ivory-colored fingers on the table.

"No," Stan said, carefully sprinkling tobacco down the length of the paper. "And even if I had I wouldn't let you score off me. You smoke too damned much, Andy."

"I feel awful, Stan." Andy's parted lips drooled as he watched Stan manipulate the tobacco.

"I'm not surprised," Stan said. "What sort of crap were you on last night?"

"They were only mandies, Stan."

"You'll kill yourself one of these days," Stan said. "But I'm not going to pay your funeral expenses." He ran his tongue down the edges of the paper and sealed the tube. "Why do you do it? Why do you feed yourself all that shit?"

"I get bored easily, Stan. I need a lift. . . ." He waved at two black girls. They came over. They sat down.

Stan lit the cigarette. He put his arm around the neck of the girl sitting next to him. "Why aren't you out and about looking for work, sweetie?"

"I want a beer," she said, pouting petulantly. "I'm tired." She was a strange-looking creature. The lobe of her right ear was missing—it looked as if it had been bitten off; her knees were patterned with blotched pink patches; a scar crossed one of her cheeks diagonally.

"Beer makes you fat, sweetie. It's bad for business. I don't get turned on by fat chicks. Not even by fat black chicks." He pulled her truncated ear. She scowled, shaking off his embrace, and snapped her fingers at a passing waiter. She ordered two beers.

"I'm not paying for two beers," Stan said.

"I'll pay for my own," the other girl said. Disdainfully, she flung a handful of coins on the table. She muttered something. Both girls laughed.

"What did she say?" Stan asked.

"Nothing."

Stan grabbed her wrist. "I want to know."

"She said that *mzungus* [white people] are all the same."

"Where'd you pick them up?" Stan asked Andy.

"She's a friend," Andy said. "I got lots of friends."

"Yeah. . . ."

"I got lots of friends," Andy said. "Lots and lots of friends." His eyes roamed the terrace. "Everywhere I go I make friends. . . ."

But Stan was not listening. He was looking speculatively at me.

"From distant parts?"

I nodded.

"What kind of currency are you carrying?"

I told him.

He clucked his tongue. "Sterling . . . that's not so good. Still, I could give you eighteen shillings to the pound."

I said I preferred to change my money legally.

He laughed. "Hear that, Andy? The guy says he prefers to change his money *legally*."

"The guy's a sucker," Andy said.

Stan leaned toward me. "How about a woman?"

"Not now, thanks."

"A boy?"

"You deal in those too?"

"I deal in most things—currency, dope, women, boys. I'll fix you up with anything you want. You could say I'm one of the pillars of the tourist trade in these parts."

"They allow you a work permit for that?"

Stan's laughter echoed across the terrace. "Hear that, Andy? The guy wants to know if we have work permits."

Even the girls were amused.

"We've got friends," Andy said. "We've got lots and lots of friends. When you got lots of friends like we have you don't need a work permit."

"In a place like this," Stan said, "you can get away with murder if you know the right people. Money *talks* in this country."

"Lots of friends," Andy said. "We've got lots and lots of friends."

"Business must be good."

"Booming," Stan said. "The only comparison is Jo'burg. Nairobi is the finest city north of South."

*

Ben wakes at dawn. His neighbor is playing his Grundig stereo at full volume. Automatically, Ben turns on his transistor radio. Lying naked beside him is his mistress, Wini. Her money enables them to go to downtown cafés and drink espresso coffee. Wini has recently risen out of whoredom and climbed a rung or two up the urban ladder. She is now secretary to a white man. Thus, her instinctive harlotry has been sublimated. Ben, dishonorably discharged from the Army, works as a casual laborer on a building site. Wini has rescued him from a life ". . . of hungriness . . . hopelessly drunken nights. . . ." Ben rises, takes a cake of Lux soap and goes to have a bath. The stinking courtyard of the tenement is strewn with junk—a wheelless tricycle, an abandoned shoe, beer bottles, a broken chair, upturned garbage cans. All the wrack of hopeless urban existence. The communal bathroom is no better. "The floor was littered with broken bits of soap, scrubbing rags, stones, cigarette filters and general trash . . . slimy green fungus grew on the outer edges of the floor and spread some way up the walls. A woman's blood-stained underpants hung on the nail behind the door. . . ."

After breakfasting on bread and coffee, he sets out for work on foot, joining the lumpen proletarian hordes heading into the city. "They walked slowly, quietly, their slow tortured boots kneading the mud and shit on the path." At the building site, the day's frenzied mechanical activities have begun. Clouds of choking cement dust rise from the concrete mixers, pickup trucks unload their consignments of sand and gravel, buckets attached to steel cables plummet through the air. Ben reports to the register clerk. The man is "hung up and dishevelled."

" 'Name?' he croaked.

" 'Ben.'

" 'Ground duties today, Ben.'

" 'Ground, my arse. Check again.' "

But ground duties it is. At lunchtime Ben risks his life crossing the streets. The motorists ". . . have made it a ritual to butcher one or two pedestrians every week as a sacrifice to the Highway Gods." He patronizes a workingmen's hostelry where he is served tea in a can that formerly contained Esso motor oil. The stale slices of bread he buys are wrapped in sheets of newspaper. Late in the afternoon he sets off home with a friend. "The empty roads lie wet and cold. The neon lights blink weakly through the streets. . . ." They stop for a drink. "Distorted music, rowdy talk and the smell of beer, cigarettes and vomit spill out into the dimly lit street. . . . A haze of foul smoke hovers ghost-like under the low ceiling." The whores buzz about the tables like flies. Ben drinks until drunk. He lurches home to his mistress, her neglected, urine-soaked child and the room that is overrun by cockroaches.

Meja Mwangi is a young Kenyan novelist, a contributor to what his publishers call "the new wave of East African writing." Ben is the "anti-hero" of his novel *Going Down River Road*, which was published in 1976. I have chosen to write about it not because it is a particularly good novel (its tough-guy realism is forced and tedious) but because of the picture, the sociological portrait, it offers of African urban man. As presented, Ben is not merely detribalized but drained clean of any memory of tribal existence. Its obligations and sensibilities, its rituals and routines—these are all utterly alien to him. Ben is the sum total of his lusts for food, for drink, for sex and for money. He grows up out of the city streets as naturally as parking meters sprout from its pavements. Transistor radios, stereo systems, jukeboxes, cement mixers and pickup trucks are the artifacts of his world, and he accepts them without question. Forty years ago, Karen Blixen could write: "The Natives were Africa in flesh and blood. The tall extinct volcano of Longonot that rises above the Rift Valley, the broad Mimosa trees along the rivers, the Elephant and the Giraffe, were not more truly Africa than the natives were."

Ben, on the face of it, has traveled awfully far awfully fast. His world is relentlessly urban; his city is universal. The unswept streets, the smoke-filled bars, the cafés serving espresso coffee, the whores, the pestilential tenements and shantytowns are the props of that vast megalopolis thrown up by industrial civilization. Ben is as bereft of "roots," of "identity," as any of his slave-descended American and West Indian brothers. He could be in New York; in Kingston, Jamaica; in Rio de Janeiro; in Soweto. When Wini, his mistress, empties her handbag, there fall out of it "a flimsy pair of knickers, cans of face powder, tubes of creams . . . a packet of aspirins." Ben's imagery is supplied by the machine world, not by elephants and giraffes and Mimosa trees. When he makes love, his mind whirls "like an electric fan." Wini, wriggling toward climax under him, "was no dynamite. She was a neatly bound bomb. She exploded." A comrade's thin legs resemble "a couple of old parking meters." Men are "guys"; women are "chicks" and "babies." This is how Mwangi renders the encounter between Ben and a bar girl:

" 'Hello darling,' a large heavy-duty wrapped her hand round Ben's.

" 'Hi!' he released himself.

" 'You have been lost,' she sang.

" 'Not me baby. Money.'

"There was no place to sit. She followed him to the juke box. He leaned on it.

" 'Where have you been?' she asked.

" 'Just around.' "

The language is cool, vaguely hip. But do people actually *talk* like that? According to Mwangi, in Nairobi they do, and we must take his word for it. He himself uses that kind of language. He dedicates his book "to the *guys* [my italics] who introduced me to Ben" and thanks other friends for the "sweet inspiration" they have given him. Despite the horrors which Mwangi parades before us, what is really being asserted, really being *celebrated*, is Ben's modernity. But is *Going Down River Road* any more authentic, any less fabricated than those numerous idylls (which, until not long ago, formed the stock-in-trade of African fiction) describing the noble simplicity of tribal ways and the corruptions introduced by the evil White Man? Is megalopolitan Ben everything his creator claims for him? It is so easy to be taken in by appearances. At night, looking out at the illuminated skyscrapers and cars and flashing neon signs, I was all but taken in.

*

How recent it is. How startlingly recent! A century ago, city life in East Africa was confined to the Islamicized, Swahili-speaking coast—to towns like Mombasa, Malindi (flourishing kingdoms when Vasco da Gama visited them at the end of the fifteenth century) and Lamu. But these towns belonged to the relatively sophisticated trading arena of the Indian Ocean and were only marginally of Africa. Up-country tribes, like the Kikuyu, living in scattered homesteads, knew nothing of urban life. Even as late as the Mau Mau emergency, the pattern persisted. For purely military purposes, a compulsory "villagization" program was adopted. Elspeth Huxley, writing in 1955, could foresee some unintended good arising out of this measure: she believed it would speed up the rate of Kikuyu cultural advance.

At the turn of the century, Nairobi could hardly be said to

exist. In 1913 it consisted of little more than the railroad, a
network of dusty lanes, a hotel or two and the ramshackle
Indian bazaar. It was in that pre-War year that Elspeth Huxley, then a child, set out in an ox-driven cart from the Norfolk
Hotel on the two-day journey to Thika—now almost a satel-
lite town of Nairobi—where her father had just acquired five
hundred acres of virgin bush ("thousands of years of un-
tapped fertility locked up in the soil," the vendor, who
sported an Old Etonian tie, had told him) on a ninety-nine-
year lease. Thika was then no more than "a name on the map
where two rivers joined. . . ." Beyond it there were "mountains and forests no one had mapped and tribes whose languages no one could speak."

A mile or two beyond the Norfolk Hotel the wilderness
began. Herds of giraffes and zebras and gazelles grazed on
the dusty plain dotted with thorn trees. They kept a sharp
lookout for lions. Itinerant Kikuyu (today's "guys" and
"chicks") trudged along the cart track. The bare-breasted,
shaven-headed women were doubled up under their burdens;
but the young braves, ". . . their locks embellished with
sheep's fat and red ochre . . . ," draped in red and black
blankets, were a picturesque sight. Juma, the Swahili servant,
was full of contempt for these people of the bush, believing
them to be cannibals, devilish people whose women gave
birth to snakes and lizards.

Thika had a small hotel and a number of Indian *dukas*
(small shops). On all sides Africa stretched away into wild
infinity, a continent of undefined threat and mystery. Having
land was one thing. Having the labor to work it, quite another.
Not far away was a Kikuyu reserve which was rumored to
be stocked with "a great supply of able-bodied young men

who did nothing all day but grease their limbs and plait their pig-tails." They were the obvious solution to the labor problem. How were they to be tempted out of the reserve to assist in the task of civilization? Huxley's father resorted to his old phonograph, working not so much on the assumption that music soothes the savage breast but on the more down-to-earth conviction that the noises it produced would lure them "as a light attracts insects." Over and over again he played "The Bluebells of Scotland" and "The Lost Chord." The natives, alas, held aloof.

A neighboring settler, Irish and resourceful, suggested a more literal application of the light–insect analogy. He advised them to hang a safari lamp on a pole. The Kikuyu, he assured them, would never have seen such a thing before. Once they had overcome the idea that there was a spirit locked up within the glass, they would not be able to resist a closer inspection of the marvel. They did as he suggested. For two nights nothing happened. The third night, however, brought success. A number of Kikuyu braves materialized out of the darkness. Not daring to approach too close to the strange object hanging on the pole, they lurked apprehensively on the outer edges of the circle of light, poised for flight should the need arise. They wanted to know if the light was a fragment of a star fallen to earth. When the lamp was brought forward for their closer inspection, they took fright and ran away. However, they returned the following night and behaved more courageously. Eventually, they grew bold enough to touch it, one of them burning his hands on the glass. The lamp was offered to them as a present. They were reluctant to take it, believing that its genie would obey only Europeans.

At the construction site, Ben is working on a skyscraper. Sixty years before, at Thika, the Kikuyu labor force had balked at having to build a rectangular grass hut. Their own dwellings were circular, had always been circular. Geometrical regularities filled them with superstitious dread; they seemed quite unable, for instance, to plow in straight lines— a failing that led the Huxleys to speculate on the relationship between geometrical regularity and civilization. The complaint is echoed even today. It was echoed by the entrepreneur I met in Nairobi. His engineering firm had been awarded a contract by one of the major state-owned organizations. To begin with, he had had an Asian work force. The job had been completed in record time; the workmanship was of a high standard; his firm was showered with praise. But then had come the first expulsions of the Asians. To keep in line with the policy of Kenyanization, he was compelled to employ Africans in their place.

"You can take it from me that Africans don't understand about straight lines. They just don't seem able to grasp the concept of a straight line." Metal plates were bent and twisted one on top of another; every screw was awry. "You must understand that these weren't people I had picked up off the street. They were *qualified*. They could show you their certificates." He had himself physically completed the job, working day and night in order to meet the deadline. "Look at me. I am not a young man. My hair is gray. They wanted to give me another contract. 'Thank you very much,' I said, 'but you can keep your contract. I've had enough. I want to lead a quieter life. You can get in touch with my competitors.'" He smiled ruefully. "The only thing to do with Africans is give them a nice chair, give them a nice-sounding

title to go with it and put them where they can do least harm."
He spread his arms resignedly. "One must be realistic. It's no
good living in cloud-cuckoo land. Most of them are less than
a generation removed from the bush. What else can you
expect?" Beyond the windows of the restaurant where we
were sitting, the lights of Nairobi twinkled with Manhat-
tanesque self-assurance; Mercedes-Benzes roamed the broad
expanses of Kenyatta Avenue; short-skirted whores, pretending to window-shop, peered at the rich displays in bright
shop windows.

Stories of African conceptual incapacity have acquired
something of the abstract quality of fable. There is a famous
one about wheelbarrows. Several versions of the story exist,
but the moral is always the same. The version I heard went
like this. Some Africans are building a road. Their European
adviser watches them running to and fro carrying basketfuls
of stone on their heads. They are quickly exhausted and have
to take frequent rests. He goes away and returns with a
wheelbarrow. He explains its advantages. Dozens of wheelbarrows are supplied. Some days later his foreman comes to
him in a state of great agitation. The workers, he reports, are
on the verge of physical collapse. Naturally enough, the
European adviser is astonished. He rushes off to the site to
see what has been happening. And what does he find when
he gets there? He finds that the African workers have been
trying to carry the fully loaded wheelbarrows on their heads.
Get that? On their heads! Imagine all those darkies (they
never managed to invent the wheel, you know) loading the
wheelbarrows, lifting them up and . . . and. . . . There follows explosion after explosion of helpless laughter. The story
is clearly apocryphal. (I have seen many Africans handling

wheelbarrows in a perfectly normal manner.) Nevertheless, certain other stories, not apocryphal, occasionally do make one pause—like that (reported in *The Nation*) which told the sad tale of three African workers who had incinerated themselves while trying to weld a tank that was full of gasoline.

The European I was with at the time burst out laughing when he read the report. "I'd have given anything to be there when it happened," he said. "Can you imagine how they must have shouted and hollered and rolled their eyes? Absolutely priceless."

The change in their relationship is unfair to both black and white. It breeds stress. This stress nourishes the impotent and puerile racism that feeds on the cycle of tales detailing native ineptitude. Hence the temptation to ignore the underlying issue and to dismiss *all* discussion of it as "racism." How much nicer to take Africans at their face value, to accept their pretensions on trust and not examine them too closely, to swallow whole the fine words about progress and development and the like. How much nicer to be able, like the visiting Premier of Nova Scotia, to exclaim over the "economic progress" which (he said) had earned Kenya "a worldwide reputation." Or to swoon, as another visiting dignitary did, over "the unparalleled progress" achieved under "the wise leadership of President Kenyatta." Words . . . words . . . words. Africa is swathed in words.

*

A certain embarrassment had so far prevented me from making use of the service offered by the shoeshine boys who line Kenyatta Avenue. The occupation had too many unpleasant associations. But observation had shown that my reservations were not shared by many people. My scruples were rapidly eroded. My chosen shoeshine "boy" was not a boy at all— though, I should add, many of the fraternity literally are. He was a gray-headed, rheumy-eyed Kikuyu. He wagged his head and clucked his tongue when he saw the state of my shoes, but praised the quality of the leather. I was reminded of past visits to my dentist who, while lauding the basic soundness of my teeth, mourned their actual condition.

"Expensive," he said, kneading the leather and nodding appreciatively.

"Not very," I said cautiously.

"But too much dust," he said. "Still, no problem. I am first-class shoeshine boy. I will make them be like new for you. They will shine just like mirror. I am best shoeshine boy in the whole of Nairobi. Many years' experience." He began loosening the laces.

"What's your charge?"

"Charge?"

"How much will I have to pay you? How many shillings?"

He waved his arms airily. "Don't worry about charge."

"But I do worry."

He blinked his rheumy eyes; he sighed. It was as though I had caused him profound spiritual pain. "Worries no good for the heart. I ask reasonable price. No need to worry." He produced a bottle containing a yellowish liquid and smelling faintly of kerosene. This he applied liberally, rubbing it in with vigor.

"Is that polish?"

"Special ingredient," he said, switching his attention from one shoe to the other. "Secret formula. Highly secret formula."

I started to feel uneasy. It occurred to me that I had behaved extremely foolishly. I should have insisted on settling what the price would be before allowing him to start.

"I don't want any special ingredient or secret formula," I said. "Just ordinary polish."

"Too late now," he said cheerfully.

I half-withdrew my foot.

"Why worry? This is extra-special ingredient." He explained that the treatment he was giving me would make any further polishing unnecessary for one whole year. "You just take a soft cloth and wipe it over. It will shine just like mirror. I give you full guarantee."

"Nonsense."

"Not nonsense," he replied equably. "True. This is Deluxe Special I give you. Not nonsense."

I withdrew my foot completely.

"Look . . ." He took a crumpled sheet of paper from his shirt pocket and handed it to me. "Read what it says there."

It was a typewritten testimonial. "This is to certify that I did not need to have my shoes polished for one year after receiving the Deluxe Special. During all that time my shoes shone like a mirror." The scrawled signature was impossible to decipher.

"Do you expect me to believe this rubbish?" I examined my shoes. The kerosene-soaked leather had gone dull and blotchy.

He watched me composedly. "You cannot meet your friends with your shoes looking like that."

I saw his point: I was trapped. I surrendered my feet to him. "Remember—no more secret ingredients and formulas. Just *polish*."

"Just polish," he repeated. "You are hard man to please,

bwana." With swift dispatch he polished and shined, coaxing out an indifferent gleam from the damaged leather. It would have to do.

I held out five shillings, thinking myself more than generous in the circumstances; I did not want to create a scene.

He looked at the money; he looked at me. "What is that for?"

"For your labor."

He laughed the way one laughs at an obvious absurdity. "Bwana . . . bwana . . ."

"Are you trying to tell me that you expect to be paid *more* than five shillings for destroying my shoes?"

He nodded.

"How much?"

"Sixty shillings, bwana." He folded his arms across his chest.

I did a quick calculation. At the current rate of exchange, sixty shillings was almost five pounds sterling. But the Kikuyu, I soon discovered, was not joking. He showed me a neatly typewritten card (I could see at a glance that it and the testimonial he had shown me earlier had been typed on the same machine) inserted in a glass-covered frame. The card—it was set out rather like a menu—listed the various services he claimed to provide and their cost. Thus:

Super Deluxe Special: 100 shillings
Deluxe Special: 80 shillings
Deluxe Ordinary: 50 shillings
Special: 35 shillings
Ordinary: 20 shillings
Quick polish: 5 shillings
Quick brush: 3 shillings

"Which one of these am I supposed to have had?"

"You had the Deluxe Special for eighty shillings. But . . . well . . . (he looked furtively at my shoes) . . . I give you discount price."

"Are you quite sure it wasn't the Deluxe Ordinary you gave me?"

He giggled. "What a thing to say, bwana."

I returned the card. "Five shillings or nothing."

"The card, bwana. Read what the card says."

"I don't care what it says. Five shillings or nothing."

He ran to the neighboring shoeshine boy. The Kikuyu, gabbling now in his native tongue, pointed at the card, then at me, then at my shoes. He was the very picture of outraged virtue. His ally glowered at me. I went over to them.

"What is he saying?"

"He is saying," the ally replied, "that you are refusing to pay him. He is saying he will call the police for you." He was grim; unfriendly.

"But he wants to charge me sixty shillings. That's almost as much as I paid for the shoes in the first place. Even you must realize how ridiculous that is."

I looked up and down the avenue. There was not a policeman in sight. The Kikuyu was gabbling again, pointing at the card and at me.

"What is he saying now?"

"He is saying that he even gave you a discount."

I too now sought an ally. I approached one of the passersby and asked what he normally paid to have his shoes shined. He shrugged and continued on his way. I asked another. He was no more helpful. An absurd panic gripped me. I offered ten shillings. The Kikuyu refused, folding his arms across his chest. I offered fifteen. He refused that too. I flung the fifteen shillings on his stand and walked away with as much resolution as I could summon. The Kikuyu pursued me down the avenue. "I call the police for you. They throw you in jail. They beat you up. They kill you. I myself kill you." I fled into the safety of the first hotel I came to.

The Kikuyu was no ordinary huckster. In the end, the vast majority of hucksters do negotiate, do bargain. The Kikuyu was different. He was not prepared to negotiate, not prepared to bargain. Why? Why carry outrageousness to the point of absurdity and even self-sacrifice? (I do believe that, having failed to extort his sixty shillings from me, he would have preferred to take nothing.) Why should he expect anyone to succumb?

His outrageousness was, I think, given a special credence in his own eyes by the typewritten testimonial and the typewritten card listing his "services" and the prices he charged for them. The *printed* word imparted legitimacy; it invested —so far as he was concerned—patent absurdity with special substance. The Kikuyu must have paid someone God knows how much to produce these documents for him. They were as much an investment as the charms which, in another age, he would have commissioned a witch doctor to concoct for him. Behind the modern vocabulary—"secret formula," "special ingredient," "discount," "guarantee"— lay more elemental beliefs. The words, attached to nothing, were mere noises plucked out of the ether. Language had been divorced from meaning. He had brought his ancient magical outlook into the new world of the city. Old wine had been poured into a new bottle.

*

The primitive world is a realistic world. Within it, vision and ambition and desire are controlled. Magic and superstition operate within a known sphere and on a familiar scale. The tribal man knows what is possible. He is at home. His means fit his ends. He is sane. It is this wholeness that we really ought to admire. His dignity arises from it. The primitive, existing within his own terms, cannot be mocked. His is a complete and undefiled self-realization. This may help to explain some of the traditional difference between the European attitudes toward the Masai on the one hand and the Kikuyu on the other.

The Masai—a condensation of the dark heart of Africa— have consistently aroused the admiration of Europeans. They have seemed (borrowing the language of Joseph Conrad) "savage and superb, wild-eyed and magnificent." Karen Blixen provides the classic summary in her well-known book *Out of Africa*: "A Masai warrior is a fine sight . . . daring, and wildly fantastical as they seem, they are still unswervingly true to their own nature, and to an immanent ideal . . . the muscles of their necks swell in a particularly sinister fashion, like the neck of the angry cobra, the male leopard or the fighting bull, and the thickness is so plainly an indication of virility that it stands for a declaration of war to all the world with the exception of the woman." Almost every trait of the Masai lent itself to panegyric: their physique (tall and slim); the Hamitic regularity of their features; their nomadism; their militaristic code; their history of conquest and their predatory relationship with neighboring tribes like the Kikuyu; their steadfast resistance to the arts and habits of modern civilization; even their diet (milk and blood) was a contributing factor.

The sedentary Kikuyu, living in closer proximity to Euro-

peans, were more adaptable—and vulnerable—to outside influence. They were condemned for their avarice and their
cunning; and they paid the inevitable price the primitive must
pay when he dilutes his authentic existence. That price is well
illustrated by an incident recorded by Elspeth Huxley in *The
Flame Trees of Thika*. One day she rides into the Kikuyu
Reserve with a party of fellow settlers in pursuit of an ab-
sconding murderer. The chief duly presents his visitors with
a young man he claims is the culprit. After the interview, the
young man turns to go.

" 'Good night, sir. Save all sinners.'

" 'Good heavens! Where did you learn that?'

" 'Good morning sir. God save the King!'

" 'A mission boy!' cried Hereward.

" 'Yes, bwana . . . I can read a book, I can write a letter.'

" 'You see?' said Hereward. 'What did I say? First thieves,
and now murderers.' "

The young man behaves like a performing circus animal,
an animal that has been snatched from its proper existence
and trained to ride a bicycle, drink tea, jump through a hoop
and dance a jig. The young Kikuyu excites scorn and deri-
sion. He is a human parrot. Authenticity has been converted
into parody. Transitional states are full of pain, riddled with
illusion. We can lose one self without gaining another. Our
development can be indefinitely arrested at the stage of
caricature.

" 'Hello darling,' a large heavy-duty wrapped her hand
round Ben's.

" 'Hi,' he released himself.

" 'You have been lost,' she sang.

" 'Not me, baby. Money.'

"There was no place to sit. She followed him to the juke box. He leaned on it.

" 'Where have you been?' she asked.

" 'Just around.' "

Ben can trace his ancestry back to the mission boy. Only the words have changed.

So often when one is talking to Africans who seem thoroughly modern, something is said that suddenly jars; that brings one up short and makes one realize that not all is what it seems to be. I think, for instance, of the modishly dressed student who told me that he was "studying literature." I asked who his favorite writer was. He said he did not have one.

"But," I said, "there must be some books, some kind of writing you particularly enjoy."

He shook his head. "I don't care much for reading," he said—not without pride.

"And yet you are studying literature. Is that possible?"

"I am very good at literature," he replied. "That is why I study it."

Our conversation ended. Communication—to put it more fashionably—had broken down. Sometimes it can be funny. *The Nation* carried a report on the troubled progress of Nairobi's new international airport: costs were rising alarmingly and, unaccountably, contractors were not being paid; for weeks at a time no visible work was being done on the site and so on. Mr. Gitonga, an under secretary at the Ministry of Power and Communications (the ministry responsible for the project), was questioned about a Commission of Inquiry that had apparently been set up to look into the mess. "Mr.

Gitonga said: 'Commission? Inquiry? There has been no inquiry. There was just a group of Government people to look
into the matter.' "

The tribal world was real; the new world, lacking definition and solidity, fades away into the dimmer reaches of fantasy. The greed of my shoeshine boy did not make sense. It
was not comprehensible. A comprehensible greed—a feasible
greed—recognizes limits. His greed did not recognize any
limits. Anything, everything, was possible: he had lost touch
with reality. This sense of people's having lost touch with
reality, of a constraining dam's having burst, arises whenever
one contemplates the lusts that disfigure African societies—
and not only African societies, but the societies of the poor
and backward in general.

"My God!" the Dutch fertilizer expert exclaims, "you have
to experience it to believe it. These people are *extraordinarily
greedy*. I've never seen anything like it. They say West Africa
is even worse. But I find it hard to imagine how anything
could be worse than this. The corruption is incredible."

"It's a disease," his wife puts in.

"That's right," her husband says, "it *is* a disease, an illness.
You know, I go to meetings all the time. I try to talk about
technical problems. They couldn't give a damn about those.
Not a damn. They fall asleep! I could sell them tinned sunshine if I wanted to. They only wake up when you mention
money. The only thing they care about is their cut."

My shoeshine boy is small fry. Desire unhinged from constraint takes on a surrealist tinge. The land grab that has followed Uhuru, the slaughtering of elephants for the ivory
trade, the tales of bribery, embezzlement, extortion and corruption that daily fill the pages of *The Nation* signal a col-

lapse of self-control verging on collective derangement. The Ministry of Health is raided. The thieves take sophisticated lifesaving machines designed for use in intensive-care units; they take, in addition, X-ray equipment, three sterilizers, two cartons of stethoscopes, three microscopes, half a dozen sphygmomanometers (whatever those are), tens of thousands of tablets, boxes of vaccines, an electric plastic cutter, surgical instruments of all kinds. Bizarre robbery! A doctor is held for questioning. What was he planning to do with these things? Open his own hospital?

It has all happened before. The insatiable appetite for slaves in the seventeenth and eighteenth centuries stimulated the equally insatiable appetite of African chiefs for brandy, beads, tobacco and guns—all the gaudy bric-a-brac of European civilization. The desire to get hold of these things unleashed an orgiastic frenzy that devastated the land and wrecked the societies of West Africa. In its essence, the nature of the ties linking the African with the European has not really changed since the first Portuguese ships went sailing down the west coast of the continent: the sophisticated magic of the white man remains irresistibly alluring to the black. Transistor radios and cassette recorders have taken the place of glass beads and mirrors. No bank clerk will deign to perform the simplest arithmetic without resort to his little electronic calculator which lights up so prettily whenever he presses one of its buttons. The genie within remains as mysterious as ever; the fear, however, has gone. The fear—and the wonder. Mungo Park, who traveled in West Africa at the end of the eighteenth century, writes thus of his guide, Karfa: "Everything he saw seemed wonderful. The furniture of the house, the chairs etc. . . . were objects of his great admiration; and he asked me a thousand questions concerning the utility and necessity of different articles . . . observing the improved state of our manufacturers, and our manifest superiority in the arts of civilized life, he would sometimes appear pensive, and exclaim with an involuntary sigh, *Fato fing inta feng*, 'Black men are nothing' . . ." Ben, automatically turning on his transistor radio when he wakes—Mwangi calls the action "a conditional reflex manoeuvre"—has neither wonder nor humility. He takes it all for granted; he is content with simple possession.

At the height of the slave trade, African rulers seemed literally to have gone mad. To get hold of the guns and tobacco and brandy they craved, some chiefs betrayed and enslaved their own people. The desire to possess had spiraled out of control. Their successors behave no differently. Slavery, of course, is now illegal. But are there any moral distinctions to be drawn between a chief who, in order to satisfy his lust for brandy, sells his own people into slavery and the contemporary politician who, coveting a Mercedes-Benz, embezzles the funds of a charity set up to help orphan children? It is no accident that Uhuru is thought of as a "fruit"—something to be eaten, something to grow fat on. Africans are content with the political kingdom. Karfa's dim vision of the intellectual kingdom that lay beyond "the objects of his great admiration" has been lost. "Progress" has been confused with possession.

*

Andrew, I would guess, was in his early twenties. We had met in the street when I stopped him to ask the way. He wore a striped suit, platformed shoes and carried a leather briefcase.

Rather than explain, he offered to escort me personally, brushing aside my objections. "I'll take you," he said firmly.

Having delivered me safely, he announced his intention to wait for me.

"That isn't necessary," I said, wary now of his generosity.

"I'll wait."

"But I don't know how long I'll be."

"That's all right. I have nothing else to do." He was quietly adamant.

He was as good as his word. An hour later I found him where I had left him. He fell in step a pace or two behind me, as self-effacing as a shadow, and followed me back to the hotel. He touched my arm as I entered the lounge. No doubt he was expecting to be paid for his services. After my misadventure with the shoeshine boy, I dreaded the prospect of another scene. Hesitantly, not knowing whether it was too much or too little or—come to that—whether he would be offended by my presumption, I offered him ten shillings. He took the note, folded it neatly and put it in his breast pocket. But he still showed not the slightest inclination to depart.

"You want *more* money?"

"I don't want more money," he said. "I want to give you this." He held out a stylishly printed calling card. "Andrew Njenga. Office Furniture Salesman." An address and telephone number were supplied.

I returned the card. "I don't need any office furniture. Sorry."

"You keep it," he said. "It's for you. If you give me your card, we could write to each other."

"I don't have a card."

This appeared to astonish him. However, ready for any

emergency, he produced an address book and a pencil. "You can write your address in here," he said.

"But why do you want us to write to each other?"

"I would like you as a pen pal," he said. "I like writing to pen pals."

I was touched, rebuking myself for my churlishness. I wrote my address in his book. Anxious now to make up for my gracelessness, I offered to buy him a drink. He accepted the invitation with alacrity.

We descended soft-carpeted stairs to the dimly lit bar, virtually deserted at that relatively early hour of the afternoon. Soon, though, it would be overrun by tourists, office workers and harlots. Canned music drifted dismally through the air-conditioned gloom. Andrew ordered a beer.

"Why don't you have a calling card?" he asked.

"I never thought of it."

"You should. All my friends have them." He took a card from his wallet and stared pensively at it. I felt he was looking at an alter ego; that the printed card helped to make him real to himself, to lend credence to his city existence.

He asked me if I was married. I said I was.

"How many cows did you have to give?"

"Cows?"

"How many did you have to give to your wife's family?"

"I didn't have to give any."

"None at all?"

"None at all."

Andrew loosened his tie knot. He looked somber. "You are a lucky man. I had to give my wife's family four cows. And what's more, one of them was pregnant." He sipped his beer.

"My real ambition," he said suddenly, "is to be a lawyer or an engineer. But for that I need a scholarship."

"Won't the government give you one?"

"I have tried. I don't have the correct qualifications." He stirred the frothy crest of his beer with a finger. "My only hope is that one day I might be lucky enough to meet some rich person who will help me. I know somebody who got a scholarship like that."

"Who gave it to him?"

"A German lady. I hear the Germans are nice people. I keep hoping I would meet someone like that. Someone who will take me away with them and give me good studies."

"Maybe you will."

"Maybe." He gazed despondently around the room. Not a rich German lady in sight. He stared at me. "You must be a wealthy man."

"Me! What ever gave you that idea? I'm not rich at all. I'm very, very poor."

"They say all you Asians have a lot of money."

"I'm an exceptional Asian. I have no money at all."

"You can't be that poor if you are able to travel all the way to Kenya. You must have a lot of *savings* in the bank." His bright, clear eyes shone with worldly wisdom. "How else could you afford to come all this way?"

"Somebody paid for me to come."

"You mean somebody gave you a scholarship?"

"Well . . ."

"You are a lucky man," he said. "I wish I could be as lucky as you."

He finished his beer; I bought him another one. The first whore of the evening had arrived. She was garbed in an ankle-length, contour-hugging dress. A white knitted shawl was draped about her bare, bony shoulders. She carried a tiny silver lamé purse suspended from a cord which was looped around her wrist. A necklace glittered on her bosom. Her severely straightened hair shone like lacquered wire in the dim electric glow. She glanced without interest at us before perching on a bar stool. The slit up the side of the dress bared an expanse of black flesh. She conversed lightly and familiarly with the barman.

"That one," Andrew said, "I know her well. She only goes with the *mzungus*." He gazed sadly at her. "She is very beautiful. The *mzungus* always get the best."

I did not know how to console him.

He finished his beer. "Come," he said, abruptly cheerful. "I'll take you for a walk. I'll show you some of the sights of Nairobi."

Kenyatta Avenue was crowded with office workers on their way home. The late-afternoon light, luminously yellow, was hazed with the fertile red dust of Kikuyuland. Spaced like sentries at regular intervals along the pavement, the shoeshine boys, surrounded by an array of tins and bottles and brushes, kept their eyes fixed on the shoes of the pedestrians. My rheumy-eyed Kikuyu was, fortunately, stationed on the far bank of the avenue. On the numerous newsstands, row upon row of the latest pornographic magazines from the West were on display. What did someone like Andrew make of these provocative displays? Did he regard it as one more token of the new-forged "equality" between black and white? More than time seems to have flown since the days when "respect" was regarded by the European settlers as a near-mystical tribute to be paid by black to white, a surer safeguard of their survival than superior firepower. Respect, Elspeth Huxley has candidly observed, was, for the European, "an invisible coat of mail . . . the least rent or puncture might . . . split the whole garment asunder and expose its wearer in all his human vulnerability."

Exposure has come in a more literal way than she could ever have imagined. That very week, at the Sombrero Night Club, Beauty Lee, "the International Striptease Artiste" (European, but of no precise provenance) was supposed to be performing on stage three times nightly. The Monro Massage Salon was enticing customers with its African, Asian and European masseuses. Naturally, not everyone approves. The long-settled British, those to whom the Norfolk Hotel is a last embattled outpost of settler civilization, remain aloof and tight-lipped. The blame is generally—and quite rightly—placed on those Europeans without adequate colonial experience—the Swedes, the Danes, the Germans, even the Swiss. One Swiss lady had caused a minor ripple of scandal when she disappeared into the bush with her African lover.

The beggars on Kenyatta Avenue, like the shoeshine boys and the stands selling pornographic magazines, had their own clearly demarcated territories. Most were maimed. Lepers with truncated arms and legs were a common sight; but even more numerous than the lepers were the victims of severe bone malformation, the result of calcium deficiency. This affliction ravages the human frame, reducing it to a tangled wreckage of atrophied limbs. Occasionally, the beggars are rounded up and sent off somewhere, hidden from sensitive tourist eyes. When I was in Mombasa just before the height of the tourist season, they lined the length of Kilindini Road like gargoyles. Some weeks later a friend of mine visited

Mombasa. He was surprised when I brought the subject up: he had not seen a single beggar and had come away with the impression that Kenya was a happy, prosperous country composed largely of polite, well-trained waiters. But the round-ups have only a temporary success. Like the shantytowns which are periodically razed, like the prostitutes who, now and again, are subjected to culling campaigns (these last can never be entirely eliminated for two reasons—their numbers are far too great, and they are an inseparable adjunct of the tourist trade: the Germans are particularly addicted to what is called the "sex-safari"), they always spring up again.

Andrew stopped and stared into the window of a shoe shop. He said he needed new shoes. "Those are nice," he said, pointing at a multicolored, platformed pair.

I pretended not to hear. We walked on, turning left up a side street lined, I noted anxiously, with clothes shops. I tried to divert his attention. "What would you do if you became a lawyer—or an engineer—and made a lot of money?"

"I'd buy a big farm and grow tea on it." He looked at me wisely. "You get a very good price for tea these days." He paused by a shop window. "Those are nice jeans."

"And what else would you do if you were rich?" We walked on.

"I would buy a Mercedes-Benz." He laughed. "Then I'd get all the beautiful women. The Wabenzi always have beautiful women." ("Wabenzi" is the pleasantly jocular term used to describe the nouveau-riche black middle class—they who have eaten well of the fruit of Uhuru. They signal their status by the acquisition, at the first opportunity, of a Mercedes-Benz. Hence, the Wabenzi—the Benz tribe.) Andrew stopped again. "That is a pretty shirt. A special offer . . ."

"What about your wife? Wouldn't she get jealous if she knew you were driving other women about in your Mercedes?"

"My wife will be looking after the *shamba* [homestead]. Anyway, I will give her lots of money." He stopped again. "That is a nice belt . . ."

"I read in the newspapers that the government was going to pass a law that would throw people guilty of adultery into jail." We walked on.

"It won't work."

"Why not?"

"If they did, they would have to throw nearly every Member of Parliament into jail. Maybe even . . ." He teetered on the verge of sacrilege. "It won't work," he said.

Before us loomed the many-storeyed tower of the Kenyatta Conference Centre, symbol of Nairobi's grandeur and aggressive contemporaneity. A few people strolled on the flagged terrace in front of it. Beds of flowers glowed in the deepening twilight. The terrace was dominated by a statue of Kenyatta raised aloft on a pedestal. He was attired in full academic regalia, his hands clasped on his robed lap. He brooded massively, portentously, over the monumental scene. However, the fountain at the base of the pedestal was not in operation, and the basin was empty.

By the time we regained the avenue, darkness had fallen. Baton-wielding watchmen warmed their hands over braziers in the doorways of shuttered shops. Neon lights flashed their inane Morse. The hour was early, but the avenue was already deserted. A curio seller was shutting up his stall; the shoeshine boys had packed up and gone home; the beggars had retreated before the chill of the Highlands night. Little groups of whores congregated disconsolately under the street lamps. They hung out their tongues at us, swayed their hips. "Want fuck? I give you nice fuck, darling."

Andrew paused by one of the pornographic displays. He picked up a magazine.

"You will buy this for me?"

I was too tired to argue. I bought it for him. He slipped it into his briefcase.

Andrew accompanied me back to the hotel. "Tomorrow," he said, "I go home to my *shamba* near Kisumu. Every weekend I go there." He laughed. "I am a different man when I work on my *shamba*. When I take off all these clothes, you would find it hard to recognize me. You will write to me?"

"I will write to you if you write to me."

We shook hands. He wandered off, swinging his briefcase, dreaming, perhaps, of the rich German lady who might stop him on the street any day to ask the way; of the "scholarship" she might offer him; of the Mercedes-Benz that might one day be his and the beautiful women it would bring. What a ragbag of fantasies must whirl in that head! Within twenty-four hours, the office-furniture salesman with his elegantly printed calling cards would, as he himself had said, become unrecognizable. He was an unstable compound of urban and peasant man.

*

"The settler's town," Frantz Fanon wrote, "is a strongly built town, all made of stone and steel. It is a brightly lit town . . . a well-fed town, an easy going town . . . a town of white people, of foreigners . . . The look that the native turns on the settler's town is a look of lust, a look of envy; it expresses his dreams of possession: to sit at the settler's table, to sleep in the settler's bed, with his wife if possible . . . there is no native who does not dream at least once a day of setting himself up in the settler's place."

Nairobi, with its broad avenues, its multistoreyed hotels, its travel agencies, its boutiques, its nightclubs, its striptease "artistes" and massage parlors, its two casinos, is not even a settler's town—not any more. It is a tourist town; and the tourist town is, by its very nature, a fantastical place, a kind of papier-mâché confection. Its quintessential expression is the international hotel. In the eyes of native and tourist alike, international hotels are dream palaces. But the tourist has this advantage: he *knows* it is a dream; he knows that at the end of two or three weeks he will fly away and return to an everyday world. The native cannot make the distinction. The abnormal becomes the stamping ground of his visions of "progress" and "development" because it is only the abnormal he sees. He is vulnerable. He is defenseless. Culturally, he is in much the same position as those aboriginal peoples who were wiped out by imported Old World diseases. Black and white meet and mingle at the point of fantasy, aggravating an already deformed vision. Fantasy is piled on fantasy. For as long as he can afford it, Andrew will sit in darkened, air-conditioned bars and dream of miraculous rescue.

CHAPTER 2

— I —

Black and White: Old Style

THE RIDGES of the Kikuyu country stretched away on all sides, wave upon wave sweeping toward the horizon. Where the land was cut away to accommodate the passage of the road, its red heart was startlingly exposed to view. Looking at that bloody redness one sensed not only the richness of the land but—more disturbingly—its visceral appeal. It seemed to symbolize the Kikuyus' fierce attachment to it, the unity of soil and tribe. In *Facing Mount Kenya* (first published in 1938), Kenyatta expressed his tribe's attitude toward the land they considered peculiarly theirs. "The Gikuyu," he wrote, "consider the earth as the 'mother' of the tribe. It is the soil that feeds the child through lifetime; and again after death it is the soil that nurses the spirits of the dead for eternity. Thus the earth is the most sacred thing above all that dwell in or on it . . . an everlasting oath is to swear by the earth." Those oaths were to surface, in a more murderous form, during the Mau Mau insurrection.

The road, which to begin with had been wide enough for two cars, narrowed to a single lane. We left behind the forest reserve through which we had been traveling and entered the coffee belt, the leaves of the neatly staked-out shrubs glistening in the soupy sunlight. "Kenya is lucky," my companion said, gesturing at the plantations on either side of us. "The Brazilian crop has been hit by frost this year."

We passed through a straggling township replete with the usual beer parlors and "ration" shops and unsightly hoardings advertising detergents, refrigerators and vacuum cleaners. The air was noisy with jukebox music. A roadside market was in progress. Long strips of colorfully dyed cloth were spread out on the ground. Young boys danced out in front of the car flourishing fruit and vegetables. Beyond the township was typical *shamba* country: small plots planted with corn; foraging goats and cows and pigs and chickens. This, even in colonial days, had been a "native" area, and it clung tenaciously to its traditional character. The coffee plantations reappeared. A veil of pearly mist obscured the more distant reaches of the open, undulating landscape. Its "English" character was emphasized by the scattered condensations of color created by stands of trees set amid the acres of coffee. The tarmac ended. Clouds of red dust billowed in our wake. We were climbing now, and after a time, the coffee country gave way to tea country. The tea gardens, emerald green, even-topped, forming an unbroken wave of cultivation, were like a scaly sheath thrown over the land.

It was almost noon when we reached the Palmers' farm. Mrs. Palmer, jovial and red-faced, her hair bunched in a scarf, greeted us amiably. It was cool enough for a sweater. The day was autumnal. Gray cloud hid the sun, and there was a vapor of blue mist in the shallow valleys. A chill, clammy wind blew. The Palmers' house—a modest-sized brick bungalow—was finely situated on a rising piece of ground. We stood for a while on the well-kept lawn surrounding it, admiring the extensive views. "In good weather," our hostess said, "you can see Kilimanjaro." We gazed in the direction she indicated, paying the invisible mountain ritual homage. Then we went inside.

A fire was going in the brick fireplace; an Alsatian was stretched out on the rug in front of it. Two high-backed armchairs with chintz coverings were drawn up in front of the fireplace. Ancestral photographs lined the walls. A piano, piled with papers, occupied a corner. Next to it was a large, brass-studded chest. Agricultural journals, old copies of *The Times* and some back numbers of the *Illustrated London News* were distributed in neat piles on a low table in the center of the room. A complete set of *Chambers' Encyclopedia* filled a small bookshelf. I noticed no other books apart from those. The wooden floor gleamed. There was not a speck of dust to be seen. It was a forbiddingly hygienic room. I felt that nothing new had happened here for a long time—just endless dusting, cleaning, preserving.

"I hear it's been a lovely summer in England," Mrs. Palmer said. "We've been reading all about it." She nodded at the pile of newspapers. "Now here you are on the Equator—and sitting in front of a fire. It must seem strange."

She rang a bell. A barefooted "boy" appeared. She ordered him to bring ice and glasses. "And Simon . . ." Simon, who had started to leave, paused but did not turn around. Mrs. Palmer smiled. ". . . when you put the ice in the glasses, do please remember to use the tongs and not your fingers. That's what the tongs are *for*. Now off you go."

Simon disappeared into the kitchen.

Mrs. Palmer was still smiling when she turned to face us.

"Simon seems to have a block about using those tongs. I can't understand it. I've told him so many times. Still, Simon has one great virtue. He hasn't been *spoiled*. Not as yet, anyway. I'm keeping my fingers crossed. It's amazing how quickly they do get spoiled, though. There used to be an old saying in this country: put a native in shoes and that's the end of him. Nowadays, of course, they've all got shoes and we aren't even allowed to call them natives." Mrs. Palmer sighed, staring out the window toward invisible Kilimanjaro. Taking a key from the pocket of her dress, she unlocked the liquor cabinet. "I'm sorry to seem so jailerlike," she said, "but pilfering, I'm afraid, is a big problem. I have to keep everything under lock and key. They take the oddest things sometimes, things they can't possibly have any use for. The other day my shower cap disappeared." She peered at the ranks of bottles. "I close my eyes to the sugar and flour they take from the larder—but I *do* draw the line at our precious Scotch. Simon is still fairly trustworthy. But you can never be sure. Leaving bottles of Scotch hanging about the place is more than a temptation. It's an invitation. And once they get a taste for alcohol, that's the end."

"Worse even than putting them into shoes," my companion said.

"*Much* worse," Mrs. Palmer replied, not catching the irony. "In the old days people used to say that to give a native alcohol was like putting a loaded gun in the hands of a child. In my opinion that's still true. But . . ." She sighed again.

She extracted bottles of whisky, gin and sherry.

Simon came in carrying a bowl of ice in one hand and three glasses in the other.

"Simon . . . Simon . . ." Mrs. Palmer wagged her head.

Simon looked at her expressionlessly.

"Why didn't you use the tray, Simon?" Mrs. Palmer relieved him of his burdens. "You can carry several things at once on a tray. That's what a tray is *for*."

My eyes strayed to Simon's bare, uncorrupted feet.

"You see what I mean," Mrs. Palmer said when Simon had left the room. "The tray is another of his peculiar blocks." She poured generous measures of whisky into our glasses.

The Alsatian sprang up, barking loudly: Mr. Palmer had arrived. He came in chattering apologies for his late arrival. He was dressed in khaki—short-sleeved khaki shirt tucked into short khaki trousers, matching knee-high socks and thick-soled brown shoes; a lean, wiry man of medium height, probably in his mid-fifties. He fondled and pummeled the fawning dog.

"Awfully sorry about the weather," he said. "Wish we could have put on a better show for you. On a fine day you can see Kili."

*

The tea gardens—the Palmers had about three hundred acres under tea—began not many yards beyond the lawn surrounding the house. The day's work was drawing to a close, and the pluckers, bent under leaf-filled nets slung from their shoulders, were filing down the aisles between the rows of bushes, slowly making their way to the weighing shed. The afternoon had become colder and gloomier. Thickening mists obscured the summits of neighboring ridges. The wind was cutting. Smoke rose from a group of huts clustered together on the shallow slope of a nearby depression. A moorland bleakness overhung the scene. The pluckers—men, women and children—crept like an army of subdued ghosts through the premature twilight, the sharp odor of the raw leaf they carried tanging the chill air. A muted murmur of conversation rose among them as they waited for the product of their day's labor to be weighed. All were equipped with shining aprons, reaching from neck to knee, made of vinyl.

"I supply the aprons myself," Mr. Palmer said. "They are very appreciative. It reduces the wear and tear on their clothing."

"They like the bright colors," Mrs. Palmer said. "They are very fond of bright colors."

The estate employed roughly two hundred people. Most of them had been brought in from outside the district—or had migrated of their own accord in search of work. The local people were not particularly interested in agricultural labor of the type offered by the Palmers. Nairobi, less than a hundred miles away, was a powerful magnet.

"The local people have been spoiled," Mrs. Palmer said. "Many actually prefer to be beggars and prostitutes in Nairobi than to earn an honest living from the soil. They consider it to be beneath their dignity." She pursed her lips.

The pluckers smiled and saluted as they shuffled past with their loads. Mrs. Palmer's scarf snapped like a flag as she surveyed the beasts of burden who marched past her. They could, with luck, earn up to a pound a day.

"I know it sounds appallingly little by English standards," Mr. Palmer said. "But by *their* standards it's a good wage. *They* don't complain. *They* are grateful that they can actually work and earn something. It's only certain left-wing journalists looking for a sensational story who come here and weep crocodile tears on their behalf."

Mr. Palmer stooped, picked up a tea leaf from the ground and stared at it critically.

"These people," he went on, "are simple, hardworking folk. They're not spoiled . . ."

"Not as yet," Mrs. Palmer put in grimly. Her scarf fluttered and snapped.

"Their needs are basic," Mr. Palmer said. "They want to have food in their bellies, to be warm, to have a roof over their heads. *I* supply those basic needs. Many of them, you know, prefer to work for us whites than to work for their own people. Their own people often treat them like slaves. They don't pay them properly, they offer no medical facilities, they house them in atrocious conditions. Paternalism like mine has something to be said for it, don't you think?" He grinned at me.

He beckoned over a boy of about ten. "Have a look at this *toto*." He squeezed the boy's arms and legs, lifted up his shirt and exhibited the well-fleshed diaphragm. "Six months ago Sammy was skeletal, covered with sores, had a bad cough. He's all right now, though. Aren't you, Sammy?" He chucked the boy under the chin. The boy, not knowing what was happening to him, gazed at us with wild, frightened eyes. His mother watched from a distance, obviously pleased to see her son the focus of her master's attention.

"In the old days we used to have an estate shop," Mrs. Palmer said. "That way you made sure they got reasonably fed. Now they spend their money how and where they like." She laughed grimly. "Maize meal isn't good enough for them these days. They want rice."

"Rice is more nutritious than maize meal," Mr. Palmer said.

"But more expensive."

"It's their money."

Mrs. Palmer sighed. We returned to the house for lunch.

*

At lunch we were joined by the Palmers' son Ralph, a gangling, graceless youth with yellowing skin and untidy hair and dirt-encrusted fingernails. He shook hands morosely. Ralph did not have much to say for himself. He sat hunched over his food, head bent over his plate, masticating with noisy devotion. I watched him shovel meat and potatoes into his mouth. There was something degenerate, something savage, about Ralph. In Africa, European civilization did not penetrate to the second generation. He had (I managed to elicit) received a certain amount of education at the minor English public school to which he had been sent; but when I asked him about it and about his feelings for England, he looked at me blankly.

"U.K.?"

I listened to his mastications.

"I have no special feelings about U.K." He shoveled more potatoes, more meat into his mouth. "This farm is home to me. I was born here."

"Ralph didn't really care much for U.K.," Mrs. Palmer said. "The cold didn't suit him at all. He is used to a more outdoor type of life. Isn't that so, Ralph?" She regarded her son with tender solicitude.

Ralph scowled.

"Ralph is very good with his hands." The look of tender solicitude did not leave Mrs. Palmer's face. "Put Ralph under a car and you'll never get him out. He has a way with machinery, Ralph has."

Rallying, it emerged, was the ruling passion of Ralph's life.
Little else appeared to interest him: when he was not driving
cars cross country, he was usually to be found under them.
My knowledge of such things being limited, I gave up my
attempts to make conversation with him. He reminded me of
my "white" Trinidad contemporaries who, as dispossessed
and as destitute as the rest of us, could only fall back on the
bogus aristocracy of color to preserve their self-esteem.

Ralph, mumbling indecipherably, fled from the room.

"No," Mrs. Palmer said, "U.K. didn't suit Ralph at all. We
should have sent him down South. That's what we should
have done."

"U.K. isn't U.K. anymore," Mr. Palmer said, dabbing his
lips with a napkin. "When I go there I feel like a stranger.
After a couple of weeks I find myself longing to get back to
my little farm in the bush."

Mrs. Palmer sighed. "It's all those strikes they keep having.
People don't want to work for things any more. They expect
everything to fall into their lap. That's the trouble. Then
there are all those Arabs buying everything up. How would
they feel if we went to Saudi Arabia, or wherever, and started
buying up everything? I don't think that sort of thing should
be allowed. It's not their country."

"At least here," Mr. Palmer said, "we don't have to worry
about the unions and strikes. Most of my workers have never
even heard the word, thank God." He dug at his teeth with
a toothpick. "I'm not saying it's Utopia. Our *friends* can be
difficult. If they really wanted to, they could kick us out
tomorrow."

Mrs. Palmer blocked her ears.

"We must be realistic, dear," Mr. Palmer said. "Our friends

can do anything they want to. I don't see U.K. sending gun-boats to protect us."

I asked what he would do if he were "kicked out."

"If I was a younger man I might go to the southern Sudan."

"The southern Sudan?"

"There's lots of lovely land in the southern Sudan. And it's virtually empty. It's like this place was seventy-five years ago. It's *crying out* for European settlers." He laughed. "I'm sorry to say I'm still a naughty old imperialist."

"They wouldn't allow it," Mrs. Palmer said mournfully.

"No," Mr. Palmer said. "They wouldn't. The lads down South have queered the pitch somewhat. A real pity that."

He poured more whisky into our glasses and began telling us a little about himself. He had been born in Ceylon, the son of a tea planter. Fifty years ago, when he was a child of two, his father had migrated to the wide-open spaces of Kenya. "As you can see," he said, "I am a naughty old imperialist who has sprung from a naughty old imperialist background. I'm not ashamed of that. I am proud. Where would our friends be without us?"

"They would still be in the Stone Age," Mrs. Palmer answered. "They would still be fighting wars and killing each other."

Simon came in. Mr. Palmer told him to bring cheese and biscuits.

"No biscuits, bwana."

Mrs. Palmer sighed. "Simon . . . Simon . . . why didn't you tell me we were running low on biscuits?"

Simon stared at his reflection in the floorboards. Mr. Palmer dismissed him.

"One of my pet theories," he said, "is that Africans lack

what I call a storage sense. The same thing occurs with my headman. Time and again I tell him to order more pesticides when stocks fall below a certain point. He *never* does. I must have told him a thousand times. But he waits until the last drop runs out and then comes running to me wringing his hands."

"They never think about the future," Mrs. Palmer said. "It has no meaning for them as far as I can see. Only today matters. *Now.* Of course, that's how it was in the old days. If their crops were good, they feasted day and night, fattening themselves up. If the rains didn't come on time, they starved. Never a thought for the morrow."

"You can't expect these things to change overnight," Mr. Palmer said. "The Kikuyu are the exception. They have learnt very quickly. They are very clever. I'm a great fan of Kenyatta's. He's really very fond of the English, you know. He respects us. It's quite amazing when you think how we treated him."

"He's not immortal," Mrs. Palmer said somberly.

"Our friends know on which side their bread is buttered," Mr. Palmer said. "They're not going to let a few hotheads spoil the party." He leveled a knife at me. "I am more confident of the future of the white man in Kenya today than I was five years ago. Things have really turned out much better for us than anyone could have expected. They know it's not in their interest to throw all of us out. You must have heard of Kenyatta's Nakuru speech."

I said I had not.

"He made it around the time of Independence. The Nakuru settlers were a tough bunch. Really hard nuts. Kenyatta went up there, to beard the lion in his den, as it were. He told them they had nothing to fear from a black government, that the time had come to forgive and forget and so on. In my opinion, it was the best speech he's ever made. He got a standing ovation."

"All the same," Mrs. Palmer said, "if some bigwig from Nairobi was driving past here one day and suddenly decided our farm was just the thing for him . . ."

"True enough," Mr. Palmer conceded. "What a Nairobi bigwig wants a Nairobi bigwig generally gets. The Old Man has a weakness for farms. If he offers to buy your property, that's virtually a compulsory order to sell. Have you noticed my brick wall?"

I said I had: the wall, nearly ten feet high, screened the road frontage of the farm.

"I built that wall to shield what's behind it from prying eyes."

"A wall isn't going to stop them," Mrs. Palmer said.

"Of course it isn't. But every little bit helps. I dread the day the road becomes asphalted. As it is, our friends feel reluctant to get their Mercedes covered with dust and mud."

I asked Mr. Palmer if he would resist a request to sell.

"No. There's absolutely no point in resisting. A stubborn proprietor might suddenly find his fences being broken, his animals poisoned, his crops fired, his workers intimidated, his house robbed. Strange things begin happening to people who refuse to play ball. It isn't worth the candle. I'd sell up and be on my way."

"To the southern Sudan . . ."

He laughed.

Mrs. Palmer tinkled the bell. Simon came in and started clearing away the dishes.

*

After lunch Mr. Palmer took us to the nursery where the seedlings were reared—a long shed roofed with polythene. Within, the air was warm and humid, heavy with the rich smells of nutrients. Beads of moisture dripped from the roof. The seedlings were planted in cylinders filled with the red earth of Kikuyuland. We returned to the cold outside air with relief and continued down the slope of the field. Mr. Palmer described the process of tea production from nursery to field to factory. To right and left the even-topped tide of his cultivation sheathed the contours of the land. Mr. Palmer swept his gaze over the emerald-green tide.

"But look across there," he said, extending an arm.

The neighboring ridge presented an altogether different appearance. It was covered with a disordered patchwork of small, irregularly shaped plots set about with dilapidated hovels. Goats grazed in the bush.

"I can remember so well how that place used to be," he said. "I hate looking at it now."

Formerly European-owned, the ridge had been vacated at the time of Independence and taken over by a group of local people. The original intention to turn it into a cooperative had come to nothing. "I believe the treasurer ran away with the money," Mr. Palmer said. "In this country, treasurers are very fleet of foot." The farm had been divided up into individual subsistence plots. Land and people had, in a manner of speaking, reverted to type at the first opportunity. Mr. Palmer looked once again at his own creation. Suddenly, one realized how fragile it all was. Nothing was assured; nothing was safe; nothing could be taken for granted. An older life pressed. Old instincts threatened. At any moment, Africa could close in. The house, the lawn, the monomaniacal acres of tea—it could all be swept away without trace. There was nothing inevitable about "progress."

We came, a little farther on, to a tract of bushland. A colony of five or six thatched mud huts came into view: dark-interiored, crumbling dwellings hemmed in by patches of corn. The settlement, at first sight, seemed to be deserted, but as we approached, groups of naked, potbellied children came out of the huts to watch us. Mr. Palmer paused, dilating on the preference of the "unspoiled" native for this traditional type of housing. He sympathized: mud huts were easier to keep clean and less cold than brick houses. However, the Government frowned on the provision of old-style accommodation for estate workers, condemning them as relics of colonialism.

"Have you ever heard anything more ridiculous? Mud huts are not *colonial*. We didn't invent them. They are native. They are traditional. Brick houses are the true colonial relics. My father lived in a grass hut for years on end—many of the early settlers did. They didn't consider it below their dignity. It's almost impossible to make our friends understand such things."

I was to come across a number of examples of this peculiar definition of the "colonial." Thus dancing is regarded by most Kenyans as an entirely respectable manifestation of their "cultural heritage." It has received the imprimatur of the President himself: everywhere Kenyatta goes he is feted for hours on end by squads of tribal dancers. So are the tourists. But to have the performers exhibit naked breasts and bottoms is not respectable. Bare bottoms and naked breasts are "colonial." Consequently, beneath the atavistic finery of feathers and beads, the women wear bikinis; the men preserve their modesty with running shorts. The effect is droll.

The people living in these huts were squatters and therefore not eligible for brick housing. They belonged to Kenya's burgeoning landless peasantry; they were the unwanted dross of what President Nyerere of Tanzania had recently described as Kenya's "man eat man" society. The Palmers allowed them to live on their land because there was nowhere else for them to go. As we stood there, more and more children appeared— I counted at least twenty—all springing from that tiny fount of dereliction. They kept themselves at a respectful distance; silent, somber presences, watching us with big, uncomprehending eyes.

"I have nightmares when I think about these children," Mr. Palmer said. "What's going to become of them? What kind of lives are they going to lead?"

Already, sixty-five percent of Kenya's population was under fifteen—and the imbalance was worsening.

Mr. Palmer skated his hand across the head of one of the children. "Overpopulation is terrifying. But there is something even more terrifying than overpopulation: the fact that nobody really gives a damn."

I knew what he meant. Not many days before, a member of the Kenyan Parliament had asserted that birth control was a plot against the black race. The attitude of the Wabenzi is reflected in the complaint about Nairobi's beggar menace written by one of *The Nation*'s lady columnists. "Again I would give a word of warning to readers [she wrote] about giving money to beggars . . . who really are not only a blot on the landscape but a complete menace. Every day they become more and more daring, and just recently a friend who had been shopping near the market got into her car and one of the boys pushed his head and hand through the window and was demanding money. When it was not forthcoming he became extremely abusive. These boys have also become adept at bag snatching, even trying to grab one's shopping baskets . . . I feel it is high time that the police stepped in again and took action . . ."

The beggars are a "blot on the landscape"—not, it will be observed, on the conscience: the lady, clutching her shopping baskets as she gets into her car, fails to make the elementary connection between social distress and the existence of widespread beggary. In the same way, the Member of Parliament who sees birth control as a plot against the black race fails to make the connection between population explosion and black degradation. To the lack of a "storage sense" ought to be added the inadequate grasp of the laws of cause and effect. The government constantly exhorts the people to leave the fleshpots of the city and go back to the land. But where is the land to be found? Everybody in Kenya, from President to bellboy, wants land. It is the national obsession. "We all feel," a Kenyan economist told me, "that we must have our own piece of land, no matter how small. A man may work in town, may live there for most of the time. But the town isn't really *home* to us as yet. We haven't evolved to that stage. Land. Land. Land. We must have it. Without it a man feels rootless, feels that he is nothing." The trouble is that most of the worthwhile land has already been grabbed. (I have driven past a farm belonging to the President: the immaculate wire fencing stretches for miles. The land opposite belongs to his daughter, ex-mayor of Nairobi.) The half-starved children watching us had arrived too late. The fruit of Uhuru had already been eaten.

We returned to the road, pausing briefly, at Mrs. Palmer's

insistence, to have a look at their herd of Friesian cows. She was hoping that they might win a prize at that year's Nairobi Agricultural Show. Cattle rustling, though, was an enormous problem.

"We have to employ an army of watchmen to keep an eye on them. It wasn't like that in the old days."

"Oh, yes it was," Mr. Palmer said. "The only difference is that they have become bolder and more ruthless. They would think nothing of murdering a couple of watchmen."

Not far away was the settlement of estate workers' houses —neat rows of unplastered brick cabins with corrugated-iron roofs. Here were more children. Their parents stood in the cabin doorways and watched us. I peeped into one of the cabins. Within—a few pieces of plastic furniture, a confusion of bedding and cooking pots, impassive faces. Food in their bellies. A roof over their heads. Warmth. Was that really all? Was there really something to be said for this kind of "paternalism" that left a man no hope? We visited the tiny dispensary, equipped to cope with most minor ailments. The girl in charge showed us her record book. Coughs of one sort or another were far and away the most common complaint.

"It's the brick houses," Mr. Palmer said. "Most of them develop chest complaints eventually."

The girl laughed and giggled.

We went back to the house. Simon served tea—the tea of the estate—and cake. Darkness had fallen when we rose to make our farewells.

— II —

Black and White: New Style

ERIC, TALL, handsome, bearded, came out of the shining sea bearing a fish in one hand and his snorkeling apparatus in the other. He held up the silver fish for our inspection.

"Bravo!" shouted Yvonne, raising herself up on one elbow from the cane-bottomed chaise longue on which she was reclining and fixing her dark glasses more securely on the bridge of her nose. The upper buttons of the loose cotton shift she was wearing were undone, exposing the pale tops of her breasts.

"Some catch," said Nathan.

Eric, the rankness of the sea strong upon him, dropped the fish on the bottom step of the veranda and walked on to the tap at the far end of the garden, where he began dousing himself with buckets of water.

The grassy garden, sloping toward the sea, was shaded by coconut palms. Banks of hibiscus and oleander, poinsettia and bougainvillea added splashes of color. To our left was the entrance to the harbor, bordered by the raised, sunlit meadows of Mombasa Island. Around the lighthouse the waves broke in a white line. A sweet, warm wind blew off the sea.

Moira, Eric's bikini-clad wife, followed him along the path leading from the beach. She too carried a silver fish in one hand and snorkeling apparatus in the other. She too dropped her catch on the bottom step of the veranda and walked on to the tap at the far end of the garden.

Eric, his body shimmering with rainbow-tinted drops of water, returned. He clapped his hands. His boy came running, collected the two fish and disappeared down the side of the house. Eric took one of the towels draped on the low veranda wall and dried himself. He gazed out to where the water broke white on the reef.

He looked at me. "Wouldn't you say this was paradise? I don't think I could ever bear to live in England again. How do the people there stand it? How did *I* ever manage to put up with it for twenty-five years?"

"For me, Israel is the paradise on earth," Yvonne said. "What do you say, Nathan?"

Nathan grunted agreement. "But this is nice too. Life is much harder in Israel. Too many taxes. Too much socialism." He played with the Star of David that dangled from the chain around his neck. His accent was clipped, slightly Germanic.

Moira joined us. She looked older than her husband: she had a narrow, raddled face; her lips were thin and pinched; the skin about her eyes was striated with crow's-feet.

"Do you think this is paradise?" Yvonne asked.

"My idea of paradise," Moira said, "is a place with lots of sunshine and an endless supply of servants. This fits the bill pretty well."

Everybody laughed.

"That is good," Nathan said. "That is very good. I must remember it." He chortled.

"I expect the Portuguese too thought Angola was paradise," Yvonne said. "And look at what happened there. This place is good for people like us now. I don't deny that. Nathan is doing very well, thank you. But one day the whites, like the Asians, will have to leave. Of that I'm sure."

"No," Eric said. "That won't happen here."

"The Asians got what they deserved," Moira said.

"Did they?" I could not help asking.

"I'll tell you a little story," Moira said. "Not long ago a friend of ours from U.K. traveled through Africa on a motorcycle. He was doing the Cape-to-Cairo bit. On his way through, he stayed with us. I asked him what had left the strongest impression on him. Do you know what he said?"

"I can't imagine."

"He said that the experience which had made the strongest impression on him was how terribly Asians treated Africans." Moira widened her eyes and nodded solemnly. "He had traveled thousands of miles. He had been everywhere and seen everything. And let me add, he had come to Africa with no preconceptions at all. He had no strong feelings about Africans one way or the other. But that was what struck him most of all—the terrible behavior of Asians to Africans."

"That's very interesting," Yvonne said.

"Your friend," I said, "had been to Rhodesia and South Africa? Did I get that right?"

"He had been *everywhere*."

"Amazing fellow."

"You shouldn't feel sorry for the Asians," Moira said. "They got what they deserved."

I watched a tramp steamer easing its way up the harbor.

"On the other hand," Eric said, "there will always be a place for white men in this country." He slid down onto the straw mat covering the concrete floor, propping his head against the veranda wall. "Everybody thought I was mad when I decided to stay on after Independence. They all prophesied doom and disaster. It was a gamble—I admit that."

He turned his head toward me. "You see, I had a feeling that for those whites who stayed behind life would get not worse but better. I figured that once the blacks got the power they wanted, things would simmer down and the situation would gradually improve. For them to get rid of us would have been like cutting off your nose to spite your face. I was right. Most of those who left are rotting away in England now. They would jump at any chance to return."

Eric had joined the Colonial Service just before Independence and been sent out to Kenya to teach English. Uhuru, he foresaw, would bring a rapid expansion of the black middle class. These people would want their children to receive a "true-blue" education. That was his opportunity. Immediately after Uhuru he went into private practice, opening up his own educational establishment, which he ran on "strictly English lines." He now owned two such schools and was planning to open a third. Business, in other words, was booming. He did not employ a single black teacher in any of his schools. The omission did not arise from any shortage of black teachers but was the result of deliberate policy. His clients were buying an *English* education from him and paying high fees for the privilege: they did not want to be taught by fellow blacks. He told the story of the Very Important Person who had openly declared (the statement had been reported in the press) that he would never allow his children to be taught by Africans.

"If you learn how to *think black*," Eric said, "there's a killing to be made in this country."

Think black. It was an arresting phrase. I asked what he meant by it.

Eric was more than willing to expound the concept. Thinking black meant understanding how the African mind worked, putting yourself into the skins of the blacks and trying to see things from their point of view. If, for instance, he had not imported his teachers direct from the United Kingdom, he would probably be out of business by now. He could so easily have made the elementary mistake of taking on black teachers in the belief that it would please *them*. His ability to think black had prevented him from taking so foolish and fatal a step. Eric warmed to his theme. "Thinking black is fairly tricky. It's like walking a tightrope. It doesn't mean behaving like a black man and saying how wonderful everything black is. They can see through all that bullshit. That's a mistake a lot of whites make. They rush around licking every black arse in sight." He laughed. "Listen! Sometimes when they make me angry I take them by the scruff of the neck and call them *niggers*. They don't mind. They laugh. They feel you are being frank and aboveboard with them when you do something like that. You can say that thinking black is knowing when and how to play the White Man. It can be hard work. If you know how to do it, there's a killing to be made."

"You are a very cynical man, Eric." Nathan smiled pleasantly.

Eric snorted. "Aren't you cynical too, Nathan? Or are you going to tell me that you're here to lift the benighted African out of his ignorance and misery?"

"I like to think that in helping myself I am also helping the country."

Eric guffawed. While speaking, he had undergone a disturbing metamorphosis. His jaw went slack; his eyes acquired a leering vacancy; licentiousness oozed from his every pore. Eric, by turning his "Englishness," his "whiteness," into a commodity, had enslaved himself. Nearly all the long-settled English I met in Kenya had succumbed to a similar degenerative process: they lived off their Englishness and whiteness. It was their chief asset. But Eric had taken it further than most. With him, the malady had entered its terminal stage. "Thinking black" had wreaked a dreadful vengeance on him. He could not "think" in any other way now. He had gone hopelessly native. Eric was what he claimed to be—the black man's White Man.

"You mustn't get me wrong," Nathan said, anxious not to be misunderstood. "I am a good Jew. I believe in profit. Philanthropy comes a poor second with me." He giggled. He turned to me—the novice in need of instruction. "I have worked in Uganda, Tanzania and Ethiopia. For me this place is without doubt the showcase of Black Africa. They are very West-minded here, and I am a very West-minded person. Here there is no socialist rubbish."

"That's the trouble with U.K.," Eric said. "Too much socialism. Too many Reds under too many beds. If they strike here, the whole lot gets clapped into jail—organizers and workers alike. The Old Man doesn't buy any of that Marxist bullshit."

"That's right," Nathan confirmed.

"But will it last?" Yvonne rubbed her fingers over the pale tops of her breasts. "Isn't it too good to be true?"

"I think it's good for at least another ten years," Eric said. "All the troublemakers have been taught their lesson."

The Luo (Eric expanded) had been taught a lesson after Kenyatta had been stoned during a visit to Kisumu: the police had fired indiscriminately into the crowd, killing an undisclosed number of people, and the leaders of the tribe had been thrown into jail; Tom Mboya, when he had shown signs of becoming too "socialist," had been taught a lesson: he had been gunned down in the street by assassins unknown; more recently, a member of Parliament who had started to ask too many uncomfortable questions about corruption in high places had been taught a lesson: he too had been murdered by assassins unknown; the Kikuyu faction opposed to the Royal Family (i.e., the Kenyatta clan) had been taught a lesson; the Asians had been taught a lesson.

"I tell you," Eric repeated, "it's good for at least another ten years."

"I'm still not so sure," Yvonne said. "It's never good to be overconfident about anything in Africa. Remember Mau Mau. What happens once can happen again. The bacillus is only lying dormant."

"At the first sign of trouble," Nathan said, "you can be sure of one thing: I won't be sticking around to see who wins. I'll be the first one out on the plane. It's not that I'm a coward. But if I have to get killed, I prefer to let that happen in my own country. I don't mind dying for a cause that makes sense to me."

"I always keep one bag packed," Yvonne said.

"For the quick getaway," Nathan explained.

"I don't intend to die here," Yvonne said. "I don't want to be cut down by a *panga* in the middle of the night."

Ghoulish fear darkened the bright day.

"They say that ——— [Nathan named a Very Important Person] has an aircraft on permanent standby at the airport."

"They also say she won't be allowed to get there in one piece." Yvonne shuddered.

Eric insisted that they were being alarmist. "It won't be

like that here—not for a while, at any rate. The big boys are on our side. They know they have as much—more—to lose than we have."

He too named a high-ranking member of the government, listing his virtues: he had his pin-striped suits tailored in Savile Row; he was married to an Englishwoman; he owned a farm in one of the Home Counties; his children were looked after by an English governess; visitors to his home were fed off silver plate and had a choice of the finest wines; he rode to hounds . . . Eric's face reddened with passion. "He isn't really black at all. The only black thing about him is his skin. People like him aren't going to let anyone spoil the party. They're in the same boat as we are."

Uhuru as a "fruit." Uhuru as a "party." Fifteen years after Independence, the imagery was as rigid as any formula expressing a mathematical truth.

Eric enlarged on his plans for the future. Kenya had shown him what could be done in other ex-colonies. Everywhere—in Nigeria, in Malaysia, in Barbados—there were black men "crying out" for an English-style education for their children. (I recalled the empty spaces of the southern Sudan which, according to Mr. Palmer, were "crying out" for European settlers.) With this in mind, he was planning to establish a recruiting agency in London for teachers who wanted to work overseas.

"All those unemployed teachers at home are a gold mine for us," Moira said.

"What we desperately need," Eric said, "is a respectable postal address for the agency. Most of our business will be transacted by mail."

"Somewhere like Bloomsbury," Moira mused. "Is that still considered respectable?"

I said I was not sure.

"West Eleven . . ." Moira said. "That has quite a nice ring to it."

"Out of the question," Eric replied. "That's Notting Hill Gate and Ladbroke Grove. Too many immigrants. They have given the place a bad name."

"If we use only the postal code," Moira said, "they mightn't make the connection."

Eric stroked his beard. "Too risky."

"Mayfair," Moira said. "The Mayfair Tuition Agency. How about that?"

"Doesn't sound academic enough," Eric said.

They went on discussing the possibilities. Nathan and Yvonne departed. Eric drove me back into town.

*

A Scandinavian cruise ship was in port, and the girls of Mombasa were out in force. Gaudy squadrons patrolled the pavements outside the bars and nightclubs. We stopped for a drink at the California Day and Night Club. As we entered, girls crowded round Eric, swaying their hips, thrusting out their breasts, begging for drinks. Eric fended them off laughingly. We plowed a path through the soliciting throng. Up on the stage a Seychellois band was playing. A muscular, jet-black gigolo leaned against the counter of the bar, resplendent in tight-fitting denim shorts, a blue sleeveless vest and platformed shoes. Scandinavians occupied the dance floor.

"When a ship like this arrives," Eric said, "nearly every other woman in Kenya seems to become a whore for a day or two. Africans don't have our sexual hang-ups. They come flocking down from Nairobi, Kisumu, Eldoret. They travel hundreds of miles to get a taste of the action. It's fantastic how the good news spreads." He looked around the room. "You get a lot of Somali girls, too."

The lights dimmed to a red glow; the band stopped playing. A moustachioed European in evening dress appeared on the stage. It transpired that he was a hypnotist—the evening's star attraction. He asked for volunteers willing to be hypnotized. Half a dozen Scandinavians offered themselves. Chairs were brought and set out in a semicircle in the middle of the dance floor. The hypnotist requested silence. In a brief introductory speech he discoursed on the seriousness and therapeutic value of his art, warned of the dangers of being hynotized by unscrupulous practitioners and affirmed his own integrity. He clicked his fingers. The Scandinavians appeared to fall asleep.

"Now we shall play games with them," he announced cheerfully. He bent toward the volunteers. "It is early morning. You have had a lovely, refreshing sleep. You open your eyes, you yawn, you stretch . . ."

The Scandinavians opened their eyes, yawned, stretched.

He prodded one of the women. "What is your name?"

"My name is Karen."

"Remember you are in bed, Karen. Why be so modest? I am your friend. Everyone here is your friend."

Karen tucked up her skirt.

"You have adorable legs, Karen."

"Thank you," Karen said.

"You are all out of bed now. It's a beautiful day. You feel full of vitality. What better than a bicycle ride into the country? Come on! Pedal! Pedal!"

The Scandinavians pedaled.

"You have come to a lake. There are boats on the lake. You decide to row a little. Pull those oars! Heave! Heave!"

The Scandinavians rowed energetically.

"After all that riding and rowing you are sweaty. Very sweaty. You begin to smell; you smell really awful . . ."

The Scandinavians crinkled their noses.

". . . the smell is so bad you feel you are going to be sick."

The Scandinavians made retching noises.

"However, the sweat dries off. You begin to feel better. You get on your bicycles again. But you have been silly billies. You have left them out in the sun. The seats are hot. Very hot . . ."

The Scandinavians wriggled and squirmed.

"It's so hot you feel you are sitting on live coals . . ."

Karen moaned, writhing off her chair onto the floor.

"This is disgusting," Eric said. "White people shouldn't behave like this in public."

"Happily, you cool down. Whew!" The hypnotist waved a handkerchief in Karen's face. He assisted her back to her chair. He stooped toward her. "Tell me, Karen, can you sing a song called 'Viva España'?"

Karen said she could.

"Wonderful. You will sing that song for us, and at the end you will shout, 'Knickers!' Will you do that for us, Karen?"

Karen said she would.

The band struck up the tune. Karen sang.

"Knickers!"

"Louder, Karen. You want everybody to hear you."

"Knickers!"

"Louder, Karen. Let the whole world hear you."

"Knickers! Knickers! Knickers!"

CHAPTER 3

Between Master and Slave

IT WAS my last day in the small lakeside town, and the Kenyan couple with whom I had been staying suggested that it would be a good idea for me, a traveler from distant regions, to be introduced to the District Commissioner. It would, they implied, be not only a courteous gesture but a modest act of homage rendered to the new Kenya whose virtues had been loudly sung during the weekend. "You will like the D.C.," my friend's wife had assured me. "He is one of the kindest, most honest men I know. You won't meet a more straightforward person anywhere."

We were welcomed with subdued official graciousness. The hand that I shook was fleshy, moist and femininely limp; the voice that spoke the formal words of greeting was fluting. The D.C., swollen rather than plump, moved with pained slowness. All that remained to him of his rumored Masai ancestry was the narrow nomad eyes—eyes born to the searching scrutiny of luminous plains. They possessed a curious goatlike intensity, and their gaze seemed disturbingly out of place in a domestic setting. But I could detect nothing in him of the angry cobra, the male leopard or the fighting bull. Civilization had had a bad effect on the D.C.

We were taken upstairs to the sitting room. The house,

overlooking the gray lake, was penetrated by swirling, water-cooled breezes. The official photograph of Kenyatta, Father of the Nation, President of the Republic—known to one and all as Mzee, the Old Man—was prominently displayed. Grouped about it were a number of reproductions of paintings with religious themes. A neatly printed placard informed us that Jesus Christ was the head of the D.C.'s household. He was the Silent Guest, the Unseen Listener. The twin pieties of Heaven and Earth, of Christ and the Mzee, hung heavy in that lake-cooled room. Coca-Cola and cake were offered by the D.C.'s wife, a small, smiling woman who, whenever she laughed, bared her gums and showed two rows of uneven, yellowing teeth. The D.C., in a piping drawl, asked if I was enjoying my visit to Kenya.

I said I was and, for a while, extolled the physical beauties of the country.

"Uhmmmm . . . uhmmmm . . . uhmmmm . . ." The distracting goatlike noise faded away only gradually.

I sipped my Coca-Cola and nibbled at my slice of cake.

"Uhmmmm . . . uhmmmm . . . uhmmmm . . . "

I looked from Jesus to the Mzee. Silent Guests. Unseen Listeners. Neither offered release.

The D.C. inquired next about the state of education in Trinidad. He wanted to know if the literacy rate was high. I said I did not know the precise figure but believed it was quite high.

"Higher than in Kenya?"

"I think it is. But . . ." I added quickly, anxious not to appear too boastful, ". . . but you have a much bigger population to cope with. For us it's relatively easy. For you . . ."

"How big is the population of Trinidad?"

"We are only one million."

The D.C. eased himself further into the depths of his armchair. He entwined his fingers. "That is *very* small. Here we are over twelve million."

I nodded humbly. "So," I said, perhaps a little too eagerly, "your problems are twelve times as difficult."

The D.C., unlacing his fingers, brought his palms together. "Uhmmmm . . . uhmmmm . . ." He seemed lost in deep reflection. "Is Fiji independent as yet?"

I was not prepared for this. I washed down the last of the cake with the last of the Coca-Cola. "Did you say Fiji?"

"Yes. Fiji. Has it got its independence as yet?"

"I believe they've been independent for some time." I smiled apologetically. "I'm afraid I don't know too much about Fiji. That's in the South Pacific—a long way from Trinidad."

The D.C. was not listening. He began to rub his palms, enmeshed in a private train of thought. The goat's eyes watched me. "What's the situation over there nowadays?"

I looked at him questioningly, wondering what "situation" he might be referring to. "Do you mean the education situation in Fiji? I'm afraid I . . ."

The goat's eyes wandered about the room. "Somebody told me that the Asians over there began to outnumber the local people. Is that true?"

Of course! How foolish of me not to have guessed. There was silence in the room. I was not an individual any more. In the twinkling of an eye I had been transformed into a spokesman for my race: one more specimen of a dangerous breed. (Later, in Tanzania, I met a man on a train who, when I told him that I had been born in Trinidad, leaned forward and whispered in a mockery of intimacy, "How is it that *you people* get everywhere?")

To the D.C. I murmured something about constitutional arrangements which ensured et cetera et cetera . . .

"Uhmmmm . . . uhmmmm . . ." He did not seem convinced; he did not even seem interested.

More Coca-Cola, more cake were offered. The talk became general. And when the D.C. heard that I was planning to leave for the Highlands later that day, he offered to arrange my transport. He levered himself up carefully from the armchair and went out of the room.

My friend's wife inclined her head toward me. "Isn't it kind of the D.C. to take such trouble on your behalf! I told you he was a nice man."

The D.C. returned. Everything, he announced, had been arranged. I had nothing to worry about.

"It really is kind of you to take so much trouble," my friend's wife said aloud.

The D.C. was self-deprecating.

My friend's wife continued to exude loud gratitude for the cake, the Coca-Cola, the trouble he had taken on my account.

As we drove down the graveled drive she said, "In the colonial days we could never have gone to the D.C.'s house for a drink. Such a thing could never have happened."

Her eyes glowed, radiant with an inner delight.

*

It was in 1972, at an abandoned army camp on the edges of Dartmoor, that I first encountered the East African "Asian" in the form in which he has since become most familiar—as refugee. Crowded together in improvised dormitories were the victims of the Ugandan expulsion. A few of the older ones were too stunned to speak. They lay on their beds, covered in blankets (it was December), gazing up at the ceiling. Others, dressed in the ill-fitting overcoats handed out by charitable organizations, roamed listlessly about the compound, staring out through the wire fence at the windswept moorland. Most had lost nearly all their property—houses, cars, businesses—and could cling only to the slender lifeline of their British passports. But the British did not want these paper citizens. Nobody wanted them. One respected front-bench Labor politician, well known for her liberal views, suggested that, on purely humanitarian grounds, the refugees should be transported to a conveniently empty island in the Indian Ocean, there to await gradual and discreet dispersal. As I moved about that wintry camp, listening to the stories of those suddenly wrecked lives, my security was shaken. Two days earlier, I had left London pleased at the thought of the article I was going to write and the money it would earn me. By the time I left that camp on Dartmoor, I could no longer take myself for granted. I could not separate myself from what I had seen.

About a hundred years ago my ancestors, peasants from the Gangetic plain, uprooted themselves and went out to Trinidad as indentured laborers. Trinidad was about as far away from India as it was possible to get: it was literally on the other side of the earth. For me, the period that covers my family's migration from Uttar Pradesh and their arrival in Trinidad near the turn of the century possesses something of the aura of prehistory. It all seems to have occurred such a long, long time ago; to belong to an infinitely remote, slightly unreal past. I see it, as it were, through the wrong end of a telescope.

Concerning my paternal grandparents, I was completely ignorant. My childhood was dominated by my mother's family. But what did I know of *them*? My maternal grandfather, who is rumored to have died on a ship that was taking him back to India, is a mythical figure. I cannot imagine him as an individual, a man of flesh and blood with a personality of his own. He is an abstraction . . . a name . . . a relationship ("your Nana") . . . the source, I was aware, of the family's Brahmanic pride. I recall—or believe I recall—a highly posed photograph taken in a studio of an unsmiling, moustachioed man attired in *dhoti* and *kurta*, caste mark pasted on his forehead, a chain of beads looped around his neck. Beside him stands the girl he married, my grandmother ("your Nanee"), someone I remember only as a blind old woman, confined to bed, swathed in flannel and smelling of bay rum.

A story or two survives about my grandfather. It is told how, when on the road to Benares, darkness fell and he lost his way. In this unhappy state he was discovered by a gang of *arkatia*—recruiters for the plantations overseas—who somehow tricked him away to the West Indies. The details are not clear; the episode refuses to come to life. That road to Benares, that pious young man lost in the dark—the scene, even now, retains its mystery, its inexplicability. I cannot make the connection between those events and my own existence. Linked with this dim prehistory was a rambling house in the Trinidad market town of Chaguanas. The house, whose facade was adorned with lions, was known as the Lion House. In my day it was a desolate, ghost-haunted place, inhabited by a couple of widowed aunts. I hardly ever went there. The house belonged to a dead, incomprehensible past.

My father, born in Trinidad, died when I was seven years old. The little I know of him—and it is very little—I have picked up subsequently. (So with him too, the connection with myself is not easy to make.) I was surprised to learn that he was intended for a pundit by his family; that for him English was an acquired language. However, my father did not become a pundit. He became a journalist. He wrote some short stories, reissued not long ago by my brother, V. S. Naipaul. The stories, exclusively about Indians, range over a period that stretches from the early years of this century to the late 1940s. The Indian Trinidad described in these stories (including those set in the later part of the period) is foreign to my experience. I approach them like a stranger. "A story like 'Panchayat,'" my brother writes in his introduction, "which reads like a pastoral romance, offers one side of the truth: the people in that story exist completely within a Hindu culture and recognise no other. The wronged wife does not take her husband to the alien law-courts; she calls a panchayat against him. The respected village elders assemble; the wife and the husband state their case without rancour; everyone is wise and dignified and acknowledges *dharma*, the Hindu right way, the way of piety, the old way. But Trinidad and not India is in the background. These people have been transported; old ways and old allegiances are being eroded fast. The setting, which is not described because it is taken for granted, is one of big estates, workers' barracks, huts."

Both these worlds—that of old India and that of the sugar estate—are unknown to me. I was a town boy: I grew up in Port of Spain. The sugar-cane fields of the Caroni plain and the villages of thatched mud huts where remnants of old India still lingered were far away. Our branch of the family, though extremely poor, had left peasanthood behind. Only at irregular intervals did I catch fleeting glimpses of that other life. There was my father's sister, a small, emaciated, deeply wrinkled woman (she always looked much older than she was), who, after a lifetime in Trinidad, could speak barely a word of English; there were the visits to my first and second cousins, still living in mud huts, still keeping a cow or two, still speaking Hindustani leavened with a kind of pidgin English, and returning from the fields at dusk carrying bundles of grass and firewood on their heads. To celebrate our visit, a chicken would be chased and killed; an impromptu meal prepared on the *choolha*—the fire pit. But these encounters were sentimental. They took place in a void. In an hour or two, after the chicken, after the swings in the hammock sewn together from pieces of jute sacking, we would go away, return to our city lives.

Life was rigidly divided into a public and a private sphere. These rarely met. The public sphere was school, the friends I made there, the democratic enthusiasms for cricket, soccer, the movies, Coca-Cola—all the anonymous assimilations of the colonial society. Black, brown and white could meet at these points without fear of mutual embarrassment, and on more or less equal terms. The private sphere was "home," my food taboos, my religion and its practices, my galaxy of cousins and aunts. This private sphere came into its own during the great religious occasions celebrated in my maternal uncle's house when, for a few days, the entire clan would be gathered together under one roof. Then we were "Indian" —Hindu and exclusive. The world outside was banished and we retreated into ourselves.

But in what sense could I be called an Indian—a Hindu? I could not speak a word of any Indian language—English was my "mother" tongue; I had been through none of the pre-

scribed Hindu *rites de passage* (an attempt was made to shave
my head in accordance with Brahmanic practice. I cannot
remember how old I was at the time, but I do remember quite
vividly the nightmarish dread the threatened performance of
the ritual roused in me. I recall a forested hillside rising above
me, the roar and splash of a nearby waterfall, garlands of
sweet-smelling marigolds, the already shorn hair of a cousin
strewn on the ground. I ran away. The attempt was never
repeated); I knew nothing of the religion of which I was a
nominal adherent; I had none of the neurotic sensibilities
associated with caste; my ancestral past was sunk in darkness
and incomprehension; the idea of India as the "motherland"
rarely presented itself to me—India was a remote, fabulous
place, a notional region of the earth lacking substance and
solidity. I never thought of our Indian community as part of
the worldwide diaspora of the Indian people—or "Asians,"
as we have since come to be called. Trinidad seemed a perfectly
natural place to be. I did not feel I was displaced or in exile.
I had no intimations of the queerness of it all. Now I look at
myself and our community with different eyes and I do see
the queerness. At the age of eighteen (which was when I left
Trinidad), I was haphazardly cobbled together from bits and
pieces taken from everywhere and anywhere. The ugly parallel
that suggests itself is one of those shantytown hovels built
up from whatever dross comes to hand—bits and pieces of
cardboard, tin, wood, corrugated iron. I had inherited no culture; no particular outlook; no particular form. Nor do I believe that the majority of my cousins—I refer to those of
roughly my own age—were any better off. When I left Trinidad at the age of eighteen I was nothing.

I am told there is an Indian revival of sorts in Trinidad; a
new self-awareness. I do not know about this: I have not

been to Trinidad for some years. But I wonder and worry about the nature of that revival, as I wonder and worry about the nature of all revivals. If it means a rediscovery and appreciation of the past, then that is all to the good. It is time our historical amnesia was ended. To rediscover a lost past is to rediscover an essential part of the self. Self-knowledge is healing. But if it is no more than an atavistic assertion of Indianness—the kind of atavism that turns young men into "pundits" and Negro-haters (and I have come across one or two examples)—then it signifies psychological disturbance, a despairing reaction to political and social stress. The past is indeed past. It cannot be revived as a living present. Our ancestors, when they crossed the black water (the *kala pani*), lost caste. Complex purification rituals would have had to be performed if they were to be cleansed of their defilement and restored to the fold. For us, their descendants, no rituals of purification will ever suffice. We are beyond restoration. There can never be any going back. I do not want to paint too dark a picture. One can also interpret what has happened to the Indian in the West Indies as a liberation. In Trinidad many Indians have achieved a material prosperity undreamed of by our ancestors. Their descendants have become businessmen, doctors, lawyers, engineers. The children of these businessmen, doctors, lawyers and engineers live in American-style houses in American-style suburbs; many, as a matter of course, will attend Canadian, British and American universities. Not long ago, my mother visited India for the first time. She paid a visit to our relatives and was distressed by what she saw—the low, dark huts, the undernourished bodies, the poor fields. "Why did you never send for us?" she was asked. Which is greater—the loss or the gain?

"You people who went out to the West Indies mixed up,"

an old Gujerati merchant I met in Mombasa said to me. "Here, we did not do that. We kept to ourselves. We held aloof." He spoke with pride. His family had been resident in Mombasa for over a hundred years, but they had remained of India. Africa had wrought no discernible changes in them. So it is with most East African "Asians": they have remained spiritually intact. *That* has been their great strength; and their fatal weakness. The old merchant's sense of caste, of community, of religion had remained unimpaired. He, though born in East Africa, had been educated in India, and it was to India he had gone to find a bride of the required purity. His sons and daughters had followed in his footsteps. I spent an evening in his household. Throughout, everyone spoke in Gujerati—except when the conversation was directed at me. From time to time I caught the merchant gazing at me with a mixture of bewilderment and disapproval. I was beyond the pale; I felt an utter stranger.

*

From a letter published in *The Nation*:

It is incredible that an Asian who has been living in Kenya for at least the last ten years and one who considers himself to be a citizen is ignorant of the true reasons why the Kenya African still has a deep resentment towards citizens of Asian origin. The Asian knows only too well what is required of him in order to qualify in the mind of the African as a true citizen, but the same Asian has so far refused to bow to reality and has instead preferred to live in the past. He not only remains the same bigot he was fifty years ago but has also become a master of pretence and a firm believer in the philosophy of eating his cake and having it . . . He must discard his bigotry and pretence. Then, and only then, should he demand that the African recognise him as an equal human being and citizen.

Not many days after I had arrived in Nairobi I was treated to a modest display of the African's "deep resentment" of the "Asian." (I dislike the term: it was coined as a convenient shorthand to lump together all the peoples of the subcontinent. However, since it is so firmly established in current usage, I shall not cavil. It has, in any case, acquired its own emotional charge. I accept it as a peculiarly East African political category—not as a universal badge of "identity.") An Asian friend came for me in his car, which he parked in the vicinity of a taxi stand. As I was stepping in, one of the taxi drivers, put out at being deprived of a fare, came rushing over and banged on the window. "That's the trouble with you Asians," he shouted. "You want to keep Africans poor. You don't want us to have anything. You want it all for yourselves."

I was a little shaken by this outburst. Ashraf, though, appeared unperturbed.

"You get accustomed to this sort of thing after a while," he observed. Ashraf was a lawyer; and he was prosperous: he owned a Mercedes as well as the more modest make of car in which he had come to meet me. "It's one of the reasons why I hardly ever use the Benz." He grinned wryly at me. "An Asian in a big car is asking for trouble. But if you look around, you'll see that most of our people still haven't got the message."

Ashraf was pessimistic about the future. "Citizen or non-citizen, it's all the same. One day we'll all have to pack up and leave—if, that is, they give us the chance to pack up." He talked about Uganda, of how traumatic an experience it had been for Asians everywhere. Uganda had totally destroyed any hope of a long-term future in Africa for the Asian. The local blacks regarded Amin as a hero. He had dared to do what they only dreamed of doing. "I live from day to day now. Life has become quite unreal." He glanced at me with sudden passion. "Do you know who have been the chief beneficiaries of all this? The whites! They are having a field day! They sit on the sidelines and watch with pleasure what's happening to us. What sticks in my throat is the injustice. We played as much part in building up this country as the whites. Yet here I am living from day to day like some damned refugee in the country of my birth. Don't you think I have a right to be bitter? We're being ground to pulp between black and white. We don't stand a chance."

He told me of his grandfather who had walked hundreds of miles through unmapped bush country, of the trade he had initiated in remote districts, of the fluency he had acquired in Masai and other native languages . . . it was only now, when it was too late, when the past was all but irrecoverable, that he had begun to recognize and appreciate the bravery, the pioneering heroism of his ancestor. "Something should have been written about people like him. There must be so many stories like that to be told." But his grandfather was dead; his story had died with him. That too was part of the injustice. Yet everyone knew of Grogan, notorious nigger-hater and sadist, whose cruelties had become part of the folklore of the country. Today he was regarded almost with affection—a "colorful" character. Everyone knew how, in a typical show of colonial bravura, he had walked from the Cape to Cairo.

His memory was still commemorated in the Nairobi suburb of Groganville. Karen Blixen too was remembered—in the suburb called simply Karen. The settler era glowed with romance. In contrast to this, the Asian contribution and achievement was consistently denigrated.

"We are nonpersons," Ashraf said. "They only see us when they want to hate us."

*

Whole books have been written about race relations in Kenya that neglect—except as a more or less complicating factor—the Asian population. The assumption has always been that it is only the relationship between black and white that really matters. The African was taught—and eventually came to believe—that his destiny was inextricably linked with the destiny of the white man. Marginality was thrust upon the Asian. Both black and white could regard him as an outsider intruding into *their* special relationship.

From the earliest days, the European has been, at best, indifferent to the fate of the Asian in Africa. The Asian represented dangerous competition: he too wanted a share in the spoils of Empire; he tended to have ideas above the station assigned to him and to make demands; he was seen as a possible source of political contamination among the "unspoiled" natives. The European could metamorphose, whenever it suited him, from depredator to the Platonic guardian of native "interests." He has always been quick to subscribe to the doctrine of Asian "exploitation" and "oppression." Indeed, he invented that doctrine.

Marginality invested the Asian with an odd kind of invisibility—"They only see us when they want to hate us." The

European settler had a highly developed image of himself as a bold pioneer opening up, with self-sacrificial courage and dedication, a savage continent to the ways of civilization. He saw himself and his actions in a heroic light. "So the settlers came," Elspeth Huxley wrote, "and found forest, bush and veld. The forest and bush had to be cleared, the veld improved and fenced; land had to be ploughed, game driven back, water supplies discovered and harnessed, buildings erected, and Africans taught the elements of farm skill; cattle and sheep imported and bred, roads made, transport organised, everything built up from nothing." The scale, the tone, is epic. It reads like a latter-day Creation myth. And that, of course, is what it is intended to be. But when Elspeth Huxley rode out on an oxcart to the wilderness at Thika, there already were Asian *dukas* established in the vicinity. The fact, however, excited neither comment nor wonder. The *duka*-wallahs constitute the most shadowy of presences. They are just *there* —like a natural outgrowth of the soil; they are excluded from the Creation myth.

Only very rarely did the Asian emerge from his anonymity, was his role as heroic pioneer lit up and highlighted. East Africa's Asians look to Winston Churchill, who visited the region during the early years of this century. He wrote of the Indian traders who ventured into bush country where no white man would go, of the Indian navvies who built the railroad from the coast to the interior, of the Indian financiers who risked their capital. Even now, this summary of their role still gives comfort. In the midst of tragedy, it soothes.

Nowadays, the Asian is portrayed as little more than a miserly *duka*-wallah who ceaselessly exploited and cheated innocent Africans. His past distorted, he is in the process of being eliminated from the present. With predictable and tiresome regularity one politician or another will rise to his feet in the Assembly and demand the liquidation of the surviving "little Bombays"—that is the ritual phrase to describe the lingering concentrations of Asian business enterprise. In a survey of Nairobi's industrial development published as a supplement by *The Nation* there was no mention made of Asian entrepreneurial and technical skills. A photograph of what the supplement referred to as a typical *duka* showed a smiling African standing behind the counter of a neat and well-stocked shop. "Kenyanization" imposes a new invisibility on the Asian.

If the Asian role in East Africa has been caricatured, so has the European role—but in a contrary direction. Nostalgic mists obscure the grimmer realities of the settler era. Spurious romanticism (shared by black and white—it is not uncommon to come across blacks who dilate enthusiastically on how "fascinating" it all was) is the order of the day. It was to be found in the English girl who confessed to me her regret that she had not been alive in the thirties.

"I can so easily see myself," she said, "married to one of those old-fashioned settler types, a real farmer's wife, living in a roomy bungalow somewhere near Eldoret. I could see myself making cakes and jams and jellies and hunting game on horseback. There was *style* in those days. And the Africans were a lot happier, too. Much happier than they are now."

("Sir," wrote Mrs. Denise Loveday to the editor of *The Times* of London, "To some of us who have lived in Rhodesia the saddest thing about the present debate is that neither the media nor the Western politicians can hear the voices of many thousands of Rhodesian blacks who beg their white friends and employers—often with tears—not to leave them to the 'mercy' of black rule.")

And what would have been the attitude of the imaginary farmer's wife toward her blacks? "I would have been very maternalistic to them," she replied. "That was how it was in the old days."

In an interview published in *Newsweek*, Sir Michael Blundell, one of the prominent pre-Uhuru settler politicians, could paint this rosy and extremely touching picture of the past and not be challenged by anyone. "In Kenya the Africans got to know the settlers and understand them. Settlers and Africans would help one another when they were ill . . . out of this grew the present very friendly atmosphere."

Is that the whole truth and nothing but the truth? Did whites and blacks really go rushing over to each other's sickbeds? (For a start, it would have meant making a special trip to one or another of the "native hospitals.") It is both sad and amusing to see Kenya's grim colonial past being reduced to such frivolous maunderings. The hymns spawned by the Mau Mau rebellion supply a corrective:

There is a great wailing in the land of the black people because of land hunger, you fools and wise people alike, is there any among you who is not aware of the overcrowding in our land.

You Europeans you are nothing but robbers, though you pretend you came to lead us. Go away, go away you Europeans, the years that are past have been more than enough for us . . .

Here is another:

Kenyatta will come with a sword for the harvest, and with a seat for our people when we receive self-government.

Because we are true servants of God we shall don the armour of war and tell the Europeans to get out.

. . . God will save us from those who oppress us and the Europeans will be driven out together with the "Black Europeans" . . .

Clearly, much water has flowed under the bridge. Not many people care to talk about Mau Mau: the uprising is regarded as a bad dream; its surviving veterans are neglected by the "black Europeans" who came to power on the backs of the rebels. For Kenya's (white) Europeans the good life goes on. In the Highlands you can still ride to hounds. "Where else in Black Africa," asks a BBC foreign correspondent, "does there exist anything like the Limuru Hunt?" The Limuru Hunt "is regarded as happily exotic . . . as a reflection in the African bush of English county pursuits . . . the point is: in Kenya, if you want to ride to hounds, you can. And such tolerance is not found everywhere in Africa." The two English expatriates he presents as his witnesses (whose "profitable hobby," incidentally, is breeding Alsatians) are no less enthusiastic about the lives they lead "in this independent black republic of which they are thriving citizens." The Africans who run the country are, they tell us, "superb gentlemen." They have "western ideals" and "western mannerisms." The browns do not enter into this happy picture. They are not even mentioned. It is as if they did not exist; had never existed. Almost instinctively, "racial harmony" is assumed to be an exclusively Black-and-White love affair.

High-spirited settlers may no longer ride their horses with

impunity into the lounge of the Norfolk Hotel and shoot the place up, but on Sunday afternoons, amid its white-walled, cane-chaired elegance, black men still move silently serving high tea to matrons who have brought their knitting along with them. In the spacious, servanted splendor of suburbs like Karen, their privacy guarded by thick hedges and malevolent Alsatians, expatriate life proceeds on its tranquil course. The voices of children are rarely heard in these enclaves: most are safely immured in schools "down South." On Saturday afternoons the old days come to life again at the Ngong racecourse. Kenya is constantly being held up to the stubborn Rhodesians as the major example of white safety, prosperity and happiness under black rule. How could it be otherwise? Think of all those quite superb gentlemen with their "western mannerisms" and "western ideals"! So friendly, so propitious is the present atmosphere that Sir Michael Blundell can confidently look forward to the day when blacks will be electing Europeans to represent them in Parliament. I have no doubt that he will be proved right: having a white M.P. can easily become a sort of status symbol. It is only on sacred occasions like Kenyatta Day that the tired old rhetoric of anticolonialism is dutifully declaimed by politicians in pinstripe suits. What is said on these occasions bears about as much relation to the actual state of affairs as the symbolic cotton-spinning performed by Indian politicians on Gandhi's birthday.

Meanwhile, the call goes out across the land for the liquidation of the "little Bombays." How is one to account for this paradox? Some Europeans are not at a loss for an answer. The potentially vengeful nature of the master–slave alliance is revealed in a letter written in response to an article I once wrote on the subject. The African, the writer says, ". . . had the *nous* to distinguish between his symbolic oppressor (the European) and his actual oppressor (the Indian). During my time in Kenya I was rarely anything but appalled by the treatment meted out by Indians to Africans—a monstrous mixture of exploitation, arrogance, disdain and blustering indifference." My correspondent, while not necessarily "condoning" what has happened since Uhuru, adds this rider: "It is hardly surprising that the African *relishes his chance to settle old scores.*"

Who banished the African from the Highlands and confined him in overcrowded reservations? Who denied him—and the Asian—an effective political voice? Whose despoliations were the direct cause of Mau Mau? On whose behalf was fought the brutal campaign of suppression that followed? I see nothing particularly "symbolic" in this dismal chronicle of settler civilization. I see only that the poacher has turned gamekeeper—with a vengeance.

The paradox remains; the answer will not—cannot—be found in rational explanations based on comparative degrees of "exploitation" and "oppression." The search must be directed elsewhere.

Dogs, I was assured by several people, *genuinely* dislike Africans. They will attack them on sight, and without apparent provocation. I was skeptical until I actually encountered such a dog—an Alsatian—who, indifferent to white and brown, reserved his ferocity for blacks. The owners swore that the animal had not been specially trained to do this. On the contrary—they had done their best to break him of the unpleasant habit: the dog was a grave social embarrassment when African friends came to the house; he had to be chained up and locked away. The animal's behavior was a profound mystery; an obsessive topic of conversation. How was it to be explained? How to account for his deep and irrational resentment of black men? Was it their smell? The timbre of their voices?

The dog's negrophobia betrays his settler provenance. His antipathy had been bred into him; it was part of his servile inheritance. He carried on his soul his creator's imprint: he had been programmed to dislike black men. The African antipathy toward the Asian possesses similar characteristics. It is part of his servile inheritance. His dislike bears the imprint of the settler—as does everything that he is and wants to be.

The European starts with an immense advantage: the African's longing to be absorbed, to lose himself in the white man's world. Out of this has been forged the black–white alliance in post-Uhuru Kenya; the forgiving and the forgetting. The African, lacking a vision of his own autonomous manhood, is vulnerable to every flattery. Between oppressor and oppressed, master and slave, there exist profound psychological bonds. (Never come between a man and his slave: the slave will surely kill *you* first!) Beyond all else, the slave yearns to be like the master; he craves his acceptance and recognition. His hatred, so full of cruelty, is often no more than a perverted adoration turned inside out. It is because of this yearning for the oppressor that slaves are never genuine rebels: the political evolution of Jomo Kenyatta furnishes ample evidence of that, as do the European M.P.s predicted by Sir Michael. The slave is a born conservative.

*

"The people who went out to the West Indies mixed up," the old Gujerati merchant had said to me. "Here we did not do that. We kept to ourselves. We held aloof."

The Asian failure in East Africa has also to be seen as a failure from within. Alberto Moravia, in his collection of African sketches (*Which Tribe Do You Belong To?*) has this to say about the Asian: "Indians and Africans. They have no social contact, they do not eat together, they do not inter-marry. Indians are racists, not of the present day but from thousands of years back; not individually and by chance, but on the basis of a centuries-old system; for that reason it is not difficult to imagine what they think of the Africans. As for the latter, their attitude is complex. Nothing could be more characteristic of this complexity than the verdict on the rich Indians given by an extremely poor, ragged African. 'They are not intelligent.' From which there emerges, not so much a political or class resentment, as a difference in the conception of life, in vision of the world."

The familiar charge of racism is misleading. Certainly, it ought not to be confounded with the European variety. The European's racism evolved out of his *contact* with the Afri-can. It was the settler's varied relationships with the African —dispossessor to dispossessed, civilized to uncivilized, guard-ian to ward—that ultimately determined his vision of himself and his work in Africa. In the process he became a White Man, a Bwana, the Heroic Creator of Order out of Chaos. The Indian in East Africa brought India with him and kept it inviolate. He never saw himself as a Brown Bwana com-peting for influence with the White Bwana. Perhaps if he had, his destiny might have taken a different twist.

As it was, he was little more than a tightly wrapped bundle of caste and group loyalties. He rarely raised his head and looked beyond the constricting boundaries of his inheritance. A Patel remained a Patel. A Goan remained a Goan. An Ismaili remained an Ismaili. A Sikh remained a Sikh. Each

looked after his own. It goes virtually without saying that
Hindu and Muslim would neither eat together nor sleep together. But, then, neither would Hindu and Hindu if they
belonged to incompatible castes or communities. It is wrong,
therefore, to think of the East African Asian in monolithic
terms. In East Africa as in India, a Patel is a Patel before he
is anything else. (There used to be a cricket team in Kenya
made up exclusively of Patels.) The caste-bound Indian is
not so much a "racist" as a "communalist." His range of vision
is severely restricted. Racism in its developed European sense
is beyond his ken; he is not capable of it. He sees only what
he has been trained to see, what he wants to see. All else lies
shrouded in darkness. Unlike the European, the Indian in
Africa did not evolve a picture of himself in keeping with his
changed circumstances. He reacted neither to the land nor to
the people among whom he lived. The African had no place
within the restricted confines of his tiny universe. There was
no room for him. He was a face across the counter of the
duka and nothing more. Out of that void of nonreaction arose
the Asian tragedy. He failed not because of what he did but
because of what he failed to do.

Typically, it took the European eye of Winston Churchill
(in *My African Journey*) to see the Asian achievement for
what it was; to point up the heroism—even the romance—of
the Asians' activities in East Africa. The traders and bankers
and navvies about whom he wrote would never have per-
ceived the larger significance of their labors. They would
never have thought of themselves as "pioneers" opening up a
continent. In their peculiar Indian way, they would have
been myopically chained to their particular vocations, co-
cooned in the claustrophobic world of caste and community

loyalty, and hence utterly incapable of the Churchillian vision. Few people are more prosaic than the East African *bania* (merchant) and have so fractional a perception of the world. Other men—and they have been few and far between —have had to sing on their behalf. But the European knew— and still knows—how to sing his own songs. More importantly, he knows what kind of songs he must sing. This near-total absence of imagination has played no small part in the downfall of the East African Asian. It has led to his losing his case by default; to his pathetic reliance on his British passport; to the lies and caricatures that now imprison him. A people without vision must inevitably perish. The Asians, blind at the beginning and blind to the point of idiocy at the end ("We are very Western," they tell you in their lilting Gujerati accents; "we like opera." "Maybe my children will marry English," a Patel told me. "We have no objections to such a thing. We will learn to go to pubs and drink beer . . ."), are doomed to further suffering and disillusionment. And not only in Africa.

While they can, the wealthier ones (many hooked into the web of post-Uhuru corruptions) stick around, living out their unreal lives. "Their wallets are their passports," a Goan civil servant complained to me. "They can go anytime they want to. But where can a man on twenty-five hundred shillings a month go to? Who wants him?" Although a citizen from the earliest days, he had no real hopes of promotion beyond the middle grades of the Civil Service. "I am trapped. This place is like a prison to me now. I can see no future."

For him and others like him—the poor, the semiskilled, the semiliterate—there is indeed no future. A slow but inexorable dereliction lies in wait—the dereliction of gradual submergence, of disappearance without trace into the land. It has happened in Jamaica; it will happen in Kenya. In time Africa will close over their heads and they will be drowned in it.

*

Toward dusk on Sundays it seems that the entire Asian population of Mombasa gathers on the seafront to take the air. The people come, young and old, to parade, to court, to gossip, or merely to sit in quiet groups and stare at the ocean. It is, to the outsider, a strange, oddly somber spectacle. The atmosphere is elegiac. I observed a similar phenomenon in Dar es Salaam, where the Asians drive out to Oyster Bay, a suburban beach, at lunchtime on Sundays. (The ritual cannot be performed at dusk because in Tanzania private motoring is banned from two o'clock on Sunday afternoons until six o'clock on Monday mornings.) "I suppose they come to commune with Mother India," an English acquaintance said to me. The explanation is romantic, and for all I know, it may be the true one.

But whatever its meaning, in Mombasa, at any rate, these clannish get-togethers are a source of irritation. I can see why. The Asians, their cars choking the narrow road that winds along the seafront, become conspicuous in terms of both number and material well-being. Given the fragility of their situation, these gatherings indicate a certain insensitivity to public opinion. They betray lacunae in the instinct for self-preservation. That is bad politics: one would expect them to behave with greater circumspection. However, these gatherings have another, even deadlier aspect. It is this: they exclude. They symbolize the impenetrability, the hermeticism of the Asian world. This inaccessibility feeds the African's "deep resentment." The Asian is irreducibly foreign; irreducibly alien. The African will always be an outsider. He can never penetrate that dense jungle of caste and blood-bound loyalties.

The European world is altogether different. It offers him if not the substance, at least the illusion of assimilation. He can consider himself to be and, up to a point, actually *be* Europeanized. The African, if he wishes to, can dress like a European, talk like a European, affect European ideas, gain entry to European clubs. He can cultivate Western mannerisms and Western ideals to his heart's content. He can never be Asianized in the same way. The Asian is the eternal "other." Consequently, the African demands his destruction —often expressed as a demand for his "integration." It is not accidental that the sexual inaccessibility of Asian women excites so much rancor. Asian integration has to be physical, to be literal. Nothing else will do. A policy of official rape was adopted in Zanzibar after the revolution there in 1964: Arab and Persian girls were abducted and forcibly married to the Zanzibari leaders.

"The Asian knows only too well what is required of him in order to qualify in the mind of the African as a true citizen . . ."

He must disappear into the land. He must cease to exist.

As I write this, the Asian whore I met in Mombasa springs to mind. "I would like to get far, far away from here," she said. "But where can I go? Who would give *me* a visa?" She had been married to a Ugandan half-caste. Her parents had disapproved of the match and disowned her. Not long after Amin came to power, her husband had been killed, and she— now stateless—had fled across the border to Kenya with her

child. Denied a work permit by the Kenyan authorities, she
had taken to prostitution.

"Africans are my people now," she said. "I live with them.
I eat with them. I sleep with them. I do not care for my own
tribe any more."

But I remember how, quite unexpectedly, she had reached
up and touched my hair and how, for a fleeting instant, as if
some nagging memory stirred within her, she had gazed at
me with the dumb sadness of someone dimly aware of an
irreparable, if indefinable, loss.

CHAPTER 4

A Highlands Adventure

I

THE TAXI that had been arranged for me by the District Commissioner was already more than half an hour late. However, I did not worry unduly. "You will get royal treatment," my friend's wife had assured me. "Remember, it's the D.C. himself who fixed it up for you. If anything goes wrong and *he* makes a complaint, you can be sure that somebody somewhere will be out of a job. Just one word from *him* and . . ." She smiled broadly and patted my wrist. "Don't you worry about a thing. You'll be treated like a king." She laughed pleasantly.

In Africa, power, whether exercised by a president for life or a petty bureaucrat, is a raw, untamed force. Men must bow before it or be crushed by it. The sophisticated civilities embedded in modern-sounding constitutions mean little. I thought now of my kingly powers and was comforted. One telephone call from me to the D.C. and somebody somewhere . . . The prospect, as the minutes ticked by and no taxi showed up, of throwing someone somewhere out of a job became increasingly alluring. Across the road from the wide, glass-louvered veranda of the hotel, red roofs showed through the dark green foliage of what I took to be mango trees. Farther on, I could see a colorless arm of the lake. A canoe, hugging the line of the shore, was being poled slowly along it. Beyond the lake, an olive-green plain faded into a rampart of bare hills. A wide-winged bird of prey soared through the blue depths of the sky. The iron silence of early afternoon had closed in over the land.

"Sit straight! Just look at the mess you are making! Your table manners really are a disgrace!"

The English voice, clear, precise, confident, traveled down the length of the veranda. Turning, I saw its source: a handsome, sun-browned woman most of whose face was hidden behind a pair of dark glasses. Sitting beside her were two neatly dressed children, a boy and a girl. A benignly smiling man—presumably Daddy—completed the party. They had come in about an hour earlier. They were a self-sufficient, entirely self-absorbed unit. Nothing, I felt, could pierce the protective bubble that seemed to enclose them. Whatever happened, they would be safe, they would be secure. I listened as the woman, oblivious of everything outside the bubble, fussed, scolded and corrected. I had been in Africa for only a few weeks, but already such echoes from Western suburban civilization rang strangely in my ears. These lessons in table manners were touching—and faintly ridiculous.

An automobile horn blared in jarring, semimusical notes. On the road below was an ancient Peugeot station wagon. Splashed across its rear window in garish lettering was the legend LOVE YOU BABY.

"Your taxi," a waiter said.

I looked at him doubtfully. "There must be some mistake," I said. "The D.C. himself arranged . . ."

He regarded me coldly. The horn blared again.

"Your taxi," he repeated.

Surely the D.C. could not have had a vehicle like this in mind. That thing standing outside the hotel was nothing but a *matatu*—a private taxi—of the lowest order. The *matatus* were notorious for their gross overloading, their mechanical defects, their unlicensed drivers. Every year scores of people were killed by *matatus*. Surely . . . Once again the horn blared. The driver screeched impatiently from the roadway. I gathered up my bags and hurried out of the hotel. My kingly status had melted away with alarming suddenness. High up in the blue sky the bird of prey soared with serene confidence.

*

The driver seized my bags and tossed them into the rear of the station wagon without ceremony. Raucous music raged from a cassette machine ensconced in the dashboard. By now I was able to recognize without difficulty the deadly harmonies of Zaïrean pop music, then enjoying a great vogue in Kenya.

"Did the D.C. arrange for this car? I think there might be some mistake . . ." It was not easy trying to make myself heard above the uproar.

The driver stared at me with sullen incomprehension.

"The D.C.," I shouted. "The *District Commissioner*. Are you sure this was the car he arranged for? Are you sure that I am the person you were meant to collect?"

He continued to stare at me, sullenness turning to irritation. Finally, he shrugged, got into his seat and slammed the door. It was an ultimatum.

"Can't you speak English?" I shouted.

He started the engine. I got in. He indicated—was it meant as a punishment?—that I should sit in the back row. I climbed over the middle seat and huddled despairingly against a window.

Africans tend to drive either dangerously fast—or dangerously slowly. This one drove dangerously fast, horn ceaselessly sounding; and, all the while, the Zaïrean music poured forth at top volume. Driving in Africa is high adventure. It is impossible to tell what your driver or the driver of the car ahead—or behind—will suddenly decide to do: for no apparent reason, any or all of these might take it into their heads to switch lanes; or stop without warning in the middle of the road to have a chat with a friend; or abruptly accelerate and overtake in an inside lane or on a blind corner or steep rise. (Pedestrians are also unpredictable. Without even a glance to right or left, they will, with utmost calmness, begin walking across the road.) The roadsides of East Africa are littered with the rusting remains of cars, buses and trucks.

We drove to the bus station, which was crowded, dirty, noisy and hot. Crammed, listing buses moved in and out, their exhausts spewing clouds of smoke. My driver moved energetically among the throng touting for custom. A young girl with a baby settled beside me; the place next to her was taken by a man in bright yellow trousers carrying an enormous transistor radio—the type of transistor radio one sees only in the underdeveloped world. Gradually the middle row of the taxi filled up. A fat, voluble woman took possession of the seat beside the driver. Pumpkins, bags of grain, live poultry, a mattress were stowed away on the roof and behind the back seat. Already we had exceeded the legal quota by two, but the driver continued to tout for more passengers. The middle row emptied; the seat was pushed forward. I watched with alarm as, somehow, a woman managed to squeeze herself in next to the man in yellow trousers. That meant there were nine of us. Another passenger was found for the middle row. Ten. A slim girl joined the fat woman sitting up front. Eleven. The middle row emptied again. A barefooted boy in short khaki trousers and a green shirt appeared out of nowhere. Without a word or even a glance at me, he placed himself on my lap. I was too stunned to protest. That had made it twelve. When next I looked, a third passenger had been able to insinuate himself up front. Thirteen—or fourteen if the baby was included. I examined the boy who sat very still and tranquil on my lap. He was very black, with the bloom of grape on his black skin. The man in the yellow trousers began tuning up his transistor radio; the Zaïrean music raged unabated from the dashboard. Somewhere a hen fluttered and squawked, sending up a flurry of down. I could hardly breathe.

"Look here," I shouted when the driver reappeared. "What's this damned boy doing on my lap?"

The boy turned to look at me. His large, black eyes regarded me with a kind of bewildered wonder. I wilted under their scrutiny, embarrassed and a little ashamed of myself.

"You want to throw him out?" someone inquired from the middle row. There was accusation in the tone.

I was aware of the boy's eyes fixed on me. He was very still.

"You want to throw him out?"

"No . . . no . . ."

"Now we go," the driver said in an unexpected burst of English.

We lurched out of the bus sation, horn blaring, pedestrians scattering. I was on my way to the Highlands.

We plunged into the maze of dirt alleys dissecting the shanty colony that fringed the town. I say "alleys"—but that is an exaggeration: there was nothing to indicate that they were anything of the sort. Much of our course took us through what looked like people's backyards—and were, I suspect, exactly that. Startled goats, chickens and children fled before us. We splashed through pools of muddy water, inches away from doorways. The driver, hunched vengefully over the steering wheel, sounded his horn without cessation. This was not meant as a warning to the unwary: it was a joyous proclamation of his daredevilry. More than once the car, in negotiating the deeper pools of water, threatened to become bogged down in the mire. No one, however, seemed in the least worried. On the contrary. They were enjoying themselves, laughing and waving at the astonished people who watched from their hovels. I tried not to think of the small item in that morning's paper which had quietly reported the *matatu* crash in which fifteen people had been seriously injured.

We arrived, finally, on the tarmac road. This, if anything, made matters worse. The Peugeot lurched and shuddered as the driver put his foot down on the accelerator. Each car we passed raised a cheer from my fellow passengers. I closed my eyes as, tires screeching, we took a blind corner, swerving across into the right-hand lane. This too raised a cheer. Did death mean nothing to them? They had slipped beyond my imaginative reach. The driver, wedged between the angle of the door and the seat, could hardly be bothered to glance at the road ahead. Frequently, he would remove both his hands from the steering wheel, the better to emphasize some point to the fat lady sitting next to him, with whom he was deep in conversation. Out of the corner of my eye I caught a fleeting glimpse of a chicken plummeting past the window. A terrific commotion ensued. We stopped, and a search party was organized. The chicken was found, alive but stunned, and restored to its place on the roof rack.

We were in sugar-cane country. To our right, the level fields stretched away to the horizon. On our left rose the blue serrated wall of the Nandi Hills, drifts of emerald-green cultivation washing up the lower slopes. We turned into the hills, leaving the sugar cane behind. The engine labored; the passengers lost their ebullience as we were reduced to a crawl up the steep gradients. I breathed more easily. At the bottom of a rock-strewn gorge lay the rusting, twisted skeleton of a truck. *Memento mori.* The passengers stared somberly at it: their sanity had been temporarily restored. As we climbed, the sky became grayer, the air cooled. The boy sat motionless on my lap; the baby slept, its fist buried in its milk-stained mouth. Ridge upon blue ridge extended about us like the waves of a petrified sea. Here and there were patches of corn. A light drizzle began to fall. The land flattened, and the petrified sea was lost from view.

We halted at the bus station of a small township. Here I would have to find another taxi for the onward journey; from this point on I would no longer be under the D.C.'s protection. Drivers descended on me from all directions, grabbing my arms, struggling to loosen my hold on my luggage, pulling and pushing me toward their cars.

"Front seat," I said. "I want a front seat. And *no* sharing."

"I give you front seat. Five shillings extra."

"All right. But no sharing."

"No sharing . . . no sharing."

I was guided toward a battered Peugeot.

"Remember—no sharing."

"No sharing . . . no sharing."

The driver, a wild-looking man—he had a woolly, tangled mop of hair, and his cheeks were deeply scored by ritual scarring—went away to tout for more customers. The taxi was as battered within as it was without: the door did not close properly; the window glass could not be rolled down because the lever was broken; the stuffing was coming out of the seats; the uncarpeted metal floor, tacky with dust and grease, looked as if it had been sprayed by a burst of machine-gun fire; the needle of the speedometer was missing. The car filled up with passengers. When the legal quota of seven passengers was reached, we set off. However, I was not at all convinced that this was due to the driver's virtuous disposition. My suspicions were confirmed when, on nearing the outskirts of the town, we were flagged down by a group of three people standing by the roadside and he stopped without the slightest hesitation.

Even from a distance, the figures composing the little group had seemed disturbingly familiar. And so they were. There, happy smiles lighting up their faces, were the man in yellow trousers, the girl with the baby and the boy who had sat on my lap. The middle row dutifully emptied. Room was made at the rear for the girl with the baby. The man in the yellow trousers squeezed himself into the middle seat. While the boy, inscrutable as ever, climbed over and placed himself on my lap.

I looked at the driver.

"Him small boy," he said. "Very small boy. Take up very little room." He held his palms parallel and close together.

"I'm paying five shillings extra for this seat."

He leaned over, thrust open the door on my side and ordered the boy out. The boy slid out and stood on the road.

An acrimonious babble erupted behind me. The driver shrugged, pointed at me and looked aggrieved.

"What's happening? What are they saying?"

"They saying you are selfish Asian," the driver said.

"Oh, God . . ."

"They say you have hard heart throwing small boy out of car."

"I didn't throw him out. You did."

"They say all Asians are same. They say African never do a thing like that. Not to small boy." The driver was enjoying himself.

I stared at the boy. He returned a blank, patient look. I opened the door. He entered and, making himself as narrow as possible, insinuated himself into the space between the driver and me.

The driver smiled broadly. He slammed the door shut. The engine wheezed and protested as we moved off. However, it took some time for the babble to die down.

The sky was lowering, a brooding presence clamped down on this high, rolling plateau. On this dank, rainy afternoon, the scene was northern, not equatorial. Dense patches of black woodland emphasized the resemblance. Sometimes the undulations would form themselves into a gentle swell of hills. Once, as in a dream, I saw a herd of giraffes. I looked at this land, so favored, so inviting to human effort; and yet, for millennia, nothing had happened. "So the settlers came, and found forest, bush and veld . . ." The primal acts of creation had to await the founding of the settler kingdom in the latter half of the nineteenth century.

The settler did, in a way, create the Highlands out of nothing. He was the first to see these upland regions for what they might be, to provide a name for—and by naming, to give form and substance to—a hitherto brute geography. The vision was entirely his. He conjured up the Highlands out of the African void and imprinted upon them his own image. That imprint persists. With the pride of creation there went, naturally enough, the pride of possession. The latter could go deeper than the simple sense of ownership and physical supremacy. "Up in this high air you breathe easily," wrote Karen Blixen, "drawing in a vital assurance and lightness of heart. In the highlands you woke up in the morning and thought: Here I am, where I ought to be."

The emptiness remains. Even today, on a drive, say, from Kitale, in the northeastern corner of the Highlands, to Nakuru, in the Great Rift Valley, the traveler, who, to begin with, might marvel at the lightness and purity of the Highland air and the spacious sweep of the landscape, is afflicted by a creeping oppression. What is its cause? It lies in the emptiness of the land; the absence of man. His works are no more than a veneer on its surface. The atmosphere of desolation is increased rather than diminished by the sudden appearance, on the slope of a hill, of a village of miserable huts, the blue smoke of cooking fires rising about the thatched roofs: a fragile human presence swallowed up in the immensity of light and space.

Ominous noises were coming from the engine. The driver frowned worriedly as we labored up a steepish slope. We

managed, I do not know how, to make the top of the rise.
It was a Pyrrhic triumph: as we were going down the other
side, clouds of acrid smoke suddenly poured into the car
from the region of the dashboard. The boy stared at me with
wild surmise.

"We are going to explode," I said. "Boom!"

I had still, I regret to say, not been able to forgive him.

"Stop! Stop!" The man in the yellow trousers panicked.
Grabbing the driver's shoulders, he began to shake him.

We stopped. We got out. We stared at the smoking car.

The man in the yellow trousers (clutching his transistor
radio to his chest) and the girl with the baby retreated to a
safe distance. They stared at the car as if it were a dangerous
animal whose next move no one could predict.

With a brave display of *savoir faire*, the driver opened up
the hood and peered inside. He came away wiping the back
of his neck with a handkerchief.

"What's wrong?"

"Overheat," he said.

"What are we going to do?"

"We wait," he said. "Engine cool—we push—we go
again."

I did not share his optimism. "How do you know it will
ever go again?"

"I know."

All about us were fields of corn, tinting the land olive-red.
There was neither house nor hut in sight, and the road was
empty of traffic. The keen air penetrated my thin sweater. I
shivered. Another twenty miles lay between us and N———.

We broke down twice more—the same horrible noises from
the engine followed by the same eruption of smoke followed

by the same panic-stricken cries from the man in the yellow
trousers. The driver, though, was gallant at the end: he waived
the extra five shillings I was supposed to pay.

II

The big signboard outside the hotel proclaimed that it was up
for auction by judicial order. It seemed an unpromising beginning. But there was no other hotel worth the name in the
town. I stood, luggage in hand, reading the notice about the
forthcoming auction. There were few people about. The
shutters were down in the shabby arcaded bazaar. Across the
road from the hotel was the wooden bungalow housing the
police station. A policeman leaned against the veranda rail,
smoking a cigarette. Pickup trucks and tractors rattled along
the streets which were stained with a powder of red dust.
N——— was a town with the look and feel of the frontier
stamped upon it.

I entered the lobby of the hotel. At one end, in a roomy
brick fireplace, a log fire blazed. A group of African laborers
was gathered in front of it. Beer bottles cluttered the table
around which they sat. A ragged bellboy relieved me of my
luggage. I followed him down a dark, linoleum-covered passage reeking with the suffocating smells of smoldering hair.
I soon traced its source: one of the rooms leading off the passage was used as a hairdressing salon. But the door was closed,
and I could only guess at the pyromaniacal techniques being
pursued behind it.

After dinner, I sat down within striking distance of the big
fire. The African laborers had gone, leaving behind a wrack

of beer bottles. I was the only person using the room. The big, high-ceilinged room had obviously seen better days. Faded curtains of red velvet, stiffened with dust and tobacco smoke, were haphazardly drawn across the windows. The scattered leather sofas and armchairs were in a state of advanced decay. Almost all of them were missing their right-hand armrests. Ash, cigarette butts, the moldering remains of sandwiches of various types were strewn across the uncarpeted concrete floor. Waiters in tattered tunics lurked with aimless menace in shadowed alcoves, clutching little metal trays to their chests.

I had come to this town on impulse; in pursuit of the slenderest of leads. Some days previously, a Kenyan acquaintance had told me the story of a young woman, a beautician by training, who had subsequently gone into public relations and then, quite suddenly, had turned her back on the glamour and ease of town life to become a farmer near the town of N———. "It was an amazing thing. Imagine a lady of the highest fashion—and I mean the *highest* fashion—who had spent nearly all her life in Nairobi deciding to do such a thing. Everybody thought she was crazy. Everybody said that she would be back in Nairobi within a month."

"And was she?"

"That is perhaps the most amazing thing of all. Alberta's been a roaring success as a farmer. The banks let her have everything she wanted. Alberta is not the sort of person to do things by halves."

"The banks let her have *everything* she wanted even though she knew nothing about farming?"

"*Everything*. And Alberta's been a roaring success. I am told everybody in N——— keeps singing her praises. She's the toast of the town. Even the whites have respect for her. You know, the colonialists used to say that we Africans would never make good farmers, that we would ruin the land. If you ever meet Alberta, you will be able to see for yourself what lies those were."

"I think I would like to meet Alberta," I said. "How do I set about doing that?"

"Oh, that's no problem. You just go to N——— and ask anybody. She's famous."

"Is that all I have to do?"

"That's all. She's famous. A *personality*. Everybody knows Alberta."

So, throwing caution to the winds (I knew my informant was a little prone to over-enthusiasm), I had come to N——— in search of a black beautician turned farmer.

*

"Alberta? Alberta who?" The reception clerk frowned at me.

"She owns a farm near here. A young woman. Very fashionable."

The eyes lit up. "Ah—you must be meaning Mrs. Wamalwa—the one who got divorced recently."

I responded cautiously. I had no desire to get hold of the wrong woman, especially one recently divorced.

"Mrs. Wamalwa is your lady," the clerk insisted. "She is just as you say—very fashionable. In fact, you just missed her. She was in the hairdressing salon."

I wondered if hers were the fiery tresses I had smelled earlier.

"I used to know her husband," the clerk said. "He often came here. I heard she gave him hell."

"Oh?"

"She kicked him out. Took all his money and kicked him out. That's what they say." He nodded somberly, lowering his voice. "They say she is a very *liberated* woman." He giggled. "Are you a friend of hers?"

"No . . . no . . ."

He tapped my wrist. "Go into the bar and ask there. Somebody there might be able to help you."

It was with a deepening sense of absurdity that I headed toward the bar.

There were about a dozen people gathered there. A group of men, perched on stools, sat around the counter arguing loudly. Nearby, listening to the discussion but remaining aloof from it, stood a solitary, middle-aged white man. He leaned straight-backed against the wall, nursing a glass of gin, fixing on the disputants a blank, blue stare. Three women in short, low-slung dresses and with shawls draped about their glistening black shoulders occupied the only armchairs. As if in calculated keeping with the tone of the establishment, they had a somewhat faded and dilapidated air. At the far end of the tobacco-colored room a noisy game of darts was being played. The girls and the white man followed my entrance without change of expression.

The barman seemed the obvious person to approach. I did so at the first convenient opportunity.

"Why, may I ask, do you want to get in touch with Alberta?"

I did not realize that I was being overheard: it was one of the group congregated about the bar who had spoken. I

turned toward the speaker, a slim young man with the beginnings of a beard, wearing bleached, skin-tight blue jeans, a
white sleeveless waistcoat and brown high-heeled leather
boots. A cowboy hat, thrust back to the perpendicular, completed the outfit. He ground his cigarette into the threadbare
carpet, slid off the stool and stood up, swaying a little as he
did so.

"Why do you want to get in touch with Alberta?"

"Do you know her?"

"I asked *you* a question."

Someone giggled. For one wild moment it occurred to me
that I might be speaking to her estranged husband. If what
the clerk had told me about Alberta was true, he was liable to
be an angry man. A very angry man. But then, I reflected, the
man confronting me looked far too young for the role my
fears had assigned him. Anyway, there was more melodrama
than aggression in the pose he had taken up.

"I don't know her," I said, "but . . ."

"Then why do you want to meet her? Why do you want
to meet somebody you don't know?" He waved drunkenly,
nearly falling over as he did so. Realizing how unsteady he
was on his feet, he resumed his perch on the stool. His accent
veered disconcertingly between "English" and "American."
His last question had been delivered in the American mode.

I started to explain. However, he did not allow me to
finish.

"I don't recall seeing your face before. Where you from?"
(This combined both the modes.)

I told him.

"So you live in London." He squinted at me, readjusting his
hat. "What part of London?"

I told him.

"D'you know the Grove?"

"The Grove?"

"Ladbroke Grove. That's what the guys called it. The Grove."

"I know it reasonably well."

"I lived in the Grove for a while. Shared a flat with some guys. Damned nice place. D'you know the Portobello Road?"

I said I did.

"Fantastic. Mind-blowing. I was doing some television work with the B.B.C. at the time." The announcement was delivered with all the casualness of a trivial aside.

I tried to look suitably impressed. "What kind of work?"

"Mainly theatrical." He stared intently at his neat pink fingernails. "I'm an actor by profession."

"Liar!" The ex–British Army intonation was unmistakable; the vacant blue eyes, unflickering, were fixed on us. "You mustn't believe a word he tells you. They're all liars."

"Cool it, Jock."

"Bloody liar!"

The actor grinned. "Pay no attention. Alcohol has softened his brain. What's your name?"

I told him.

"Mine's Stephen."

We shook hands.

"Damned bloody liar! He's never seen a stage in his life. They're all bloody liars."

"Who's he?"

"He's the manager," Stephen said.

"The manager of what?"

"Of this hotel. That's why it's going bust. He drinks most of the booze himself."

Stephen raised his voice tauntingly. "Why don't you go

back home, Jock? If you hate us all so much, why don't you go back and leave us in peace?"

The manager did not react. He seemed not to have heard; to have forgotten about us. There was something cataleptic about his immobility.

Stephen took a book out of his pocket and handed it to me. It was a dog-eared copy of a Wole Soyinka play.

"Africa's Shakespeare," he said. "I'll be playing the leading role in this play in a few weeks' time."

"Congratulations."

"I'm also producing it, directing it and designing it. The fact is I'm the only real professional they've got around here."

"Still," I said, returning the book, "there can't be too much work in a town like this for someone like you. It seems a strange place to find a professional actor."

Stephen's eyes darkened with alcoholic gloom. In Kenya, he replied, no artist could hope to earn a living. To avoid starvation, he had become a farmer; he had been lucky enough to inherit some land from his father, on which he grew corn and sunflowers. "For someone like myself, someone with an artistic temperament, this is a very frustrating kind of life. I feel my talents going to waste here. They're all philistines here. I drink to drown my sorrows." He gulped a generous mouthful of beer. "My great ambition is to play Othello."

"Maybe you will one day."

"I don't mean *here*. I mean on the London stage."

"About Alberta . . ."

He waved the interruption away. "Let's talk about London. How's Oxford Street?"

"Fine."

"And Trafalgar Square?"

"Fine."

"I love London, you know. It's my spiritual home." He closed his eyes sleepily; he swayed dangerously, righting himself with a start.

A small, very drunk man with tousled hair lurched between us.

Stephen pushed away the interloper. "Go away, Noah. This gentleman and I are having a serious intellectual discussion."

Noah staggered off.

"Peasants . . . !" Stephen muttered. "Don't go away." Easing himself off the stool, he disappeared in the direction of the toilets.

A heavy hand descended on my shoulder; a beery breath enfolded me. "You're thinking I've got European blood. I know. I know what you are thinking." Noah wagged a finger in my face.

I examined him more closely and realized that, beneath the dirt, Noah was copper-complexioned; he was a half-caste, a man without tribe.

"I know what you are thinking. But don't be fooled, my friend. I am a Negro. Like Joe Louis. Like Muhammad Ali. Like George Foreman. They are all Negroes like me. I think Joe Louis had the same sort of complexion like me." Noah danced around me, punching the air with his clenched fists. "I don't want you to think that I have any European blood in me. I am a Negro. Like Joe Louis, like Muhammad Ali, like George Foreman." He brought his face close to mine. "Who are you? What are you after?" His finger wagged in my face. "Take care, my friend. I can be dangerous. Nobody makes a fool of Noah . . ."

I looked up with relief at the sound of Stephen's voice. Noah lurched away, looking full of menace.

"I want you to meet a good friend of mine," Stephen said. "He's someone you can exchange ideas with."

A man I had not noticed before lurked reluctantly in his wake. His nose, curiously truncated, resembled a pig's snout. His name was Tobias, and he was the headmaster of the local secondary school. "I don't want to meet anybody now," Tobias grumbled. He cast a longing glance toward the girls.

"You will find this gentleman most interesting to talk to," Stephen said.

Tobias glanced sourly at me.

"The trouble with Tobias," Stephen said, "is that he is sex-mad. Booze doesn't go to his head. It goes straight to his genitals."

Tobias smiled with wan pride.

"I would like to hear you two exchange ideas," Stephen said.

"Why can't we exchange ideas tomorrow?" Tobias was plaintive now.

But Stephen was not to be denied. "This gentleman might not be able to see you tomorrow, Tobias."

Tobias stared at me resentfully.

"Is he really a headmaster?" I asked.

Tobias, affronted by my skepticism, wrenched himself into a more dignified pose.

"Go on," Stephen urged, "exchange ideas." He looked at me. "Give us your ideas on education."

I suggested that it might be more fitting if Tobias were to give us *his* ideas on the subject.

"Damned good idea," Stephen said.

We both looked at Tobias. Noah, I observed, had taken up a crucifixion pose in front of the dart board.

Tobias fidgeted.

"You must have some ideas, Tobias," Stephen said. "What would you say is the purpose of education?"

"To educate," Tobias replied.

"And how do you set about doing that?" I asked.

"Good question! Damned good question!" Stephen clapped his hands enthusiastically.

Stephen appeared to be taking the charade seriously. He puzzled me.

But our exchange of ideas was short-lived. Noah was now shouting at the manager, dancing about him and waving his arms. "You white people have Amin on the brain. Why is that?"

"I don't have Amin on the brain," the manager said. "You have."

"Why are you always talking about him, then? You must admire him." Noah was the picture of alcoholic frenzy. "Everybody is afraid of Idi Amin. The whole world is afraid of him. He is like Joe Louis, George Foreman and Muhammad Ali rolled into one." Noah boxed the air. "When he's ready, he'll kick all the whites out of Africa. He'll drive them into the sea."

Noah went berserk. Uproar broke out as he started slapping everyone within reach. Glasses smashed; the girls screamed. A number of men, including Stephen and the manager, converged on him. He was overpowered and dragged out of the room. Tobias—I believe he was one of those slapped

—smiled ruefully. He walked out arm in arm with one of the girls. The barman began pulling down the shutters. Stephen and the manager returned.

"About Alberta . . ."

"I don't really know her as such," Stephen said. "Didn't I tell you?"

One of the girls tugged at Stephen's waistcoat.

"Coming straightaway, sugar-pie."

The other girl looked hopefully at me.

"You want her?" Stephen asked.

I declined the offer.

"We'll meet soon. I want to have some more intellectual talks with you." He disappeared through the door.

Only the manager, the unutilized girl and I were left.

"Savages. They're all bloody savages. Civilization doesn't go more than skin deep with them." He pinched and lifted the skin on his forearm. "*That* deep and no deeper." His face was dead white. "I married one of them. I *know*."

The girl rubbed her hand invitingly against his thigh.

"Scat!"

I went out.

*

Chairman Mao's death was splashed across the front page of *The Nation*. I tried to read the agency reports, but concentration was an effort. In this place the noise of the outside world was muffled. I put the newspaper aside. It was nearly ten o'clock and I was the only person having breakfast. At the far end of the dining room was a rostrum. A mural, depicting a number of modishly dressed African men and women dancing what I assumed to be the twist, provided a colorful, if somewhat dated, backdrop. The mural, I suppose, had been commissioned in the first flush of Africanization that followed Uhuru: a hotel like this would have been one of the bastions of settler supremacy.

My plans were in disarray. It seemed unlikely that I would ever meet the elusive Alberta Wamalwa; and I had no intention of walking about the streets of the town asking after her. I stood at the entrance to the hotel gazing out at the red streets, the clattering tractors and pickup trucks. Outside the blank, modernistic facade of the bank, two armed security guards leaned on their rifles. An olive-red sea of cultivation encircled the town. I thought I would take a stroll.

These Highland townships are charmless places, purely functional settlements. Bazaar, hotel, bank, police station, courthouse—they offer little more than the elementary building blocks of urban existence. The Highlands had attracted a breed of settler who sought to re-create in an African setting the kind of landed-gentry existence that was becoming increasingly unfeasible in crowded, industrialized Britain. "It was not the society that had thrown them out," Karen Blixen (the spokesman of the type and herself an aristocrat) wrote of two of her friends, "and not any place in the whole world either, but time had done it, they did not belong to their century . . . they were examples of atavism, and theirs was an earlier England, a world which no longer existed."

For such people, the Highlands provided an opportunity to reconstruct a type of existence ruined by creeping suburbia, labor unions and general elections. It stimulated elemental dreams of master and servant and wide, untrammeled acres. Primitive Africa invoked primitive dreams of overlordship. It was like going back to the beginning of the world: Africa was a clean slate on which anything could be written. Displaced and debased aristocratic longings could take root and flourish here. Everything lent itself to the fulfillment of this type of settler fantasy: the climate, the spaciousness, the beauty of the land, the people, the wild animals. The last two provided a kind of ready-made heraldry. In Karen Blixen's imagination, the implicit heraldry occasionally became literal: "In approaching we were a little lower than the carcass; the lion stood straight up over it, dark, and behind him the sky was now all aflame. *Lion Passant Or.*" Even today there is a tendency among the long-established white families—the remnants of the classic settler elite—to regard their Rhodesian kith and kin with condescension, as being of a generally inferior social and cultural standing. (Also, many white Rhodesians are not even English: they include many postwar Greek and Italian immigrants.) This attitude does not, of course, preclude a silent sympathy with their cause.

Not that Kenya itself was free of less desirable elements. Toward the end of her own time there, at the beginning of the 1930s, Karen Blixen was already becoming distressed by the new breed of settlers coming into the country. These were the true men of the age. They had no rarefied ideas about themselves, the country, or its people. ". . . The country had been the Happy Hunting Grounds," she lamented; "now it was slowly being turned into a business proposition."

Yet the aristocratic vision of the Highlands has shown remarkable staying power. It has survived white expulsion and black possession. Nostalgia clings to its rolling hills; the dreams of a would-be aristocracy lie buried close to the surface. It is amazing how many whites (even those who left long ago) still speak of it with a quasi-mystical assumption of a special "belonging."

"I live in Africa not because I want to be called *bwana* by black men. Nor do I live here simply because I happen to have been born in the country. I live here because it's so extraordinarily beautiful. The beauty of Africa gets into your bones . . . it becomes part of you. It's awfully difficult to explain . . ."

Beauty—the word rarely fails to crop up in conversation with the long-settled expatriate. But it is not an ordinary "beauty" that is being referred to; not a straightforward aesthetic response that is being described. It is a special form of perception, of yearning, that is almost an illness.

In 1963—the year after Uhuru—Alberto Moravia visited Kenya. In Nairobi he met an English girl who was soon to return to England for good with her family. "What you need to see," she said to Moravia, "is a free lion walking amongst the bushes on the plain; a free elephant standing still, lurking amongst the foliage of the forest; a free rhinoceros as it raises its black head above the yellow grass." Seven years after the launching of Sputnik, we are back in the primal heraldic world of Karen Blixen and her friends. When all else has been taken away, there remains the pure vision of noble man and noble beast. The Highlands have once again ceased to be a business proposition.

"I could not help picturing her," Moravia writes, ". . . in a foggy, gloomy Nordic winter . . . even there, her eyes would from time to time have a look of enchantment when instinctively, amongst the foul industrial murk, they sought the green outline of the hills of Africa, the sunlight on the plateau, and the small, black elegant figures of the Masai wandering over the pastures with their cattle."

The nostalgia, though alluring, is anything but *innocent*. A morbid melancholia pervades the passage. What Moravia is really describing is an act of arrogation, an assertion of implicit overlordship. The heraldic vision, growing out of a pre-sumption of a special relationship with the land and its creatures (human and animal), makes claims that go far deeper than those bred by vulgar economic and political con-siderations. When the eyes of the English girl seek "the green outline of the hills of Africa," a sense of ineradicable divine right is also being asserted. We, she is saying, are of the blood royal; you, who have come after us, are upstarts and usurpers. We alone, because we are what we are, can properly compre-hend the spirit of the place and be comprehended by it. This assertion of a mystical kinship with the land and its creatures achieves, not surprisingly, its most flagrant expression in the work of Baroness Blixen.

When her lover, Denys Finch-Hatton, was killed in a plane crash, he was brought to be buried, as he had previously indi-cated he would like to be, in the Ngong Hills not far from Nairobi. "As it [the body] was placed in the grave, the coun-try changed and became the setting for it, as still as itself, the hills stood up gravely, they knew and understood what we were doing in them . . . it was an action between them and him . . ." Nor was that all. Some time after she had left Africa she received reports of certain curious events ("the like of which I have never heard") that are supposed to have oc-curred at the burial site in the hills. The local Masai are alleged to have reported (reports apparently corroborated by more prosaic sources—Indian truck drivers) that on several occa-sions, at dawn and dusk, they had seen a lion and a lioness reposing on Finch-Hatton's grave. The Baroness's astonish-ment did not last long. "It was fit and decorous," she remarks, "that the lions should come to Denys's grave and make him an African monument . . . Lord Nelson himself, I have reflected, in Trafalgar Square, has his lions only made out of stone."

Primal Africa pays homage to the English nobleman. Displaced aristocratic yearning has achieved its apotheosis. Nowadays, when educated Africans pause to exclaim over the beauties of a Highland view, it is not easy to rid oneself of the suspicion that they are looking at it through ghostly settler eyes. They seem at such times to be struggling to re-create within themselves the perceptions of the people in whose footsteps they tread; to be asserting as much to themselves as to others that they are where they ought to be, that they are worthy inheritors.

*

"I hear you want to meet La Wamalwa," Elaine said.

"If she exists."

Elaine giggled. "La Wamalwa exists, all right. Once you meet her and her three cars and her two lorries and her two tractors and her two deep-freezes, you won't have any doubts about that." Elaine, wearing a frilly gym slip and holding a squash racket, was sitting on the counter of the bar, swinging her legs.

It was film night at the Club. The whites had retreated from the "upper" to the "lower" bar, surrendering possession of the former to the more adventurous black and brown townsfolk.

"Does she really have *two* deep-freezes?" It was Tricia, the magistrate's wife, who asked the question.

"So I've heard," Elaine said.

"What does she want with two deep-freezes?"

"Search me, darling."

"I believe the bank is threatening to take at least one of the cars back," the magistrate said. "Africans, as a rule, don't seem to understand that when banks lend you money, they expect something back in return. She's about to go bankrupt, by all accounts. Bye-bye motorcars and tractors and deep-freezes. Oh, well—easy come, easy go."

I expressed surprise, saying that I had come all this way because I had been told that Alberta was a highly successful farmer, the toast of N——— and the surrounding districts.

Viljoen, the Afrikaaner soil-conservation expert, laughed. "Who told you that?"

A friend of hers I met in Nairobi."

Viljoen laughed louder. "They say she used to be in P.R. before she took up farming, and you can take it from me that she remains one hell of a lot better at P.R. than she is at farming. When you meet her, she'll tell you what she tells every-body—that she became the first woman ever to finish the course on the East African Safari Rally. I know for a fact she dropped out after the first day. That sums her up."

"Is she really going bankrupt?"

Viljoen became serious. "Do you know anything about maize?"

"No."

"If you did, you wouldn't doubt it. Alberta reckons she's going to get about twenty-six bags an acre this year. She'll be lucky if she gets twenty. Have a good look at her maize. See how spindly and yellow it is."

"Her maize isn't her only problem," Konrad put in with quiet satisfaction. Konrad, a veterinarian, had been sent out from West Germany—part of that country's technical-assistance program. Earlier, I had listened to him shouting at the waiters in the Club restaurant. He had an extremely bad reputation among the black farmers: it was said that he confined his attentions to the animals owned by the *mzungus* and generally neglected his duties because of his passion for big-game hunting. "A couple of weeks ago, she lost half her herd of Friesians. She went out of her house one morning and there they were. Dead."

"How did she manage that?" Elaine asked.

"Poison," Konrad said.

"Who would do such a thing? And why?"

"She claims people have it in for her because they're jealous of her success."

Everyone roared with laughter.

The secretary of the Club—a retired British Army major—staggered into the bar. He began to complain about the laziness and insolence of his African staff. "Every time I give those boys an order, the buggers laugh in my face."

"You mustn't call them *boys* any more, Major," Elaine said. "That could get you into trouble."

"Damn it! They're boys and always will be boys as far as I am concerned."

"Boys will be boys." Elaine giggled.

I looked at the African barman. He was inscrutable. Alberta had temporarily been forgotten.

A crowd gathered about Tricia, who was sitting on a stool in the middle of the room. She was telling funny stories about "them." Collecting tales of native folly was one of her hobbies. She had, over the years, filled several scrapbooks with her anecdotes. These she sent Home, where, apparently, they gave rise to much hilarity. Her latest scrapbook lay open on her lap. One of her stories was about some "boys" who had planted corn on the courthouse lawn—Africans plant corn everywhere; another was about a case dealt with by her husband, involving the theft of lengths of drainage pipe.

"What on earth would they want lengths of drainage pipe *for*? That sort of acquisitiveness simply defeats me . . ." Elaine simulated extreme bewilderment. "Like that woman and her two deep-freezes . . ."

"We should run a competition," Viljoen suggested. "A bottle of Scotch for the person who can work out what a native would do with a piece of drainage pipe."

"He can shove it up his arse-hole." The major guffawed, showering spittle. He staggered out onto the lawn. Chill night air rushed in through the door, which he had left wide open. I listened to him being sick.

Europe in Africa—it had all gone terribly wrong.

III

The reception clerk called me over.

"I have good news for you."

"Have you?"

"Do you see that gray car over there?" He pointed toward the bank. Nearby was parked a mud-spattered Citroën. "That car belongs to Mrs. Wamalwa. She will be over here in a few minutes."

The clerk told me that she had come in earlier that morning and deposited her two daughters in the hairdressing salon. "Those little girls are as fashionable as their mother," he said. "Mrs. Wamalwa keeps them looking very nice."

I sat down in the decrepit lounge and waited. I stared at the mud-spattered car: it bespoke such confidence. Its owner had begun to assume a formidable aspect in my imagination. Alberta . . . the liberated woman who had recently discarded a husband; Alberta . . . the big, brave spender, owner of two deep-freezes; Alberta . . . the lady of high fashion; Alberta . . . the farmer doomed to bankruptcy. I was almost nervous at the prospect of meeting this prodigy.

A swirling current of sweet, heavy scent heralded her arrival; a slightly hoarse voice spoke behind me. I stood up.

"Sit down . . . sit down . . ." Alberta, carrying many parcels, slumped into a chair. She was a big, generously proportioned woman, probably in her mid-thirties. Her dark brown skin was smooth and taut and shining. A multitude of glistening ringlets formed an intricate pattern across her skull. Her long fingernails, painted scarlet, were studded with constellations of tiny blue and yellow stars. She was accompanied by her two daughters—plump girls, not quite in their teens, dressed in shorts and T-shirts. Their hair was done in exactly the same style as their mother's.

I introduced myself.

"You write like Robert Ruark?"

"I can't say. I haven't read any of his books."

Alberta raised her severely plucked eyebrows. I had shocked her. "But you must read him. He's a great writer. I have nearly all his books at home."

Throughout East Africa, among black and white and brown, the works of Robert Ruark are greatly admired.

Alberta lit a cigarette. She asked after our mutual acquaintance, and I passed on the messages of love with which I had been entrusted. Alberta, exhaling streams of smoke through her nose, listened abstractedly.

My eyes kept returning to her distractingly ornamented

fingernails. She dropped the remains of her cigarette on the floor and, stretching out a sandaled foot, crushed it beneath her heel. It was only then that I noticed her toenails were decorated in similar fashion to her fingernails.

She looked at her watch. "I must love you and leave you," she said, rising hastily. "I must go and see some insurance people. They're being very difficult. But I'm having a little lunch party tomorrow. Will you come?"

It was arranged that she would pick me up from the hotel at midday.

*

The rain was heavy now, sheeting the land, and the Citroën, skidding alarmingly on the slippery surface of the track, seemed to have acquired a life, a will of its own. Alberta peered into the watery curtain.

"Relax. You couldn't be in safer hands." She swerved to avoid a puddle. The car lurched sideways, toward a green blur of bush. Alberta yanked the steering wheel. Red mud spattered the windshield. "I love driving in weather like this. It's a real challenge." She glanced at me. "I entered the East African Rally last year—the toughest driving test in the world. Everyone laughed. They said a woman had no business being there. But I showed them."

"You won something . . ."

"I didn't actually win anything. But I finished the course. Naturally, that made people even more jealous of me."

We swerved to avoid another puddle—and all but careered off the track and into the bush. Red mud flowed like blood down the windshield and windows. The track was lost to view. Alberta slowed to a crawl in the thickening ooze.

"The people here get terribly jealous if they see you doing well. Just the other day, someone poisoned seventy-eight of my cows. Not one or two. Seventy-eight! They'll stop at nothing. Even my ex-husband was jealous of me."

Her husband, she said, had been a "very top" civil servant, earning an excellent salary. Unfortunately (as it turned out), her own progress in the world of public relations had been nothing less than meteoric. Her fame was such that firms began to compete with one another for her services. "I got to the point where they would tell me to name my salary. Can you imagine that?" Soon she was earning more than her husband. Alberta glanced at me. "And his salary wasn't peanuts, let me tell you. I'm not boasting. But facts are facts. What's the good of denying facts?"

A pair of headlights loomed through the watery curtain. A truck roared past, spewing up more mud.

"Mind you," she went on, "it didn't bother *me* that I was earning more than him. It didn't affect my estimation of him as a man. But it bothered him. Boy, how it bothered him!" She peered with grim concentration into the milky obscurity ahead of us. "He wanted me to give up work so that I could sit at home and have his babies. No way, I said. No way! I wasn't going to be a child-producing machine just to please him. No way!" She laughed. "He was a male-chauvinist pig." She slapped my arm playfully. "I bet you never expected to meet a women's liberationist in Darkest Africa. You thought we were all backward and behind the times, didn't you? Come on. Be honest!"

Our imminent arrival saved me from having to reply.

Alberta gestured expansively. "From now on, everything you see belongs to me."

The rain had lost much of its intensity: the clouds were higher and whiter; the green blur had receded; the outlines of trees were visible in the middle distance. The gentle rise and fall of the land, the mist, the verdancy—these were all of England. Only the acres of corn spoiled the illusion.

Alberta must have read my thoughts, for she said, "You could be in Kent or Sussex, couldn't you?" It was half statement, half appeal for confirmation. "The resemblance was one of the things that made me buy the estate."

We turned off the track and came to a stop before a white farmyard-style gate. Alberta sounded the horn impatiently. A man in yellow oilskins emerged from an outbuilding and hurriedly opened it. We drove at speed up a curving graveled drive, at the top of which was an extensive half-timbered bungalow: mock Mock Tudor. By the time I stepped out of the car, the drizzle had ceased. Patches of blue had appeared in the sky, and the dripping leaves of the trees and bushes surrounding the house had started to glisten with the first hints of returning sunlight. An elderly, uniformed maid opened the brass-studded front door.

I was led into a long and narrow sitting room, whose ceiling was crisscrossed by crooked, dark-stained beams. The furniture was imposing. High-backed, deep-sided armchairs of antique inspiration were ranged about a carpet of Turkish design. Accompanying each were a footstool covered in red velvet and a little nest of mahogany side tables. At the far end of the room a fire blazed in the depths of an elaborately carved fireplace. Above it hung a huge reproduction, in an ornate gilt frame, of Rubens's *Allegory on the Blessings of Peace*. At the other end of the room was a crescent-shaped bar with a Formica top. Stools were grouped convivially around it. Ornaments of brass and glass glimmered in recessed niches. Everything—even the fleshy Rubens in its gilt frame—looked new, untouched . . . virginally intimidating. Nevertheless, the most striking thing about the room was not its absurdity—the childishly random juxtaposition of conflicting styles—but the total absence of Africa. Most of the European and even Asian houses I had been into had had on display at least token African *objets d'art*.

The armchairs were unexpectedly hard; unexpectedly uncomfortable. Alberta stationed herself behind the bar. Her daughters appeared. They put on a record of "Afro-American" soul music and started to dance.

"You can have beer, gin, whisky, wine, sherry . . . you name it. I've got everything."

I said I would have some whisky.

"How would you like it? With soda? With water? On the rocks?"

"With soda."

She brought over a full bottle of White Horse and a soda siphon. "Now I'll go and change into something a little more comfortable."

I had the eerie sensation that I was taking part in a film. Alberta disappeared through a doorway veiled by a bead curtain. I drank whisky and watched the girls gyrate. Alberta reappeared. She had changed out of her skirt into slacks. She poured herself a sherry. I stared at her impeccably ornamented fingernails.

The doorbell chimed musically; the maid scuttled toward it. She conducted two men, one African, the other European, into the room.

"I hope you don't mind me bringing Bertie along," the African said.

"Of course I don't mind, Joe. Not in the slightest. It's a

pleasure, a real pleasure . . ." Alberta, hastening forward to shake Bertie's hand, radiated genuine delight.

Joe, short and rather unprepossessing, smiled jovially at me. A white cap adorned with two emblematic golf clubs crossed like a pair of swords sat rakishly on his unbarbered head. Bertie was dressed in typical European style: short trousers, short-sleeved shirt and knee-length socks. His shoes and legs were mud-stained.

Alberta turned to one of her dancing daughters. "Beatrice, be a darling and tell Cook to set another place at table."

Beatrice skipped out of the room.

Alberta beamed at Bertie. "It's a pleasure, a real pleasure . . ."

Bertie sank diffidently into an armchair, staring about the room.

Alberta offered drinks. Bertie said he would have a beer.

"Are you sure? I've got everything. Whisky, gin, wine, sherry . . ."

"Beer will be fine," Bertie said.

"Honestly?"

"Honestly." Bertie stared at the Rubens. "This is a nice place you have here . . ."

"Alberta has done wonders with this house. It's the sort of place you would find in Wiltshire." Joe moved familiarly about the room.

Alberta was deprecating. "I haven't finished with it as yet."

"It must have cost a lot of money to get it looking like this," Bertie said.

"Ten thousand pounds to date," Alberta said.

Bertie whistled.

"You should have seen the state it was in when I bought

it. The man who had owned the estate before me had gone bankrupt or something like that, and one day he just disappeared into the blue. What happened next doesn't bear thinking about. The locals moved in and divided it up among themselves . . . you know what *they* are like." Alberta widened her eyes conspiratorially at Bertie. "There must have been half a dozen families living here. Naked *totos* running about and peeing everywhere . . ."

Bertie assumed a shocked expression, but remained silent.

"It was *horrible*." Alberta, closing her eyes, shuddered. "Even now I get nightmares whenever I think about it. They used to make their cooking fires in this very room. The ceiling was black with soot and grease, huge chunks of plaster had fallen out . . . they'd even chopped up doors and furniture to make firewood."

"Vandalism," Joe said. He adjusted his golfing cap. "What is one to do with such people?"

Bertie gazed into the fire.

"People might think I'm extravagant spending so much money to restore this place," Alberta said, "but I feel that if you decide to do something you must do it properly. I don't believe in half measures. No way! That causes a lot of jealousy, believe you me."

Joe exclaimed. "Where did you pick this little gem up?" He was examining an old-fashioned windup phonograph.

"In London on my last trip. Isn't it quaint?"

"This prehistoric machine brings back my youth," Joe said. "I used to play Xavier Cugat records on a windup like this." He did a few dance steps. "I cut my teeth on Latin American dance music."

The uniformed maid announced that lunch was ready.

Alberta led the way down the corridor into the dining room. Here too the furniture was of mildly antique inspiration, but framed reproductions of works of the Impressionist masters and a William Morris wallpaper lent a more modern touch to this room. The dining table was spread with an array of cutlery of Scandinavian origin and slim-stemmed wineglasses. White damask napkins were coiled into silver-plated rings. A pair of red candles flamed from tall, pewter-colored candlesticks. Green velvet curtains were half-drawn across the French windows, which opened on to a well-tended lawn planted with rosebushes. When we had all been assigned our seats, Alberta tinkled a tiny bell. The maid entered with a tray of prawn-filled avocados.

"This is how it must have been in these houses in the old days," Joe said with sudden feeling. "It's why I like coming here."

Alberta acknowledged the compliment with a smile. Without thinking, I picked up my fork. Joe stayed my hand, nodding toward our hostess. Alberta, hands clasped, head lowered, eyes closed, was moving her lips soundlessly. She was saying Grace.

The possibility of wine was canvassed, but rejected on the ground of the lethargy it would induce: for no clear reason, we seemed determined to remain alert. We worked through our slightly unripe avocados. Alberta tinkled the bell. The maid reappeared, took away the used plates and returned with the main course: stewed chicken and rice.

Joe, it emerged, had political ambitions: he had run for the district of N——— in the last election—but had been heavily defeated—and was planning to offer himself again. He was confident that he would do much better the second time around.

I asked him what he would do if he won the election.

"I would clean the town up."

"Metaphorically or literally?"

"Literally. You must have noticed how filthy the streets are. In the old days people weren't allowed to throw their rubbish just anywhere. I would try to restore civic discipline."

Apart from restoring N——— to its former hygienic splendor, what else would he do?

He began to rail against the peasants who were infiltrating into the Highlands, enlarging on the concomitant dangers of soil erosion. His golfing cap had warned me not to expect too much radicalism. All the same, I was surprised by his relentless conservatism. The voice I listened to was that of reincarnated settlerdom. Soil erosion had been one of the great settler obsessions. The battle against it had become part and parcel of the battle for civilization, providing a powerful argument for the preservation of the status quo in the "White" Highlands. The Mau Mau had reacted by agitating against soil-conservation programs. Joe, in effect, had taken up the White Man's burden.

"Joe has a brilliant political future," Alberta said. "He has a double First in law from Cambridge. And he knows all the important people in Nairobi."

The maid brought in dessert. When we were done, Alberta tinkled the bell once more. We would, she said, be having our coffee in the music room: Beatrice and Emma were planning to give a little recital on the piano. The announcement was greeted with cries of anticipation.

Alberta led the way down the corridor to the music room. The two girls, dressed in skirts that swept the floor, were already installed at the piano.

"You're getting terribly Victorian in your old age, Alberta," Joe said.

Alberta tilted her head and smiled.

The presiding bust of Mozart on the piano seemed to intimate that something classical was in the offing. I was wrong: the girls proceeded to pound out "Lullaby of Broadway" in a spirited honky-tonk rendition. The applause at the end was fervent.

"Encore! Encore!" Joe danced about the room.

"Such a sense of rhythm," Bertie said.

The girls obligingly repeated the performance. They then sang a couple of Gilbert and Sullivan songs. The recital was brought to a close with "Chopsticks."

We "repaired"—as Joe put it—to the sitting room. Alberta offered a choice of liqueurs. She began to talk of the decline in educational standards that had occurred since Uhuru.

"There is not a single decent girls' boarding school left in this country now."

I asked what had caused the decline.

"The answer is simple: Africanization."

I did not know what to say: I appreciated that for people like her, Africanization had been a mixed blessing: on the one hand it had given her access to a farm in the White Highlands; on the other, it was ruining the education of her daughters.

"We have only one African teacher at Parklands," Beatrice said, speaking up in defense of her school.

"Not true," Emma replied. "There're two Africans teaching there now."

The girls started to squabble.

It was unnerving to listen to them talking about "Africans" as if they were referring to a species of humanity utterly distinct from themselves.

"I'm hoping to send Beatrice to a boarding school I heard of in Lincolnshire from next year," Alberta said. "If she likes it, Emma will follow. When all is said and done, you can't beat a real English education."

"Those cold baths build character," Joe said.

"Won't that cost a small fortune?" Bertie was looking bemused again.

Alberta laughed. "I'm looking around for a rich man to marry. I'm being quite serious. The man I marry next must be richer than me. I could never have any respect for a man who has less money than I have. It might sound harsh—but that's the way it is with me."

I looked up at her in some surprise. The statement did not square with her earlier declaration when we were driving through the rainstorm. Then she had said, and with equal seriousness, that her estimation of a man was not related to his earning power. With her, one sentiment did not necessarily connect with another; one moment did not necessarily connect with another. This was not because she deliberately set out to deceive: Alberta, I felt, could not help the contradictions with which she was riddled. She was able to combine the peasant belief in her neighbors' jealousy and their use of poison against her cows with "Victorian" sophistication. She wanted, as her hairstyle indicated, to be proudly African and at the same time, as the skin-lightening creams in her bedroom indicated, to abolish Africa. She was harsh and cynical about the husband she had dismissed and pathetically pleased to entertain Bertie in her house. So, like nearly all the rest—

like Andrew, like the student of literature who did not read
books, like Stephen with his keenness to "exchange ideas,"
like Joe with his golfing cap and rigid settler politics—she
would suddenly fade out of focus, slip beyond imaginative
reach. None of them could, properly speaking, be said to have
a stable personality. They were made up of a number of
separate and warring selves. Hence the wild veering between
farce, piety and up-to-date cynicism.

"Would you like to see the rest of the house?" Alberta
looked supplicatingly at Bertie.

Bertie said he would like nothing better.

Alberta showed us the conservatory she was building; the
study, with its Victorian-style lamps and rolltop desk; her
bedroom, furnished in what she called "French Imperial"
style and dominated by an extravagantly wide bed decorated
with a high, padded, heart-shaped headrest; the kitchen, with
(I was sorry to see) its two deep-freezes; the dank scullery,
where a ragged houseboy crouched on his knees scrubbing
pots and pans. Bertie, gushing admiration, was soaking in the
detail: the Club was going to be royally entertained the next
time he went there.

We returned to the sitting room. Joe and Beatrice were
gyrating to Afro-American soul. We sat close to the fire.

"I'm so glad Joe brought you along. I can't tell you how
refreshing it is to meet someone like you who can appreciate
what I'm trying to do here." Alberta gazed at Bertie with
naked gratitude. "Of course, I've accumulated debts doing it,
debts I'm not sure how I'm going to pay back . . ." A sudden
fear made her eyes lustrous.

"Are you talking about debt?" Joe joined us. He squatted
in front of the fire, warming his hands. "I accumulate debt as
a matter of principle."

He was, he said, a gentleman, and a gentleman's good faith, his honor, ought never to be doubted. "I never carry any cash on me. I always insist on having credit. A gentleman should never be asked to pay in cash. That's the ultimate vulgarity, I think."

"It's not for myself alone I'm doing all this," Alberta went on, pursuing her own private train of thought. "It's for Beatrice and Emma. I want them to be proud, to hold their heads high. Other people must know we don't all live in grass huts and swing from trees . . ."

It was an unexpected and startling confession.

Bertie blushed, gestured awkwardly, stammered rebuttals. He did not think of Africans in that way. Maybe in the past a few ignorant people had . . . but not now . . . not anymore . . . "After all, look at you, look at Joe . . ." The younger generation like himself, a man born in the country, hardly knew what color prejudice was . . .

"You were born here?" Alberta stared at him with joyous surprise.

"I grew up in Kitale," Bertie said.

"So," I said, "you're a native."

There was an awkward silence. I had blundered.

Alberta looked reprovingly at me. "That is not a word we use here," she said.

I apologized.

"People like us ought to see more of each other," Alberta resumed, "we ought to get to know each other."

"Sure," Bertie murmured, "sure . . ."

Alberta complained about the difficulties of social life in N———, lamenting the lack of true contact between black and white. "Here we both are living in a small town and this is the first time we actually meet each other properly. Isn't that strange, Bertie? We speak the same language, appreciate the same things . . ."

Bertie shifted about uneasily.

As she talked, her loneliness, her isolation rose to the surface. Alberta had risked bankruptcy and mockery to make herself and her house ready—only to find there was nothing to be ready for. The Rubens waited to be looked at, the deep-sided chairs to be sat on, the piano to be listened to, the drinks to be drunk. It was all such a shameful waste and betrayal. In this wreck of a society, nothing would ever happen. She would be remembered only for her two deep-freezes. One day she too, like the previous owner of the house, might disappear into the blue and abandon it all. What then would happen to her Rubens? Would it be used for firewood? Poor Alberta.

The day had begun to darken. A band of purple cloud stretched long and low across the horizon. In the fading light, the cornfields looked somber. Alberta drew the curtains. The girls put on a record and started to dance once more. Joe dozed, his golfing cap covering his face.

Alberta was reluctant to let us take leave of her. She clutched Bertie's arm. "You must drop in again . . . feel free . . . you don't have to stand on formality with me, you know that . . . don't feel you need an invitation . . ."

She accompanied us out to the drive. The night was starless, heavy with impending rain. A cool wind was blowing across the cornfields.

"You'll come again, won't you?" It was to Bertie she spoke. "Sure . . ."

"Promise that you will."

Bertie started the engine. We moved slowly down the drive.

"The next time you come, bring all your friends with you," she shouted. "We'll have a party . . ."

Her voice faded behind us. At a bend in the track, the lights of the house suddenly vanished. It was as though it had ceased to exist.

*

"Hi, there!" Stephen, dressed in his cowboy outfit, leaned negligently against the reception desk. "I've come to take you home with me. I want to exchange a few ideas."

"What sort of ideas?" I was tired and irritable; I had been hoping to leave for Nairobi earlier that morning, but the transport I had arranged had, after several hours of waiting, failed to materialize.

"You'll see when we get there," he answered mysteriously. "Will you come?"

It was difficult to refuse.

Stephen lived about ten miles out of town. His house was approached by a long, miry lane bordered by sunflowers. A girl in a pink satin dress opened the door. She was, I learned with some surprise, Stephen's wife. Her name was Cynthia.

"Cynthia is not an intellectual like me," Stephen said. "You can't exchange too many ideas with her."

Cynthia, smiling vacuously, led the way inside. The house was in a state of extreme dilapidation. Windowpanes were cracked and broken; the walls were full of holes where chunks of plaster had fallen out; the ceiling was stained brown from the rainwater that had soaked through. The air reeked with the odors of damp and decay. I was taken into a room empty of furniture. Bits and pieces of clothing were scattered about on the floor. Records and paperbacks, mugs and plates and spoons were piled on a tattered window seat. Cynthia went away to make tea. Stephen cleared a space on the window seat for me. The squalor was astonishing; but even more astonishing was the wooden bar counter, brand-new, that curved across the far end of the room. On the wall behind it were tiers of shelves. In front of the counter, a number of low-slung easy chairs were piled one on top of another. They too were new. Stephen followed my bewildered gaze.

"I am planning to open a club," he said.

"What kind of club?"

"A cultural club. That is what I wanted to talk to you about." He handed me a sheet of typescript. "The draft constitution," he said. "I wrote it myself."

I read the preamble. "The N——— Humanist Club is intended to advance the cause of culture. We, the founding fathers, believe in peace, in freedom and racial harmony. We pledge ourselves to the service of all the community rich and poor, literate and illiterate . . ."

"Who are the other founding fathers?"

"I'm the only one so far. What do you think?"

"The ideals are certainly very noble."

Stephen stroked his meager beard. "Go on," he urged. "Read some more."

I went on reading. Members would have to be nominated by at least three people of "suitable professional standing"; they would have to be well dressed; they would have to refrain from using bad language; they must have no previous criminal convictions. There was to be no discrimination on grounds of race, religion or sex. Women of "immoral turpitude" were strictly barred . . . It was a forbidding document.

Stephen looked at me anxiously. "What do you think?"

"It's a little stern, isn't it?"

This comment appeared to please him.

"But what about members? Don't you have *any* apart from yourself?"

"Not as yet. That's why I built the bar and put up shelves and bought chairs and so on. I did that to show people I am serious. I feel that if they see a bar and chairs and shelves, they might begin to believe in it. Do you see what I mean?"

"I see."

Cynthia brought in the tea.

"What about your wife? What does she feel about it?"

"I told you—she's not an intellectual. She can't really understand."

Laughter was stilled by the fact that he had actually spent money on this fantasy club of his.

"I can see it all so clearly," Stephen said. "People will come here to read and listen to poetry, to put on their plays; we will have concerts."

"Are there any playwrights and poets and musicians in N———?"

"There will be—in time."

"Suppose there are no more founding fathers? Suppose no one wants to join?"

Stephen winced.

"Come," he said, "I'll drive you home before it gets dark. Finish your tea and we'll go."

We drove all the way back in silence.

Early the next morning I left for Nairobi.

CHAPTER 5

A Spell on the Coast

FROM NAIROBI the tarmac road and the railroad wind down from the temperate uplands to the equatorial heat of the Indian Ocean coast, a distance of some three hundred miles. In between are thorn scrub and savanna, stray Masai, dying cattle.

Up-country and coast—they have so little in common. Everything—climate, vegetation, religion, language—is different. And yet the Kenyan flag flies over both. For hundreds of years, the coastal people have looked to the East—to Arabia and the Persian Gulf. The monsoonal highways of the Indian Ocean were more familiar to them than the tenuous trails leading into the hinterland of the continent that lay, mysterious and threatening, behind their backs. Now they must pay obeisance to the Kikuyu state centered on Nairobi. It is all of a piece, however, with the irrationality of the various statehoods imposed on Africa by the colonial past and clung to so tenaciously by its black inheritors—an irrationality that, for example, makes "Kenyans" out of one half of the Masai and "Tanzanians" out of the other. The coast brings home the nonsensical nature of African nationality.

Four hundred years before, Malindi had been the first Swahili town to give Vasco da Gama a friendly welcome on his voyage to India. "Our joy was great," Camões wrote in his great epic *The Lusiads*, "to come at last on a people that knew the art of navigation . . . They were Negroes too, but apparently they had dealings with some more civilized race, and in their speech an occasional word of Arabic was recognizable." Here the Portuguese rested and repaired their ships. "The pagan king was at pains to give the brave seafarers such entertainment as might win him the friendship of the King of Portugal and of so powerful a people. It grieved him that his lot had been cast in a spot so far removed the fertile lands of Europe . . . He regaled them accordingly, in the best traditions of Malindi, with games, dances and other festivities day by day, with agreeable fishing expeditions—so Antony was wont to amuse and beguile Cleopatra . . ." The kings of Malindi have vanished; but the regaling of foreign transients goes on unabated. At night my sleep had been disturbed by the wandering whores who had stopped below my window, whistling and susurrating. The locals who tried to sell me trinkets spoke their pidgin English with a German accent.

After a couple of days I decided to push farther north along the coast, to Lamu: this tiny island, I had been assured, was one of the last surviving strongholds of Islamic culture on the Kenya coast. But that was not the only reason I had decided to go to Lamu. I had had its Circean attributes hummed in my ear. Lamu, I was warned, seduces and corrupts. Sirens sang there, luring unsuspecting men to their doom. It was an island inhabited by lotus eaters, homosexuals, houris. Beware! Beware! Naturally, I decided I must go.

*

The bus is crowded. Suitcases, boxes, bundles of many sizes and shapes cram the roof racks. Live poultry flap and squawk under the seats, releasing downy, asthmatic vapors. The warm, steamy air is like a thick soup. I am thrust up against a window, my solitary item of luggage jammed between my legs. In the aisle people are pushing and shoving, shrieking at each other and threatening to come to blows. I sit absolutely still, trying to work myself into the trancelike state of mind which, I have discovered, is the *sine qua non* of long-distance journeys in this part of the world. It is a state of mind that combines fatalism, self-surrender and a steely determination to maintain one's toehold of possession. I have come a long way since my first *matatu* ride. No more do I easily give way to either outrage or compassion.

It is raining hard, streams of water gushing down the window glass. Through the blur I can see there are many more people fighting for the right of admission. Some, in desperation, are scaling the sides of the bus, vainly attempting to haul themselves up onto the roof. Agonized faces peer at me through the blur. In all poor countries the boarding of trains and buses provokes similar frenzies. Otherwise polite and kindly people suddenly seem to lose their sense of proportion, to panic and run amok. The mood is highly infectious. It forces on one a realization of the horrors implied by the phrase "the struggle for existence." For a moment or two, the struggle for existence and for admission into bus or train must become virtually indistinguishable to those involved. Life concentrates itself into a single overwhelming desire; the single, overwhelming fear of being left behind.

The bus is, perhaps, more crowded than usual. Id, the feast which breaks the austerities of Ramadan, is close at hand, and, no doubt, many Lamu expatriates are returning home for the occasion. There is a fair sprinkling of tourists on the bus—a party of well-dressed Germans carrying expensive cameras;

a sedate English couple; a scattering of American hippies. The rain eases. Gradually, the civil wars that have been raging in the aisle subside. Those who cannot find a seat resign themselves to having to stand. Punctually at 10:15, the bus pulls out of the station yard. The ride from Malindi to Lamu is a long one. It can last between eight and ten hours—or, if the bus breaks down, one may never arrive.

The woman sitting next to me is tending three children, one of them a babe in arms. They are being kept quiet by an endless supply of food. The baby's mouth is permanently clamped to its mother's breast. The toddler chews and sucks a piece of sugar cane. The eldest child dips chunks of bread into a plastic cup filled with milk; the sludge oozes out of the corners of her mouth and drips down the front of her red dress. The rain dies away. I open the window a crack, inserting my nose in the gap. Casually, the woman leans over and slides the glass shut again. It is something I have become accustomed to, and I do not contest the issue: Africans, when traveling, seem to have an aversion to fresh air. A man in a cream-colored, ankle-length shift begins to sing. The refrain is taken up, and the atmosphere, so recently rancorous, becomes mildly festive. The toddler looks up hungrily at his mother; he has finished his stick of sugar cane, whose mangled remains lie scattered about our feet. She takes out a banana from her basket, peels it, drops the skin on the floor and presents it to him. A congenial little slum is being created around us. She smiles happily at me.

At first the coastal plain had been covered with a moss-green scrub. Gradually, that skein of verdancy had faded away; color had been sucked out of the landscape. The marshy soil is baked hard and white and fractured by fissures.

Leafless, intricately stemmed bush blankets the land in a cloudy web, the color of ash. There is no movement; no life. A pall of negation, of death envelops the sun-stunned vacuum. Here and there the bleached skull of some animal—a cow, a goat—provides a kind of hideous sculptural ornamentation. The singing grows weak, revives, grows weak again. Ahead of us stretches the unpaved road, narrow and potholed. The midden grows apace about my feet. I think of the sea, of its coolness and color.

Toward midday, in the middle of the wilderness, there suddenly appears a fairly extensive settlement of huts. Its sighting is the signal for renewed panic among the passengers, some of whom begin to scramble for their possessions. Is it possible for human beings to live in this nothingness? The place is marked on my map. It is called Garsen. I stare in disbelief at the collection of weather-beaten hovels scattered across the ugly, life-denying plain. The map shows Garsen to be located near the marshy mouth of the Tana River. Obviously, the land here must be able to sustain some measure of physical well-being. Even so, I still cannot conceive how men can fail to recoil from this desolation.

We halt near a row of ramshackle shops. Women and children parade down the sides of the bus offering peanuts, sun-blackened bananas, hard-boiled eggs. Lepers drag themselves through the dust, making toward us. A lunatic, waving a staff, howls and shrieks. The Germans take photographs. More passengers pile on, bringing with them fresh consignments of livestock. Heated arguments break out as those who have stepped outside to stretch their legs return to find their places usurped by the newcomers. The lunatic begins to beat the sides of the bus with his staff. Waking, the baby screams.

The woman removes the milk-exhausted breast it has held in its mouth for hours and presents the other. The Germans continue to take photographs.

A mile beyond Garsen is the ferry across the Tana, and we are required to disembark—a cause of further uproar. The ferry is elementary: a metal platform that has to be propelled manually by means of ropes. When we arrive, it is moored on the opposite bank, taking on a cargo of three Land-Rovers carrying a party of tourists decked in sun hats, bush jackets and dark glasses. Getting across is going to be a slow, tedious business. I climb a muddy mound overlooking the river. At this point in its course, the Tana is unimpressive: a brown, sluggish stream, not very wide, pushing itself toward the sea between low banks. I am joined by a pair of American hippies. The man is wearing a silk jacket and loose white trousers. His hair, long and tangled, falls to his shoulders. The girl wears a long skirt of crushed velvet and a short, tight bodice glittering with sequins. She has a festering sore on her ankle.

"When I went to school," the man says, "I didn't learn many words. Then one day I figured I'd learn some. Now I know a lot of words. But I find I don't need to use them."

She, staring at the river, does not reply.

"You get to the stage when words are just noise. Just so much noise."

She, staring at the river, still does not reply. A fly settles and feeds on her sore. But she does not seem to notice.

The ferry bumps lightly against the bank; the Land-Rovers speed away toward Malindi.

Beyond the Tana, the character of the land changes dramatically. It becomes greener, lusher, almost jungly. Palms, branched like candelabra, abound. The land is more thickly populated, and our progress is slowed by frequent stops. Beds, stoves, radios, tables and chairs are taken off the roof and borne away into the bush like trophies. At each stop it seems that the entire population of the locality comes out to watch: men, women and children materializing out of the bush. At one of these stops, the woman departs with her three children. The sky clouds over as dusk approaches and we zigzag from *shamba* to *shamba* along tortuous sandy lanes. A mosquito whines close to my ear. Then a sudden lightening of the skyline heralds the appearance of the sea and journey's end.

A battered launch is tied up at the water's edge. It is drizzling as I negotiate the perilous transition from gangplank to deck. The drizzle turns into a tropical downpour as we chug out into the strait that separates Lamu Island from the mainland. The awning which, perhaps, might be an effective shield against the sun is a useless defense against the rain, and within a minute or two I am soaked through to the skin. After about ten minutes, the white houses of the town come into view. As we touch the sides of the jetty I surrender myself into the hands of a "guide," who leads me the few yards along the waterfront to the warmth, the food and the rest that I crave.

*

The morning is fine and clear. I look out across the sparkling water to the low, green shoreline of another island. Uninhabited Manda is well known for its ruins. The sea flows benignly, like a river, between the two islands. A dhow, its sail lit up by the sun, drifts with apparent aimlessness—a prodigious, prehistoric bird afloat on the water. Below me, a group of *kekoi*-clad men (the *kekoi* is an ankle-length wrap-

around lower garment traditionally worn by Swahili men)
sit astride the seawall, talking softly. A man rides past on a
donkey, his feet scraping the ground: the donkey is the only
means of transport on the island, there being no automobiles
or even bicycles on this roadless paradise. Close by is the
museum, guarded by a pair of antique cannon. The Kenyan
flag droops on its pole. The tide is out, and the shoreline
reeks with rank marine odors. Piles of mangrove logs are stored
along it, awaiting shipment by dhow to the Persian Gulf,
tangible reminders of an ancient trade and ancient ties.

The main thoroughfare of the town is little more than ten
feet wide. Donkey droppings steam in the heat; dead cockroaches float in the gutters. Black-veiled ladies, some in platformed heels, wander about in groups, dark eyes boldly
staring, voices querulous and uninhibited. Their public display
is connected with Ramadan; during this period, I have been
told, women are given greater freedom than at any other
time of the year. Facial features range through all the grada-
tions from the African to the Arab. A maze of shadowed
passageways leads off the main thoroughfare. These are barely
wide enough to accommodate two people walking abreast.
Sleepy-eyed men lounge on the steps of small, unremarkable
mosques. Many of the older houses are in ruins. I stand in
insect-humming bush and look at mounds of fallen masonry,
at crumbling archways, at rotting timbers, at the eroded remnants of fine molding on walls. In some of the ruins, betel
plantations have been established. The stone-built town peters
out into colonies of mud huts lining twisting, muddy lanes.
Beyond are rubbish dumps, guarded by long-legged,
protuberant-chested scavenger birds.

Lamu is bound to be a disappointment to the casual tourist.

The blank facades of the houses, adorned with elaborately carved doors—these doors are the glory of Lamu culture—tell nothing; the ill-lit shops that look so promising from the outside turn out, on closer inspection, to sell Palmolive soap, Colgate toothpaste, Surf washing powder and Cadbury's chocolate. The people of Lamu no longer make anything; they simply endure among the relics of a dead past. Bad reproductions of the old doors are made on commission from the richer tourists—that is all. The young men have nothing to do. They become "guides" and beachboys.

I return to the waterfront, to the heated glare of sea and sky. On the summit of a hill is the official residence of the District Commissioner—an up-country man, a Kikuyu. Its remoteness is forbidding and imperial.

"They tell us that one day they will drive us back to Arabia," one of the beachboys who hung around the hotel had said to me. "They say that we hunted black men and made them into slaves."

I looked at him—woolly-haired, flat-nosed, thick-lipped: "Arab" here was a state of mind.

I am beyond the town now. The sandy track is bordered by groves of coconut palms. Boys frolic in the surf. I pass a gang of prisoners, dressed in blue shirts and shorts, supervised by an armed, khaki-clad guard. The prisoners are sawing logs. A sign forbids the taking of photographs.

I skirt a rocky headland. The sand dunes at the northern tip of the island glisten in the sunshine. In the eighteenth century, a bloody battle had been fought on those sand dunes between the people of Lamu and the city-state of Pate to the north. The invaders, their dhows stranded by the ebbing tide, had been routed. It is said that their bones can still be seen.

I try to picture the scene but cannot. Too much has been altered.

I come to more houses—and a hotel. With the wind skimming off the sea, it is cool—almost too cool—on the hotel's shaded patio. Pleasure boats rock on the water. A party of elderly Americans—from their conversation I gather they are day-trippers from Malindi—is sitting at a nearby table drinking Cinzano. They are accompanied by a "guide." They are talking about Ramadan and its strictures.

"I find religions from hot countries are all the same," a sprightly lady with baby-blue eyes observes. "Take this Muslam the natives here believe in . . ."

"*Islam*," the white-haired gentleman sitting next to her corrects gently.

"*That* started in a hot country, didn't it? Then there is . . . what do you call it? . . . the . . . the Jewish religion . . . they're all based on hygiene. It's the heat. You have to be very careful with food in a hot climate. It's the same with all native religions, in my opinion." She turned toward the guide, exuding goodwill and sympathy. "Would you like to travel abroad one day and see how other people live? In my country we don't worship . . . what's his name?"

"Mohammed," the white-haired gentleman says.

"We don't worship Mohammed. We believe in someone called Jesus Christ. We believe that he is the true son of God." She raises her voice. "Have you ever heard of Jesus Christ? We don't believe in the . . . the . . ." She snaps her fingers.

"Koran," the white-haired gentleman says.

"We have a book called the Bible. Have you ever heard of the Bible?" The baby-blue eyes engulf the guide with compassion.

The guide stares wildly toward the sea. Everyone around the table is smiling relentlessly at him.

"Maybe, though, you wouldn't like it in our country. Where I come from, it's full of noise and busy people. Hurry, hurry, hurry. That's how it is in my country. You wouldn't like that, would you?"

The guide, all too willing to please but not knowing precisely what is expected of him, alternately nods and shakes his head.

"I tell you what." The lady pats his wrist. She hands him an address book. "If you write your name and address in here for me, I'll send you a copy of the Bible instead."

The guide scribbles.

'Wonderful! Wonderful!" The guide wilts under the ecstatic gaze of those baby-blue eyes.

They rise. A plane awaits them on the airstrip on Manda Island.

"You stick to your palm trees and sunshine," the lady says. "You don't know how lucky you are."

*

"I hear you have traveled abroad," I say.

"Yes," Hassan replies. "My girl friend took me with her."

"Who was your girl friend?"

"She was a lady from Switzerland."

"Did you ask her to take you abroad with her?"

"No. She invited me."

"What did she say to you?"

"She said she liked me. She said she was lonely and wanted me to be her friend and companion. Her husband had just died, and she had a lot of money from him."

"Did you think it strange?"

"No. Many *mzungus* offer to take beachboys like myself home with them. I have had many invitations."

"How old was your girl friend?"

Hassan hesitates. The question embarrasses him.

"Was she much older than you?"

"Much."

"How much?"

"She was fifty years old."

"How did you meet her?"

"As I meet all the other *mzungus*. They come, they ask for a guide. If they pick me, I take them around and show them what there is to be seen. Most of them, though, do not only want a guide."

"What do they want?"

"I am sure you can guess. Germans are the worst."

"And you give them what they want?"

"Why not? They pay me well."

"Men too?"

"Yes. Men too." Hassan smiles. "It is all the same to me—men or women."

"Tell me more about your girl friend from Switzerland."

"She was not a human being. Very few *mzungus* are human beings."

"Why do you say that?"

"Because of the way they treat us."

"How do they treat you?"

"Like animals. Most of them only want one thing from us."

"Why, then, did you go abroad with your Swiss girl friend?"

"Because I wanted to see the world and she was giving me

the opportunity. Because I didn't think she would be like all the rest who wanted to take me with them." Again Hassan hesitates. "She said she wanted to adopt me."

"To adopt you!"

"That was what she said."

"Did you see something of the world?"

"Yes. We spent many months traveling. She took me to Italy, to France and to Spain."

"Did you enjoy it?"

"To begin with. I liked seeing all those different places and learning how other people lived. But then it got harder and harder for me."

"What went wrong?"

"She turned out to be of a very jealous disposition."

"How did it show itself?"

"In many ways. She would get very angry if she saw me talking to another girl. She would even get angry if she saw me looking at another girl. She wanted to have me all to herself. Once—I believe it was in Paris—she threw a glass of wine over a waitress who smiled at me. In Spain it got very bad. She wouldn't let me out of her sight; she wouldn't let me leave the hotel room to go out for a walk. I was like a prisoner. Also . . ."

"Yes?"

"She became very demanding. Day and night she wanted me. An old woman like that—it was disgusting. She wasn't human at all by then."

"What did you do?"

"I was a prisoner. She had all the money—she would never let me have any in case I ran away from her. Finally, it got so bad I said I would call the police for her; I refused to make any more love with her . . ."

"What happened?"

"She would come after me crying, shouting, cursing. She would crawl after me, begging me to make love with her. When she saw my mind was made up, she quieted down. She said how much she loved me, that she wanted to marry me, adopt me . . ."

"How could she adopt *and* marry you?"

"I don't know. By then she was completely crazy, I think. In the end, she realized it was no use trying to keep me with her. She gave me some money and sent me back home."

"Have you heard from her since?"

"I get letters. Crazy letters."

"Do you write back?"

"No. I have a new girl friend now."

I had seen Hassan, dressed stylishly and immaculately, strolling along the seafront with his new girl friend—she was young and American, a discharged Peace Corps worker. A week or two before I came to Lamu, she had been the center of a minor scandal: she had been set upon one night by assailants unknown and knifed. She had run screaming through the darkened passageways of the town. Now, fully recovered from her injury, she was daily to be seen strolling along the seafront with her lover as if nothing at all had happened.

*

I am to go by dhow to the ruins of Manda Island. My guide is a man called Ahmed (everyone here seems to be called either Mohammed or Ahmed). Ahmed does not like to be thought of as a mere guide. He has participated in a number of archaeological expeditions investigating coastal ruins—though in precisely what capacity I am not sure—and so regards himself as something of an expert in antiquarian matters, befriend-

ing only those visitors to the island whom he considers to be
of "serious" intent.

"I do it as a favor only," he explained to me on our first
meeting; "that you must please understand."

However, he does accept—and expect—payment for his
services.

"Please," he had murmured, clasping his hands together
and looking pained when I had brought the delicate subject
up, "how much you give is up to you. I have no fee. Some
give two hundred shillings, some a hundred, some even less
than that. You give what you can afford. Whatever you give
I shall be happy to accept. Please."

Ahmed's "please" could be used to express pleasure, deference, irritation. At times, it was used as a straightforward
command. He came from one of the older Lamu families and
was proud of the fact. Excessively so.

Ahmed, clad in a *kekoi*, turns up at the hotel punctually at
one o'clock. However, he stands on the road and refuses to
come in.

"Please," he says, "I would not care to."

I hurry down to meet him.

"I do not feel it is right for me to enter such places during
the fast," he explains as we walk the few yards to the jetty.
"I see many bad things going on in there. I leave such places
to beachboys." Ahmed droops his lower lip. He walks with
measured steps, his hands clasped behind his back, looking at
all he sees with severe, if vague, disapproval.

An American couple is waiting for us on the jetty.

"Please," Ahmed says, "you will allow these people to come
with us." It is not a request, but a declaration of settled intention. "They are good friends of mine. Scholars. They too

have a great desire to see the ruins in my company." He beckons to a boy standing at the top of the jetty. "Also my relative. He also will come with us, please."

The boy clucks like a chicken, grins and turns a somersault.

Ahmed gazes severely at him.

"Hi!" The American man shakes my hand. "I'm Dean, and the lady over there is Carol—my better half. Hope you don't mind our muscling in on your trip. We figured a ride by dhow was just too good to miss."

Dean, dressed in shorts and striped cotton shirt, is heavy-framed and bland of feature. Carol, round-shouldered, long of face and homely, smiles pleasantly in my direction. I learn, without particular surprise, that they are both anthropologists and have been resident in Lamu for some months collecting material for the theses they are writing. Carol is investigating divorce procedure; Dean is investigating the music played in the mosques.

It is impossible to be in Lamu for any length of time without encountering the professional researcher: Lamu has more researchers per head of population than doctors. Already I had met a German academic, a specialist in Swahili poetry, who was scouring the island in the hope of finding hitherto unpublished manuscripts; a photographer who was compiling a detailed visual record of the interiors of the finer Lamu houses; a sociologist who was studying the hapless descendants of fishermen who had migrated to Lamu from the Comoros Islands. Fecund island! There seemed no end to the dissertations to which it could give rise, the modest academic careers it could support.

There is no sign of the dhow Ahmed has arranged for us.

"This is bad," he says. "This is very bad." Shielding his

eyes from the sun, he scans the dhowless expanse of water. Ahmed scowls. He stamps his foot. After half an hour, he gives up hope. We will have to go by motor launch instead.

"Please forgive," Ahmed says. "It is not my fault. I will see that those wicked men are punished."

I take a puerile pleasure in his embarrassment.

Five minutes after we start, the dhow is spotted rounding the headland. Ahmed, jumping up excitedly, waves his arms and shouts. The two craft come together in the middle of the strait. Ahmed chatters indignantly; the two men in the dhow chatter indignantly; our boatman, fearing redundancy, chatters indignantly. For a while, all three aggrieved parties seem on the verge of coming to blows. Dean and Carol are delighted by this impromptu folksy display, following with scholarly neutrality the frenzied antics of the disputants. The crisis passes. Somehow Ahmed manages to pacify the boatman who has brought us this far, and we transfer ourselves to the dhow.

The dhow glides smoothly and silently through the water, a light wind slapping the sail. I listen to the quiet swish and suck of the water along the sides. We are absorbed into the slow, stupefying rhythm that binds together earth and sea and sky. Manda Island's mangrove-fringed shoreline looms closer as the white houses of Lamu recede astern. Far away to our right the sand dunes glisten in the shimmer of heat and light.

We leave the open water and enter a mangrove-fringed inlet. Ahmed, eyes closed, head tilted up toward the sun, squats meditatively in the bow. His *kekoi* is drawn tight across his thighs. He has a fine "Arab" cast of feature: prominent, hooked nose, high cheekbones, firmly molded mouth. Black-brown hair curls stiffly back from a broad forehead. His skin, smoky bronze in color, seems to be irradiated with the sullen heat of the coast. His young relative claps his hands; the sound echoes across the stillness of the inlet like a burst of gunshot. A cloud of tiny birds wheels upward from the depths of the mangrove, their panic-stricken twitterings momentarily livening the stagnant air. When the birds attempt to resettle, the boy claps again, causing them to wheel about once more. He laughs.

Ahmed looks at him reprovingly.

The inlet narrows. On either side, the latticework of twisted roots and branches recedes into green gloom. The water is black and smooth as glass. There is not a breath of wind, and the odors of the swamp close in about us. The sail being useless, the boathands begin to pole the boat along. The inlet narrows; it becomes a creek. Soon the men stop poling— they are worried that the boat will run aground. Ahmed, stripping off his *kekoi*, announces that we must wade the rest of the way. He lowers himself gingerly over the side. The black water laps his knees. One by one we follow suit. I sink well beyond my ankles in the cloying ooze. Ahmed's relative makes gurgling sounds; the black water closes about his shoulders; he flails his arms wildly; he rolls his eyes. Ahmed wrings his ears: the boy is only pretending to be trapped in quicksand.

When we reach dry land, we follow a twisting path through sun-withered grass. Walking is a torment: the ground is littered with tiny thorns that work their way through the thin soles of the rubber slippers I am wearing. The nests of weaverbirds hang from the branches of tall, spreading trees. After about ten minutes we come to the ruins: crumbling stone walls, the foundations of houses, a few tombs, a roofless mosque. The heat is intense. Close to the entrance of the mosque is a water trough, now filled with earth. Ahmed stoops, digging with his fingers. Buried within is a plate of blue-and-white Chinese porcelain. Great quantities of Chinese ware were imported by the Swahili towns: plates such as this were often used to adorn the walls of mosques and tombs. Ahmed covers over the plate carefully.

"Tell no one what I have shown you," he says.

Ahmed leads us from one pile of rubble to another. "Here," he says, slapping the flanks of a sloping stone wall; "here must have been bathroom." Ahmed's knowledge seems to center around the location of bathrooms. He has no idea who built the town or why it was built where it was, when it was finally abandoned or why it was finally abandoned. These coastal ruins reflect, on the whole, a modest cultural achievement, echoing, a trifle forlornly, distant civilizations across the Indian Ocean. Yet it *was* an achievement. Ibn Battuta, the fourteenth-century North African traveler, when he visited the East African coast, found himself in a world which, if distinctly foreign and exotic in many ways, was also recognizably Islamic. He was impressed by Kilwa (a town farther south, on the coast of present-day Tanzania) ". . . amongst the most beautiful of cities and most elegantly built . . ." Above all, he admired Swahili religious fervor. "They are a people devoted to the Holy War," he wrote of the citizens of Kilwa, "because they are on a continuous mainland with unbelieving Zunuj [blacks] . . ." Nevertheless, he was in Africa. "Most of its [Kilwa's] people are Zunuj, extremely black. They have cuttings [i.e., tribal scarring] on their faces . . ."

Islam and Africa had coalesced; they had made something of each other which, however modest and provincial the scale, was authentic. Their contact had ended in neither recoil nor parody. (Africa's "independent," revivalist churches do nothing but caricature Christian teaching. The Alice Lumpa church in Zambia and the hymns of the Mau Mau are good examples of this.) The Swahilis were not imitation Arabs. They were Swahilis, participators in a great current of civilization. They evolved an architecture, a poetry, a music, a style that was quite unique. If their speech was interlarded, as Camões remarks, with Arabic vocabulary, their grammar was Bantu-based. They had succeeded in fashioning a personality of their own.

A dog growls somewhere close by. I jump back, startled not only by the sound but by its ferocity.

"It is nothing," Ahmed says. "It is only him playing the fool."

His relative, who has been crouching in the grass, leaps to his feet and runs away.

We follow the path which leads across the narrow neck of the island to the east-facing shore. From some way off, we hear the roar of the surf. This side of the island, exposed to the raw blast of the Indian Ocean, presents an entirely different aspect. Bottle-green breakers, welling high and treacherously, explode violently, hissing and foaming up the steeply shelving shore. Away to our right, they pound the banks of coral, shooting upward stinging jets of rainbow-colored spray which the wind blows into our faces. A wrack of rotting tree trunks, palm fronds and seaweed litters the beach below us. We stand there for a while, watching the dramatic spectacle of wind and wave. Dean says he will return one day and have a picnic here.

"Please," Ahmed urges. "It is time for us to go back."

A cock crows from behind one of the tombs as we retrace our steps.

Ahmed's relative bounds through the grass like a wild creature.

*

The new imperialism comes complete with settlers. Lamu looks nervously across to the mainland, to that advance out-post of Kikuyu-style progress, the Lake Kenyatta Harambee Settlement Scheme, which has infiltrated thousands of up-country people into their midst.

It was in 1970 that the Coast Provincial Commissioner launched the project which, it was claimed, would grow cotton. (It has, in fact, grown very little cotton.) "He appealed," the official Report on the Scheme says, "to the Coast people to take up the challenge and accept to be settled in the Scheme . . . This was unfortunately met with very poor response if at all as very few people of Coastal origin showed any interest." The Report accuses them of laziness. Laziness may indeed have been one factor. But there were other, more concrete reasons for the lack of enthusiasm shown by the "people of Coastal origin." The Report itself provides a few clues. The nearest source of water was three miles away; there was no dispensary, no school; housing conditions were atrocious. Nevertheless, by the middle of 1971 it was clear to those in charge that the cotton project would come to nothing "if it were only to depend on the unreliable local labor." It was decided "to tap human labor from wherever it may be available in the country."

In October 1972, Lamu watched anxiously as a group of fifty families from Nairobi answered the call. They were given twenty-acre plots. The invasion had begun. The provincial authorities announced plans to build a dispensary, set up a primary school, construct roads and install a water pump at the lake. To crown it all, the settlers were to be provided with assistance from the Famine Relief Fund. The national ideal of Harambee—self-help—had been turned on its head. Settlers poured into the Lamu district. By the end of 1975, over three thousand families (carefully described by the Report as drawn from a "cross-section of tribes") had been absorbed into the Scheme. To accommodate the invasion, the land grant was reduced to ten acres. The Report predicts a rapid expansion of population ". . . as more and more children are expected as settlers bring more of their relatives from up-country." Lamu is paying the price of the post-Uhuru land-grab: dispossession breeds dispossession.

The war between Coast and Interior takes many forms. Nairobi's representatives look with hostility upon those Europeans who are buying up the old Lamu houses with a view to their restoration and preservation. Their antipathy is partly political—the fear, not altogether unjustified, that Lamu will become an expatriate enclave—and partly the product of self-interest: they do not want Europeans to snap up all the valuable property before others are given a chance. However, there is also a certain bewilderment and incomprehension. Are those old houses really beautiful? They should be pulled down, not preserved. Their retention is unprogressive. A new, a proper, town should be built on the mainland.

The Kikuyu take their civilizing mission seriously. One day I was shown a letter from the Coast Provincial Commissioner—a Kikuyu—that had been sent to all the hotels on the island. It forbade the wearing of the *kekoi* by hotel employees. This garment, worn for centuries by the Swahili, was condemned as a colonial relic which was not in keeping with the "progressive image" of modern Kenya. Hotel staff were to be issued *trousers*.

In 1938, Jomo Kenyatta wrote:

> When the European comes to the Kikuyu country and robs the people of their land, he is taking away not only their livelihood, but the material symbols that hold family and tribe together . . . When he explains to his own satisfaction and after the most superficial glance at the issues involved, that he is doing this for the sake of the Africans, to "civilise" them, "teach them the disciplinary value of regular work" "give them the benefit of European progressive ideas," he is adding insult to injury . . .

*

When the new moon was spotted last night, people rushed from their houses and gaped up excitedly at the sky: the austerities of Ramadan were over.

This morning the children appear dressed up in new clothes. On a piece of open ground some goats have been slaughtered. Severed hooves and bits of fur lie on the blood-soaked earth. Ahmed, attired in a *kanzu* robe and embroidered skullcap, arrives and invites me over to his house.

The room in which I am entertained is small, square and dark, furnished with Morris-type armchairs. Worn linoleum covers the floor. Indian calendars decorate the walls. There is a framed photograph of Ahmed at his most magisterial.

"Today is full of pleasure for us," he observes morosely.

Ahmed, who has taken care to hide his womenfolk away from my profane gaze, offers me Coca-Cola and a tacky confection (*halwa*). Flies buzz in the stuffy warmth of the room and settle greedily on the *halwa*. While I drink and eat, Ahmed discourses on the virtues of self-denial and laments the cultural decline of Lamu.

In the afternoon, I pay a visit to the fair that is being held on the grounds of the primary school. There I run into Dean and Carol. Dean is equipped with a tape recorder. The fair is a tawdry business—the stalls offer only primitive games of chance: in Lamu every creative instinct has atrophied. The island's womenfolk are out in force. Beneath their black robes they wear sumptuous new dresses. I stare at platformed heels; at hennaed, jeweled hands. The afternoon's chief attraction is a belly-dancing display by a transvestite homosexual. Nearly the entire audience is female. During the performance, the women are unable to restrain their excitement. They climb onto the benches, clapping and screeching with delight. Dean is a mine of information on the role of the transvestite homosexual in Lamu society. I foresee the beginnings of a paper on the subject.

It is twilight as I walk back through the alleys of the town, past those blank facades with their intricately carved doors. From one of these houses comes the raucous roar of beer-fed male voices singing an American pop song.

I escape to the cooler air and silence of the seafront. The riverlike sea flows serenely; wavelets lap the piles of mangrove logs awaiting shipment to the Persian Gulf. A bugle sounds. Passersby stand to attention as Kenya's flag is lowered over this distant outpost of its sovereignty.

PART
TWO

CHAPTER 6

Taking the Socialist Road

I

"You WILL like Tanzania," the Asian girl had said. "You will find it totally different from Kenya in almost all respects."

The girl had described herself as "committed" to Tanzania, and knowing she had recently returned from a pilgrimage to Cuba, I was not surprised by the categorical recommendation.

"But if she's so committed," an unkind acquaintance of hers said to me afterward, "why does she come all the way to Nairobi to buy her underwear? Why isn't she content with the Chinese underwear they must sell in Dar es Salaam?"

I could find no reply to the cruel question.

*

Over the years, President Julius Nyerere of Tanzania has adopted something of the character and style that Nehru affected in the first years of Indian independence, claiming a special place in the moral firmament for himself, his policies and, by extension, his country. But there are other, more down-to-earth reasons for the esteem in which Nyerere is held: with the possible exception of Kenneth Kaunda of Zambia, he is just about the only African head of state one can

contemplate without immediate sensations of outrage or embarrassment. After Field Marshal Idi Amin, Emperor Bokassa,
Sese Mobutu and Dr. Hastings Banda, after the gross corruptions of Nigeria and Kenya, after the genocidal manias
of Ruanda and Burundi and Equatorial Guinea, one turns
with relief to Julius Nyerere. Here, astonishing as it may
seem, is an African leader with pretensions to intellectual respectability. He has translated Shakespeare into Swahili; and
his collected speeches and writings fill three fat volumes. Even
confirmed Tanzanophobes will pause at his name and dole out
the ritual praise. Nyerere is a good man. Nyerere is a sincere
man. Nyerere does not feather his nest. See how simply he
dresses. See how simply he lives. The "Mwalimu" (Teacher)
reinforces faltering faith; he makes it possible to believe—if
only for a little while—that Africa can be taken seriously,
that Africa really wants to "liberate" itself.

In response, the philanthropists and the aid-givers pour
into the country, bringing in their baggage a burning "commitment," a burning idealism, all seeking to do something
worthwhile with their lives—if only for a year or two. Living with the poor and starving (you will be told) is a soul-
enriching experience.

"To the peasants of Tanzania," runs the dedication of one
of the scores of academic treatises devoted to the country's
socialist endeavors, "whose livelihood and environmental
situations have become the laboratories for some intellectuals
and the theatre for some politicians." Predictably enough, the
author, C. K. Omari (his book, *Strategy for Rural Development*, is published by the East African Literature Bureau),
has written a book far beyond the comprehension of any
Tanzanian peasant. Mr. Omari, nevertheless, makes a good

point. For if the Highlands of neighboring Kenya stimulated to fresh life outmoded and frustrated aristocratic longings in a certain type of European settler, then, and with much the same justice, it could be said that Independent Tanzania has stimulated the fantasies of a certain type of outmoded European socialist—men and women of a somewhat pastoral and utopian turn of mind—whose socialism fades by imperceptible degrees into a kind of benevolent, condescending patronage of the backward and deprived. They are different sides of the same coin. For both frustrated patrician and frustrated philanthropist, it is like going back to the beginning of the world. The African soul is a blank slate on which anything can be written; onto which any fantasy can be transposed. Much of the blame must rest with Nyerere.

The pleasant northern Tanzanian town of Arusha has lent its name to the "Declaration" that is generally considered the theoretical fount of Tanzanian socialism. It is a small document—about the size of the *Communist Manifesto*—but lacking the latter's stark, apocalyptic appeal. The prevailing tone is inspirational, not chiliastic. It reads in some parts like the American Declaration of Independence, in others like a Sunday-school homily, in others like a stern missionary tract. Sometimes it is sweetly reasonable; sometimes a naked authoritarianism breaks the surface. Now the pastoral vision of a virtuous, hardworking peasantry dominates; now incipient Third World paranoia. It is a thoroughly African piece of work, veering as it does between realism and fantasy, between piety and tyranny.

The Declaration begins with a statement of the Creed of the Tanganyika African National Union—the sole legitimate political party: the equality of all human beings; the right of every individual to "dignity and respect"; the right of free expression, religious belief and association "within the context of the law," and so on. It also asserts the State's right of control over "the principal means of production" in order to prevent "the exploitation of one person by another or one group by another," either or both of these things being "inconsistent with the existence of a classless society . . . A truly socialist state is one in which all people are workers and in which neither capitalism nor feudalism exists . . ." No one must be allowed to live off the work done by others except the very young, the very old and the crippled. Because Tanzania is a state composed of peasants and workers, the government must be chosen and led by peasants and workers.

The Declaration proclaims that the Party is "at war" with Poverty and Oppression. It is at this point that it rises to something approaching a truly rhetorical flamboyance. "We have been oppressed a great deal, we have been exploited a great deal and we have been disregarded a great deal. It is our weakness that has led to our being oppressed, exploited and disregarded. Now we want a revolution—a revolution which brings to an end our weakness, so that we are never again exploited, oppressed or humiliated." That is well, and movingly, said.

But how is that Revolution to be brought about? The Declaration castigates the obsession with Money. "It is as if we have said, 'Money is the basis of development. Without money there can be no development.'" Tanzania, however is a poor country. Some money, of course, can be found by taxation. That, though, is hardly feasible. "We realize that the cow has no more milk—that is, that the people find it difficult to pay more taxes."

The Declaration attacks the emphasis usually placed on industrialization and the towns. All such development is generated from external sources and has to be paid for in foreign exchange. Where does that foreign exchange come from? It comes from the country's agricultural earnings—and hence from the sweat and toil of the peasants, who derive little benefit from their exertions. The peasant's labor pays for the town's hospitals, tarmac roads, electric lights, water pipes and hotels. Salvation—of body and soul—must be found on the land, in the physical and spiritual uplift of the peasantry.

Switching now to its Chinese manner, the Declaration lists the "four prerequisites of development." These are (1) The People; (2) The Land; (3) Good Policies; (4) Good Leadership. It lavishes praise on the virtue of hard work. Tanzanians waste far too much energy on "gossip, drinking and dancing." The people must be taught the meaning of "self-reliance." They should be able to make their own clothes, build their own houses, grow their own food. "In our country work should be something to be proud of, and laziness, drunkenness and idleness should be things to be ashamed of . . ." And then the paranoia—"it is necessary for us to be on guard against internal stooges who could be used by external enemies who aim to destroy us . . ."

Under the heading "Good Policies," the Declaration returns to its favorite theme—exploitation. If exploitation is to be avoided, it is necessary that every man and woman should live off his or her own labor and use no one else as an instrument for gaining his or her livelihood. "Nobody should go and stay for a long time with his relative, doing no work, because in doing so he will be exploiting his relative. Likewise, nobody should be allowed to loiter in towns or villages without doing work which would enable him to be self-reliant without exploiting his relation . . ." Then follows one of those thought-numbing passages so characteristic of this kind of exhortatory rhetoric: "If every individual is self-reliant the ten-house cell will be self-reliant; if all the cells are self-reliant the whole ward will be self-reliant; and if the wards are self-reliant, the District will be self-reliant; if the Districts are self-reliant then the Region is self-reliant, and if the Regions are self-reliant, then the whole Nation is self-reliant and this is our aim."

Nowhere in the Arusha Declaration is *ujamaa* explicitly mentioned—a surprising omission considering what a fundamental concept it is in Nyerere's philosophical and political speculations. We have to look elsewhere among the Mwalimu's speeches and writings to discover what he means by it.

Ujamaa he defines as "familyhood." It was, he tells us, the basis of traditional African society—a society he describes in glowing terms. "In traditional African society *everybody* was a worker . . . Not only was the capitalist, or the landed exploiter, unknown . . . but we did not have that other form of parasite—the loiterer or idler . . . Capitalistic exploitation was impossible. Loitering was an unthinkable disgrace." In this utopia, land ("God's gift to man") was a community and not an individual asset: landlordism was utterly foreign to the tribal mentality. The social system offered security from the cradle to the grave.

Colonialism destroyed this idyll, planting the seeds of individuality. Sin, in the guise of capitalist yearnings, entered the African's simple soul and corrupted it. Falling from grace, he was driven out of the Garden of Eden. It was not long before the first loiterers appeared on the scene. These were the land-lords who ". . . usually are in the same class as the loiterers I was talking about: the class of parasites." The African's soul was becoming as black as his skin. "In the old days the African had never aspired to the possession of personal wealth for the purpose of dominating any of his fellows . . . But then came the foreign capitalists. They were wealthy. They were power-ful. And the African naturally started wanting to be wealthy too." The capitalist serpent sang seductive songs telling of the rich fruit to be gained from exploitation and domination, de-forming the natural goodness of the African. "In our tradi-tional African society," Nyerere laments, "we were individ-uals within a community. We took care of the community, and the community took care of us. We neither needed nor wished to exploit our fellow men." The belated emergence of the African into history brought, according to him, noth-ing but tragedy. A way must be found back to lost primeval innocence. That can be done only by recapturing the spirit of *ujamaa.*

Africans must reconstruct, must rediscover the spirit that charged their prehistoric communities—though, it should be added, Nyerere is not quite so fundamentalist as to suggest that they should do without the benefits brought by tractors and fertilizers and other modern aids to production. How-ever, modern knowledge must be acquired without any of its sinful accompaniments. "Inherent in the Arusha Declara-tion . . . is a rejection of the concept of national grandeur . . . It is a commitment to the belief that there are more important things in life than the amassing of riches, and that if the pursuit of wealth clashes with things like human dignity and social equality, then the latter will be given priority." If the price of goodness is backwardness, then Tanzania will remain backward.

II

. . . on the morning of the ninth, my friend Demba, with a number of people, came to see me, and said that they were sent by Tiggity Sego for my present, and wished to see what goods I had appropriated for that purpose. I knew that resistance was hopeless, and complaint unavailing . . . I quietly offered him seven bars of amber and five of tobacco. After surveying these articles for some time very coolly, Demba laid them down, and told me this was not a present for a man of Tiggity Sego's consequence, who had it in his own power to take whatever he pleased from me . . . Demba and his attendants immediately began to open my bundles, and spread the different articles upon the floor, where they underwent a more strict examination than they had done at Joag. Everything that pleased them they took without scruple . . . Upon collecting the scattered remains of my little fortune after these people had left me, I found that as at Joag I had been plundered of half, so here, without even the shadow of accusation, I was deprived of half the remainder.

Travels in Africa by Mungo Park

*

One tends to think of Africa, before the full-scale imposition of European administration, as an essentially borderless place. That is not altogether true. Africans have known about borders and their possibilities for a long time. Park's account of his travels is, by and large, a chronicle of frontier tribulation; a sad tale of a gradual but unremitting dispossession. Throughout his journey he was harassed by the border officials of the petty chiefdoms through which he passed. At the end of it all, he had (almost literally) nothing left. Something of that eighteenth-century atmosphere of rapacity persists at the border posts of the modern states.

I traveled by bus from Mombasa to the Kenya–Tanzania border town of Traveta. We had left Mombasa at dawn, and it was past noon when we arrived at Taveta, a dusty, disordered collection of mud huts and wooden shacks roofed with corrugated iron, scattered across a plain ringed by volcanic hills. We crowded off the bus with our luggage and were shepherded into a small brick building housing Immigration Control. The officer in charge ordered me to take off my hat—in deference, I assumed, to the portrait of Kenyatta hanging on the wall behind him. He barely glanced at my passport.

"Do you have any Kenyan currency on you?"

I said I had two hundred shillings.

"Show me your wallet." He thrust out an importunate hand.

I handed over my wallet. He extracted the two hundred shillings, turned the wallet upside down and shook it vigorously. Satisfied there was nothing more to be had, he returned the wallet, carefully folded the Kenyan notes and put them into his shirt pocket.

I protested. I was intending to return to Kenya and wished to keep at least a hundred shillings with me.

"It is a crime to take Kenyan currency out of the country," he said. "A serious crime—don't you know that? If I reported you, you could be in a lot of trouble." He handed me two hundred Tanzanian shillings. "If you have any Tanzanian money when you come back," he said with a smile, "I'll change it for you."

There was nothing I could do. I was aware that Kenyan currency was in great demand in Tanzania: on the black market it was possible to get twenty Tanzanian shillings for fifteen Kenyan shillings. When I came back through, he would give me the unfavorable black-market rate. A painless profit.

I stood beside my suitcase in the white afternoon glare awaiting Customs examination. That, however, proved to be a mercifully brief and desultory episode. I was nearly last in the queue, and the searches of the Customs Officer, which, I had noticed with dread, had been ominously thorough to begin with, had gradually lost their zest as the heat sapped his energy.

"Coming back this way?"

I nodded.

"Good." He grinned as he scrawled his chalk across the canvas.

We climbed back into the bus and set off for the Tanzanian post, a few hundred yards farther on. The building, an architectural counterpart of the one we had just left, was shabbier and dirtier. Once more we crowded out of the bus with our luggage. An official pointed to a concrete platform and directed that we haul our belongings up onto it. The passengers —nearly all of them Tanzanian peasants—looked visibly tense as they carried their boxes, baskets and cloth-wrapped bundles up onto the platform. There they began opening them up for inspection. Gathered anxiously about their possessions, they looked for all the world like a group of refugees who had no idea what their fate was to be. It was clear that Customs inspection on this side of the border was no mere ritual. Were these cowering individuals "the People" so often invoked, so often wept over, by the ideologues of the Tanzanian Revolution? Was it to these peasants, staring about them with the frightened eyes of children, that Mr. Omari had dedicated his book?

Hat in hand, I went over to the Immigration Office. The officer in charge, smartly dressed in a green uniform, was young and good-looking. On the wall behind him there were not one but *three* official photographs, Nyerere (his photograph, admittedly, slightly larger than the other two) flanked by his lesser luminaries of state: the Mwalimu's modesty compels him to share his personality cult. I had ample leisure to contemplate this robed and tasseled Trinity, because the officer, who was speaking to a friend on the phone—I assumed it was a friend because the conversation was giving rise to much thigh-slapping laughter—paid not the slightest attention to the queue that was building up in the room. A full five minutes elapsed before he was ready for business.

When I returned to my luggage on the platform, the Customs Officer was about halfway down the line. Those who had been cleared were busily repacking. The officer stooped to examine the bundle of an old peasant woman which seemed to contain mainly clothes. He lifted up each item, held it up to the light, went through the pockets, fingered the seams. What was he looking for? Was it just petty bureaucratic harassment? Not entirely . . . one corner of the platform was occupied by a small but growing pile of confiscated goods. The woman stared dazedly at him. He said something to her in Swahili. She put a hand into her bosom, brought out a

knotted handkerchief and undid the knot. Within were a few
crumpled banknotes and some coins. He returned the handkerchief and its contents to her. For a moment, the woman hesitated: she seemed afraid to take it back; to be offering it to
him. He pushed her hand away and moved on. His hand
delved into a cardboard box. He took out a cooking pot (he
removed the lid and peered inside), a bottle of cooking oil
(which he uncorked and smelled), a packet of detergent (he
opened it and shook out some of the blue powder into his
palm) . . . nothing escaped his scrutiny. Then it was my turn.
With a small grunt of triumph, he fished out from my suitcase the half-bottle of whisky I was carrying.

"And what is this?"

"Whisky."

He revolved the bottle. "You cannot take this into Tanzania, bwana."

"Why not?"

"It is not allowed. It is illegal to smuggle spirits into Tanzania."

"I wasn't smuggling . . ." I gazed at him indignantly.

"Then you should have declared it. Instead you have given
me all this trouble . . ."

"Show me where it says a tourist cannot take half a bottle
of whisky into Tanzania."

"I do not make the law, bwana." He shrugged. "I only do
what the law says I must do." He handed the bottle to a
minion, who ostentatiously bore it off toward the pile of
confiscated material.

The bus driver appeared at the foot of the platform. He
shouted, tapped his watch and pointed at the bus.

"Go," the plunderer said. "I don't want you to miss your
bus."

Some days later, I picked up a volume of Nyerere's speeches and writings and read, with the greatest interest, a charming little disquisition—delivered at a state banquet in Peking—on "The Supremacy of the People."

*

The mountains, higher summits draped in cloud, lay away to our right. Among them was snow-capped Kilimanjaro, but I was unable, because of the clouds, to identify it with certainty. The plains at the foot of the mountains were golden with the trash of harvested corn. But the land, though beautiful, had a stricken look. The road wound through settlements of crumbling houses. Faded green-and-black TANU flags fluttered over doorways and roofs. These would be the homes of the active Party workers, the so-called "ten-house cell" leaders (because they were in charge of ten houses) who formed the base of the Party pyramid. On the grounds of a school, a detachment of the People's militia was being drilled, legs kicking high as they goose-stepped around the compound. Why, I wondered, the goose step? Did it represent a vestigial memory of the German occupation? I did not associate the formalized goose step with Socialist Liberation of the Tanzanian variety. So, within minutes of crossing the border, I had had a taste of the confused rhetoric that fuels and sustains the Tanzanian Revolution. Still, after Kenya, these indications of militancy came as a shock. In Kenya, the Party claimed no idealism and had none—it was simply a careerist organization based on the Kikuyu tribe. Officially inspired devotion was not to a cause but to a man. Rhodesia and South Africa were far away and mattered to no one. *The Nation* expended more editorial space on the Middle East than it did on Southern Africa: it hardly ever ceased fulminating against the Palestinians and calling for tougher measures against terrorists. In Tanzania, however confusedly, the focus shifted back to Africa and its problems.

At Moshi, a nondescript town in the shadow of the mountains, I had to change buses. Two young men grabbed my suitcase and hustled me into the waiting Arusha bus. They demanded seven shillings for their services. I refused, offering them three. They became abusive. I raised my offer to three *Kenyan* shillings. Their eyes lit up at the suggestion. They scraped up the coins from my palm and vanished.

We moved across the sunlit plain, the mountains always on our right. The driver bent over me conspiratorially: he too wished to be paid in Kenyan shillings. But I had been warned about *agents provocateurs* and did not oblige. The bus toiled through the warm, golden afternoon. Several times we had to stop and allow the engine to cool. I caught glimpses of the enduring pastoral life that lay behind the Party flags and the goose-stepping People's militia: a naked youth, wet and shining, poised with arms outstretched on the edge of a pool; women bathing themselves and washing clothes in a rushing, rock-strewn stream; a boy with shaved head sitting on a rocky outcrop staring dreamily at a flock of goats.

I was sinking into my usual trancelike state when I was jolted back to full consciousness by a sudden grinding of brakes, the unmistakable thud of metal impinging on yielding flesh, followed by a tumbling forward of the passengers standing in the aisle. A great gabbling commotion broke out on all sides. I soon discovered what had happened: we had hit a wandering cow. The animal, its flanks still heaving, lay in the middle of the road, blood oozing in a crimson stream from its mouth, staining the asphalt. Its owner was kneeling beside it, staring at the blood, as if unable to grasp its meaning. Then he rose and uttered a piercing wail. Peasants streamed out of the fields and gathered round the dying animal. The driver mopped his sweating forehead and looked frightened. Maybe he feared a lynching; maybe he feared for his job; maybe he feared the arrival of the *polisi* who had been sent for. Maybe he feared all these things: in a society like this, a man must have so much to fear.

He began to harangue the passengers, speaking in Swahili. From his gestures and expression of aggrieved innocence I gathered that he was appealing for their support and explaining that the accident had occurred through no fault of his, that the cow should not have been where it was, that the blame must rest with the owner. Eventually, the *polisi* arrived. They took numerous statements, measured distances, drew chalk lines on the road, removed the dead animal. After about an hour, we were allowed to continue on our way. The driver, subdued and mournful, drove with exaggerated caution. Later, I was told by one of the passengers that he would have to appear before his cell leader.

"Is that serious?"

"It can be *very* serious."

"What can they do to him?"

"If they think he is at fault, they might send him away from the town to work on a development project somewhere."

That sounded unpleasant. I extended my silent sympathy to the unfortunate man.

We were crawling across a shimmering, uncultivated plain strewn with boulders. The sun, burning and very yellow, poured into the bus. Its heat, coalescing with the exhalations of the laboring engine, had a stupefying effect. It seemed to me that I had left Mombasa in some dim and distant past. Dazedly, the sun beating full on my face, I stared at an insect, wings frantically whirring, struggling to scale the interior surface of the window. All its efforts were in vain. As I watched, its exhaustion merging into my own, a hand stretched forth and snuffed out the wretched creature's existence, leaving only a smear.

A traffic circle, bright with flowers, signaled our entry into Arusha.

CHAPTER 7

Three Portraits

I

PIETER'S HOUSE, approached up a narrow, tortuous dirt track, occupied the summit of a hill commanding a fine view of the plain dotted with the cones of extinct volcanoes. From the top of the hill they looked like anthills. The walls of the spartanly furnished sitting room into which he led me were decorated with blown-up photographs illustrating the various afflictions brought on by malnutrition—children with bulbous bellies, deformed limbs, shrunken torsos.

"You find my wallpaper shocking?" His narrow, pudgy-lidded eyes glinted with faint amusement behind his thick, rimless lenses.

"A little . . ."

"Most of my foreign visitors are shocked. Most of them prefer not to know. I think it is good to know, good to be reminded every hour of the day."

He clapped his hands; his "boy" came running into the room; tea was ordered. Pieter had been living in Tanzania for nearly five years, working for a Dutch charity. He was a strict Calvinist: within minutes of our meeting he had informed me that he did not smoke or drink alcohol—and dis-

213

approved of those who did. Looking around the room, I observed that many of his books were theological works.

"When I was a student," he said, "I lived a bad life. I smoked. I drank. I went with girls. The Devil had possession of my soul."

"You believe in the Devil?"

"If God exists, the Devil exists. I was very unhappy while the Devil had possession of my soul. One day I tried to kill myself, I was so unhappy. They took me to hospital and I recovered. I thanked God. It was then I decided to dedicate my life to Him by serving the poor. Albert Schweitzer became my hero. I model my life on his."

"Why did you choose Tanzania?"

"I did not choose Tanzania. It chose me. The people I work for told me I must come here. But I am glad I came here. Nyerere is following the right policies." He stood by the window, his back to me, staring out at the plain. "Here I feel so much more free than I do at home in Holland. I feel I belong here." He turned to face me, his face made almost invisible by the glare. "I find Africans a very spiritual people. They have remained closer to nature than we have, closer to God."

"You mean they have remained more primitive . . ."

He scowled. "I do not like that word. I prefer to say 'simple.' That is how I wish them to remain."

The boy brought in our tea on a tray, rested it carefully on a low cane table and went out again.

"In that case you do not wish to see them 'develop'?"

A flicker of irritation momentarily disturbed the taut cast of his face. "I do not want them to repeat the mistakes we have made in Europe. Why must they too have factories and pollution and political parties? If *that* is what you mean by development, then, no, I do not wish to see them 'develop.' To be frank, speaking sociologically, I do not believe they are truly capable of such things. Why make them try for the impossible? It will only lead to unhappiness."

"You do not think their brains are up to it?"

"I think their brains have been conditioned in a different way from ours. Not better or worse. But *different*. It is foolish not to recognize that difference." He knelt by the cane table and poured out the tea.

"What do you wish for them?"

He took off his glasses and polished the lenses on his shirt sleeves. "I wish for them to have enough to eat, to be free of disease, to be happy and contented with their lot." He warmed to his theme. "The greatest asset of these people is their naturalness, their simplicity. When we give them our ideas and our machines, we destroy that."

"So you would not give them machines . . ."

"I personally would not. Why give a man a hydroelectric dam when a waterwheel would serve as well? Why give him a tractor when he can use an oxcart?"

"Why bother to give him anything at all? Why not just leave him alone? Why teach the primitive how to be primitive?"

He waved an arm at the photographs. "There is a great deal of suffering to be overcome. They must be taught to keep their population down so that they will not starve. It is a Christian's duty to help and to see that they follow the right path and are not led astray. But I fear it is already too late. They see what we Europeans have and they want to be like us. If I had my way I would not let them read newspapers, or go to the cinema or look at the television. But to do that now is like . . . what is the saying? . . . something about a stable and a horse."

"Shutting the stable door when the horse has already bolted."

"That is it. The horse, I think, has already bolted."

II

Mr. Henckel, a management expert, had been sent out to Tanzania by the United Nations. Mrs. Henckel, after three months in Arusha, was close to breakdown.

"Listen," she said, "it was traumatic for me when I moved sixty miles from my old home in upstate New York. Can you imagine what coming out here has been like for me? I tell you, it's driving me crazy. If I stay here another three months, I'll go out of my mind. I know it."

She was in her middle forties. Graying hair blended with gray eyes. Her freckled skin looked as if it had been soaked in formaldehyde.

"What's driving you crazy?"

"Everything. I can't get butter. I can't get milk. I can't get cheese. I can't get frankfurters. What do the people here *live* on?"

I knew what she meant: the shelves of the shops were bare. Only bottles of locally processed fruit juices, Chinese canned goods and out-of-date Eastern Bloc magazines seemed to be readily available. Arusha was a ghost town.

"The other day I had some painters in. They took one week to do a job that a New York painter would have done in one day. One whole week! Just having to sit here and watch them nearly drove me crazy. My dear husband tells me their slowness is probably the result of protein deficiency. Well, I try my best to be sympathetic. But there are limits even to my sympathy. How does protein deficiency explain the fact that there's nothing to buy?"

"Protein deficiency doesn't explain it. It explains protein deficiency."

She laughed. "Yeah, I guess it does. It's fantastic. I never imagined anything like this in my wildest dreams. You know, when our boy saw the refrigerator we had got for ourselves, his eyes popped right out of his little head. He didn't believe things like that existed. Why, back in New York State I have *two* refrigerators, and both are bigger than this one we've got here. I tried to explain, but I don't think he's taken it in."

"People here don't have refrigerators as a matter of course."

"People here don't have anything! It's driving me crazy. The car they've given us has a gearshift. I've never used a gearshift. In the State's it's all automatic transmission. So the car remains in the garage and I can't go anywhere. My *askari* [watchman] is always drunk, and burglars have tried to break in three times. I tell you, I'm going out of my mind."

"Before you came here you must have had some idea what it would be like."

"I never gave it a thought. I suppose I assumed everywhere was like the United States."

"You had never heard about underdeveloped countries?"

"Sure I had. But I never reckoned on there being no food in the stores and cars without automatic transmission . . ."

"Still," I said, "there are compensations."

"Name one."

"Well . . . there's the beauty of the landscape . . ."

"Give me the Grand Canyon any day."

"And the wild animals and the game parks . . ."

"I've been to a game park. I didn't care for it one little bit."

"Why not?"

"It was so dirty."

"Dirty?"

"Yes. So much dust, you know. I've never seen so much dust in my life. Why can't they build proper roads? I had to keep washing my hair. I hate having dirty hair. From now on I'll be quite happy to see my animals behind bars in zoos. The fact is, I was never much of an outdoor person. We went once to the Virgin Islands with some friends. The moment we got down to the beach, these people we were with kicked off their shoes and started walking along the sand. I couldn't do that sort of thing. I remember I was wearing a new pair of shoes that day which cost me sixty-five dollars. They were *ruined* in a few minutes. It nearly drove me crazy. They were such lovely shoes. Black with silver straps and open toes. I've never been able to find a pair like that again." She gazed down sadly at the shoes she was wearing. "Do you know what I'm going to do when I get back to the United States?"

"No."

"I'm going to get right down on my little old knees and kiss the ground. That is what I'm going to do. Get right down on my little old knees. Never again am I going to roam too far from upstate New York . . ."

III

The Masai girl lay huddled under a gray blanket. She had given birth two days previously and was exhausted. Her close-cropped hair emphasized the gauntness of her face. The baby slept on her bosom. The bed was without either sheet or pillow: the clinic did not run to such refinements. The room, like the bed, was elementary—no curtains, no table, no chair: just a bare concrete cubicle with a bed in one corner. When we entered, the girl drew the blanket up to her chin—she was naked under it, having no clothes suitable for the occasion—and stared impassively. The German volunteer, a trained nurse, smiled cheerfully. She asked a couple of questions in the local dialect. The girl's replies were barely audible. Mother and daughter were, apparently, as fine as could be expected in the circumstances. This was the girl's third confinement. Of the two previous children, one had died. The volunteer reckoned she was about twenty years old.

"Tomorrow she will have to leave." The volunteer picked up the sleeping baby and looked at it. "She shouldn't really. As you can see, she's still far too weak to feed it. But somebody else needs the bed. What can we do?" She returned the baby to its mother.

Outside, in the bright sunshine, women wrapped in colorful cloths queued patiently, waiting to have their babies weighed by the Swedish volunteer. Those who had completed the ritual sat on the grass in the shade of the jacaranda trees, talking softly, eating and drinking; a few were washing clothes at a standpipe. They were mostly Warusha, a branch of the Masai who had been converted to sedentary life. Some of them had walked many miles to attend the clinic (held once a week). It had become a bit of a social occasion.

There were flies everywhere, settling around the eyes of the children and their mothers, feeding greedily on sores, spreading the infections which the clinics sought to combat.

No attempt, I noticed, was made to brush the flies away: their victims seemed untroubled by their depredations. I watched the Swedish girl weighing the babies presented to her. Roughly half were below the recommended minimum weight for their age. The mothers of these starvelings were doled out rations of cooking oil, soya flour and cornmeal—gifts, as the cans and boxes and sacks in the storeroom proclaimed, of the people of the United States of America. It was a slow, arduous business.

"One of the strangest things," the Swedish volunteer said, "is that we cannot get well-off and educated Tanzanians to come and help us out. I know many middle-class women who sit at home all day with nothing to do but polish their nails and read foreign fashion magazines they buy from Kenya. If all we expatriates had to leave the country tomorrow, this clinic would probably have to be closed down. They just don't seem to care. They sit back and let us do everything. How do you account for that?"

She cradled a child in her arms, staring at its shrunken limbs; the head—grotesquely large in relation to the rest of its body—whose weight it did not have the strength to support; the flies that clustered around its half-closed eyes. It lay motionless in her arms, like something already dead.

"This child may not be alive in a month's time," she said without emotion. "Why should I care when they don't? Why do I bother to come here? That is a question I ask myself all the time."

CHAPTER 8

Animals and Men

THE GOANS of Arusha had organized an expedition to the Ngorongoro Crater. However, it was not the Goans but Mr. Mukerjee, himself neither a Goan nor a member of the Club that was organizing the outing, who invited me to come along.

Mr. Mukerjee's influence over the Goans stemmed from the fact that it was he who had arranged for the charter of a bus at a special concessionary rate: Mr. Mukerjee prided himself on having strange friends in strange places. I was a little reluctant to accept, having heard that there was some anxiety about the Club's being able to accommodate all its bona fide members who wanted to go.

But Mr. Mukerjee was insistent. "If I say you can come, then you can come. You mustn't let these spineless colonials frighten you off. Nobody is going to argue with *me* if I say that I am bringing you along as my guest."

His belligerence confirmed what I had heard about him— that Mr. Mukerjee thrived on "confrontations." I began to feel that his invitation was motivated less by a desire to do me a favor than by a compulsion to exercise and test the limits of his power over the Goan Club.

Mr. Mukerjee, who was fond of describing himself as an "Indian national," worked in some mysterious capacity for

the (now defunct) East African Community which had its
headquarters in Arusha. The silolike towers housing the Community occupied the side of a hill overlooking the town.
What actually went on within those towers never became
clear to me, though I visited the place a number of times. As
Swift wrote of the Academy of Lagado, "Every room hath
in it one or more Projectors; and I believe I could not be in
fewer than five hundred rooms." Arusha's Projectors—nearly
all supplied by the United Nations—seemed hardly less fantastical than their Laputan equivalents who labored at con-
verting ice into gunpowder or proving the malleability of fire
or inventing a device for plowing the ground with hogs (that
has echoes of Tanzanian self-reliance). Much of Mr. Mukerjee's time was spent in acrimonious dispute with his colleagues.
He had achieved a genuine notoriety when, fed up with the
failure of his employers to provide him with suitable domestic
accommodation—as he put it—he had gone on a hunger
strike: an event which, months after it had occurred, was
still the talk of Arusha. The Tanzanians, who had never witnessed anything of the kind before, were stupefied. Mr.
Mukerjee got his house.

As our expedition headed out of Arusha one Saturday
afternoon, Mr. Mukerjee relived his exploit with undisguised
glee.

"These people had never seen anything like it. They had
no idea what to do with me—and I was wearing a *dhoti*, which
confused them even more. Their trouble was that they didn't
know the kind of man they were dealing with. They thought
I was another spineless Asian who they could kick around
like a football." He waved contemptuously at our Goan com-

panions. "They must have thought I was like one of those. But I'm no *Asian*. Not by a long chalk. I'm an Indian national, and I showed them what a nasty customer I could be." He giggled. "I can be a very nasty man when I want to. I can turn very ugly indeed."

Mr. Mukerjee was accompanied by Mrs. Mukerjee, a plump, pale-skinned woman, who, while her husband spoke, pondered his countenance with benevolent satisfaction, and by his two sons, both of whom bristled with safari para- phernalia—binoculars, cameras, dark glasses, sun hats, thick- soled walking shoes—and both of whom treated their Indian nationality no less seriously than their father did his. Our little group occupied the rear of the bus, where we spread ourselves comfortably. The Goans up the front were more tightly packed. From the very beginning it was obvious that the Mukerjees (and I) were considered by the rest of the party as forming a separate—and hostile—camp. I dreaded the confrontations that lay ahead of us.

"My husband tells me you are a writer of books," Mrs. Mukerjee said."

"Occasionally."

"I am a writer too." She smiled graciously at me. "But not of books."

I asked her what she wrote.

"I write shorti stories. Do you write shorti stories?"

"Sometimes."

"How many shorti stories have you written?"

"Not many. About six or seven."

Mrs. Mukerjee looked at me pityingly. "I have written over a hundred shorti stories."

I congratulated her.

"My wife writes shorti stories of high excellence," Mr. Mukerjee put in. "She has great talent."

"I am sure she does. Are her shorti stories written in English?"

"Some," Mrs. Mukerjee said—I thought a trifle evasively.

"She has an excellent English style," Mr. Mukerjee said.

"But mostly I write in the vernacular," Mrs. Mukerjee said. "In Bengali. That is a very poetic language. Much more poetic than English."

"What sort of things do you write about?"

"I have many themes. But mainly I write about poor people. I think there is much beauty in our Indian poverty. Much spiritual value."

"What about African poverty? Do you write about that too?"

Mrs. Mukerjee played with the gold bracelets that ringed her fat forearm. "African poverty is different. It does not inspire me. I do not find it so spiritual."

The conversation lapsed. Mr. Mukerjee was nodding off to sleep. Some of the Goans started to sing. Mr. Mukerjee, coming to with a start, commanded silence. An elderly lady glanced disapprovingly at him.

"What is wrong with their singing?" she asked. "You have no right to behave like that."

"Damned colonials," Mr. Mukerjee muttered.

"What did you say?" The lady glowered at him.

Mr. Mukerjee did not reply. Instead he, Mrs. Mukerjee and the two Mukerjee boys ostentatiously stuffed their ears with pieces of cotton wool.

"Some people really have a nerve," the lady observed loudly to a friend of hers.

War had been declared.

We were crossing a treeless plain. The withered grass had been cropped so close that it could hardly be said to exist. Bleaching light and heat rained from an incandescent sky. A haze of dust stained the remote horizon. That vast, desiccated expanse lay perfectly still and silent under the high, white sky. Here, within living memory, there had been trees. But the trees had all been cut down for firewood and the land was slowly turning into desert. Fire-blackened hillsides were spiked with the leafless, twisted skeletons of a dying secondary vegetation. The Masai periodically roamed these plains with their herds of cattle, squeezing what little sustenance they could from the desolation. Masai cattle were particularly damaging to the land over which they passed, more damaging even than goats: they had a tendency to pluck out the grass by its roots. In a short time even the Masai would be driven from these plains. The ruined land was austerely beautiful.

Mrs. Mukerjee offered me a beef sandwich: the singing having stopped, the Mukerjees had removed the cotton from their ears.

"I'm afraid I do not eat beef."

Mrs. Mukerjee was astonished. She prodded Mr. Mukerjee awake.

"Did you hear what he said, Dilip?"

Mr. Mukerjee stared sleepily at me.

"He says he does not eat beef."

"Holy cow!"

The two boys laughed.

"You people from the colonies are very old-fashioned," Mrs. Mukerjee said, biting with deep relish into her sandwich.

"Progressive ideas travel slowly," Mr. Mukerjee said.

Pride stirred. "Trinidad is not a colony."

"You mean you people are independent?" Mrs. Mukerjee, jaws working, cheeks puffed, stared wide-eyed at me.

Mr. Mukerjee laughed outright.

We left the tarmac, turning on a dirt track. Thornbushes covered the stony plain. Ranges of hills appeared. Some miles ahead, a cliff rose sheer from the plain, a black wall against the white sky. It was a dramatic sight. From time to time, wandering herds of lean cattle strayed onto the track, the tiny bells strung around their necks tinkling pleasingly. The herdboys, lean as the animals they were tending, followed our passage impassively, leaning on their staffs. There was a flurry of excitement when a pair of giraffes was spotted loping across the plain, their long, floating strides taking them rapidly away from us. The Mukerjees, however, remained studiously calm, refusing to rise from their seats. Mr. Mukerjee grimaced at the excited Goans who had stampeded to the windows.

"All this fuss over a giraffe," he said. "I have never seen such foolish people in my life."

The cliff wall loomed closer; the road started its climb toward the summit. It was a steep, perilous ascent, the outer curves of the narrow track swinging out into blue vacancy. Mr. Mukerjee closed his eyes: he said he did not have a head for heights. The plain fell quickly away below us and the shrunken, shining body of Lake Manyara took shape, a silver glare edged with an area of mossy green marking the extent of its dehydrated bed. Beyond it was the brown, oceanic sweep of the plain, the brown becoming tinged with pink toward a horizon bounded by the barely discernible serrations of remote mountain ranges. In all that vertiginous expanse, there was no sign of human presence. Awesome emptiness. Awesome beauty.

The land flattened, becoming greener. Here were banana groves and patches of jungly forest. We drove through a township. The road was lined with stalls heaped with basketry and animal carvings. Splendidly coiffed and greased Masai warriors brandished their spears, scowling sulkily. They were waiting to be photographed. Then we were in exquisite open country, moving through a cool, translucent dusk glowing with soft color—yellows, browns and blues. Scattered groups of huts stood amid fields of wheat and corn and sisal.

The pastoral beauty of the land hinted at the ideological backwardness of its inhabitants. In this area, according to a Party official who had done a political survey, the life of the community was "torn between two opposing forces, traditionalism on the one hand and modernization on the other." Despite the Party's best efforts, "traditionalism" seemed to have the upper hand. The peasants here displayed little or no understanding of TANU policies, being ignorant "of the concepts contained in the Arusha Declaration and the paper on Socialism and Rural Development." Their enthusiasm was restricted to those government projects they considered immediately relevant to their needs. Thus, they had set to work willingly enough on a godown for their crops and a schoolhouse; but, the official complained, they showed not the slightest interest in the erection of a TANU office. ". . . the foundation is now spoilt due to neglect . . . They say it benefits only the Party officials."

Not only were the peasants ignorant of the Arusha Declaration and the paper on Socialism and Rural Development; they were often downright hostile to the Party and its representatives. They had reason to be unfriendly. TANU zealots would not allow anyone to sell livestock in the market unless he or she bought a Party membership card. Similarly, only Party members were allowed to brew *pombe*—the local beer. Worse still, they looked back longingly to colonial times. "They said that during that period even the most junior members of the local administrative staff had command over certain goods and services. One very conservative leader said, 'A leader like me got certain things freely, such as pombe and labor on his shamba . . .'" The ten-house-cell leaders were illiterate and did not understand their revolutionary duties. Because they did not receive "material reward," they did not bother to exert themselves: out of twenty-five cell leaders interviewed by the official, not one had ever called a meeting of his members. "The task of bringing change in the countryside [was the sad conclusion] is not an easy one."

Darkness fell on the recalcitrant land. A yellow moon rose, lighting up the sky. Sheet lightning flashed among the hills. The bus went slowly, its headlights illuminating the dusty track. Someone shouted. I was startled to see a man, bathed in the glare of the headlights, standing in the middle of the track with arms upraised. He was holding a rifle. We stopped. An agitated murmur swept the bus. More men—perhaps half a dozen—emerged out of the bush, surrounding the bus. They were all armed, and all were dressed in everyday clothes.

"Soldiers . . . are they soldiers?" Mrs. Mukerjee gazed fearfully at her husband. "If they are soldiers, why are they not in uniform?"

"These are not soldiers," Mr. Mukerjee replied.

"Dacoits? Guerrillas?"

"It is possible."

"Those are not regulation rifles," the older of the boys said.

The remark cheered no one.

One of the men entered the bus, ran his eyes over us and went out again.

"Do not be afraid." Mr. Mukerjee comforted his wife. "They won't be interested in us. They are after bigger fish."

And he was right. The men, after consulting among themselves on the roadside, waved us on. After the adventure, everyone was gay. The Mukerjees consumed the last of their beef sandwiches; the singing started up again.

We drove on slowly through the dark, climbing steadily. The cool air turned distinctly chill. Mr. Mukerjee talked of his addiction to thin, cold air; Mrs. Mukerjee talked of Gulmarg, the Himalayan holiday resort.

"Do you people in Trinidad have high mountains with snow?"

I said we did not. She gazed pityingly at me.

An hour later, the lights of the lodge came into view.

*

That night there was a discotheque, the music played on a scratchy, battery-operated record player supplied by the manager of the lodge. The poor reproduction did not dampen the ardor of the Goan girls (they outnumbered the boys), who danced dedicatedly with each other, "bumping and grinding." The German tourists who, at the beginning of the evening, were gathered in a circle in front of the log fire were driven out. Mr. Mukerjee, seeking a confrontation, complained to the manager about the noise. The manager—a big, bearded but unturbaned Sikh—stood his ground.

"You can always go to your room if you do not like," he replied, politely obdurate.

"I have no desire to go to my room. My family and I have every right to stay here if we wish to."

"So have they."

"But do they have a right to kick up such a racket? It is disgraceful behavior. I have not come all this way to watch a bunch of colonials making fools of themselves—and disturbing the peace of the night into the bargain."

The manager shrugged. "If you don't care for it, you know what you can do." He turned his massive back on Mr. Mukerjee.

This was more than Mr. Mukerjee could bear. He chased around his adversary so that they were facing each other again. "Look here—do you know who you are talking to?"

"I don't care who you are." The manager stared insolently. "It is I who am boss here, and what I say goes."

Mr. Mukerjee's bulbous eyes started out of his head.

Mrs. Mukerjee tried to restrain her husband. "Please, Dilip. It is no good arguing with him. Let us go to our room."

Mr. Mukerjee pushed her aside. "I'd have you know, sir, that you are not talking to a spineless Asian colonial. You are talking, sir, to an Indian national, a citizen, born and bred, of the Republic of India. I won't be treated in this way."

The manager remained unimpressed.

"Calm down, Dilip." Mrs. Mukerjee took hold of her husband's arm. "Let us go to our room." She looked reproachfully at the manager. "You have no right to speak to him in that rude way."

Although still protesting, Mr. Mukerjee allowed himself to be led away. The two Mukerjee boys followed their parents.

The manager heaved himself into the seat beside me. "You meet all types in this business," he said.

"I expect you do."

"From the moment I set eyes on him I knew he was a troublemaker. I can spot a troublemaker a mile off." He examined me closely. "You play poker?"

I said I did not.

He sighed and called to the bar for a bottle of *konyagi*—the Tanzanian equivalent of gin.

I asked whether he enjoyed looking after the lodge.

"I used to enjoy owning it much more." He poured himself a generous helping of the *konyagi* and drank it at a gulp.

"My family built this place up from nothing." He watched the bumping, grinding girls. "We used to have fingers in lots of pies—transport, gemstones, sisal . . ."

"And it's all gone?"

"All gone . . . all gone . . ."

His family was scattered over the face of the globe. He had two brothers in England, a brother and sister in Canada, another sister in the United States; his parents had retired to the Punjab.

"Why didn't you go too?" I asked.

"Me? I couldn't be bothered. I like the slow pace of life here." He laughed. "And they were kind enough to let me stay on here as manager after they nationalized it. If they had put an African in charge, it would have closed down a long time ago."

His eyes strayed toward a khaki-clad African sitting at the bar. The man was looking at us assessingly.

"You mustn't misunderstand me," the manager said in a louder voice, a voice intended to carry. "These things take time. I am all for socialism. Our people used to exploit the Africans very badly."

He downed his *konyagi*; he rose. "I must go and do my accounts," he said—and hurried away.

*

In the morning a damp, gray mist, driven by the wind, smoked and eddied about the lodge. The sun was nowhere in sight, and the cold was piercing. A smell of wet grass and leaves permeated the icy air. The guests were wrapped up in thick sweaters; faces were pinched and drawn. There was much excitement when an elephant, its gray bulk blending into the shifting mist, was discovered feeding in the high grass at the rear of the lodge. Cameras and binoculars appeared. The Mukerjees held aloof from this vulgar exhibition of enthusiasm. Mr. Mukerjee stared grimly about him, tilting his head in unsmiling greeting when he saw me: the events of the night before still rankled.

The mist thinned as the sun rose higher; the morning warmed up. Sweaters and scarves were discarded. Soon the mist had cleared completely. After breakfast the Land-Rovers that were to take us down to the floor of the crater arrived. The Mukerjees immediately staked their claim to exclusive use of one of the vehicles.

"Spread yourselves and scowl if anybody comes near," Mr. Mukerjee ordered. "I'm not having any of these colonials in our Land-Rover."

The Mukerjees spread themselves and scowled. As it was, no one challenged our occupation: a glance within seemed sufficient to frighten them away.

"Look at them," Mr. Mukerjee giggled, "packed like sardines. Not much room for a discotheque, eh?"

Regrettably, we were not allowed to leave without a further confrontation.

The younger Mukerjee boy asked our Tanzanian driver if the viewing trap in the roof could be opened.

"It is not going to be opened now," the driver replied brusquely. "Why be in such a hurry? There are no animals to see up here. Have some patience, bwana."

The boy was silenced.

Mr. Mukerjee immediately leaped to his defense. "He didn't ask you to open it *now*," he said. "He asked you if it *could* be opened. That is a different question."

The driver did not—or would not—grasp the subtle distinction. "It will be opened in the crater," he insisted. "I am not opening it up here."

"That is not what he asked," Mr. Mukerjee retorted with rising heat. "He asked if it is *capable* of being opened. He wanted to know if it works. That is an entirely reasonable inquiry, and it deserves a reasonable reply. Can't you understand English?"

"Dilip . . . Dilip . . ." Mrs. Mukerjee tried to soothe her husband.

The driver stared at him mulishly. "The roof will be opened when we get to the crater. Not before." He folded his arms across his chest.

Mr. Mukerjee was, by this time, beside himself. He raged at the driver, saying that he was not a man who took insults lying down, that he could be a very nasty man indeed if he wanted to, that he was no damn-fool Asian but an Indian national, a first-class and not a second-class citizen.

While this was going on, the other Land-Rovers had left. I watched the driver anxiously. Would he abandon us? Would he, goaded to fury, strike Mr. Mukerjee to the ground? Amazingly enough, he showed no sign of wanting to do either of these things. Instead, he listened intently, his arms folded peaceably across his chest. Astonishment had displaced anger. Finally, Mr. Mukerjee having temporarily exhausted himself, he said with utmost mildness, "I thought you were an Asian. Like the others."

"Me! Like the others!" Mr. Mukerjee hopped about. "In what way am I like the others? I have a backbone. I have nothing in common with those invertebrates. I am a citizen of the Republic of India. Would you like me to show you my passport?"

The driver laughed. "I understand. It is all clear to me now." He said something in Swahili to the manager, who had come out to see what all the fuss was about.

Mr. Mukerjee rounded on the manager, who was wearing a bathrobe. "I demand to know what he is saying about me."

"He says," the manager replied reluctantly, "that you are a man to be feared and respected."

Mr. Mukerjee was too overcome to say anything. He seemed confused, stunned by the unexpectedness, the ease of his triumph.

"Are you sure that is what he said?" He stared distrustfully at the manager.

"Ask him yourself," the manager answered sourly—and returned inside.

Mr. Mukerjee glanced at his wife; he rubbed his hands; he giggled. "It shows you what a little firmness will do in your dealings with these people. You have to stand up to them. It is what I have always said."

"The roof will be opened when we reach the bottom of the crater," the driver said. "It is not safe to open it before."

"Fine." Mr. Mukerjee smiled pleasantly at him. "If it is not safe, it is not safe. You see, I'm a very reasonable man."

We set off.

*

Suddenly, the crater opened out below us. Its floor, yellow-white and smooth, was encircled by the purple mountain wall crowned with a band of cloud. It lay there like a dream spawned by the earth, defying the senses; a vast bowl floating amid the mountains. We started the descent.

"So," the driver said conversationally as he guided the Land-Rover down a winding, stony ledge, "you from Bombay?"

"Calcutta," Mr. Mukerjee replied. He was gripped by vertigo and looked pale and tense.

"Is that near Bombay?"

"No. It is very far. Hundreds of miles. India is a big country."

"Bigger than Tanzania?"

"Much bigger."

"Ah . . . But do you have such a thing as this in India?" He swept out an arm toward the immensity below us.

"No."

The driver grinned. "That is what I thought."

It took about twenty minutes to complete the descent. A worn patina of brown grass covered the floor of the crater. The Land-Rover moved easily over the hard, smooth ground, throwing up clouds of dust. Zebras and buffalo and antelope browsed placidly in scattered groups. A pair of ostriches fled before us. Hyenas skulked through the grass. The Masai herdsmen who lived on the floor of the crater trailed self-absorbedly after their flocks, ignoring our presence. The crater was shot through with an air of theatricality: it was as if the animals were aware of their importance, of the spectacle they were supposed to provide. All about us I could see the explosions of dust produced by other Land-Rovers, emphasizing the artificiality. The crater had been transformed into a kind of Disneyland.

In East Africa, the concern with wildlife has become obsessive. The animals of the region cannot be ignored for long. They press in on the visitor; they command attention. Or perhaps I should say that it is the *obsession* that presses in on the visitor, that commands attention. At every turn one is reminded of their existence by the army of tourists in their safari outfits, the flotillas of zebra-striped vans, the convoys of dusty Land-Rovers returning from upcountry expeditions. Over sundowners on the terrace of the Norfolk Hotel, rich American voices discuss the sightings of the day and the prospects for the next. Notice boards in the bigger hotels inform patrons of the numbers and types of animals seen during the previous twenty-four hours. Animal themes dominate decor. In the window of a Nairobi bookshop, out of forty-five books on display, thirty-one (I counted) were devoted to wildlife and related themes.

Speeches by prominent politicians refer to the animals as "our heritage"—virtually a "cultural heritage." When a rumor was spread in Nairobi that there was starvation at the "animal orphanage," the city's hotels responded with generous, widely publicized donations of food. Editorials brimming with outrage appeared in *The Nation*, a newspaper famed for its long-running campaign against the slaughter of elephants.

"Our heritage" was being destroyed. But it was odd to read elsewhere—almost, as it were, in the same breath—of a child who, while drawing water from a well, had been savaged to death by a hyena.

Animals are frequently at the center of major political controversy. Tanzania quarreled with Kenya, which it accused of siphoning off too many tourists. Relations between the two countries became so bad that Tanzania sealed off its borders. Tanzanians will tell you that *their* animals are the best. "It's only here you see lions sleeping in trees," I was assured. "In Kenya lions don't sleep in trees."

The obsessive concern with wildlife leads insidiously to the degradation of the human population. In the eyes of the beholder, the more backward tribes become mere adjuncts to the animals. ("If you ever go to Ngorongoro," I had been advised, "make sure you don't miss the Masai in the crater. They really are value for money.") Indeed, they are often treated, if they are sufficiently exotic and sufficiently primitive, as their equivalents. Side by side with all the lavishly produced books describing the animal population, are the no less lavishly produced books describing the human fauna of the region. Ocher-painted Masai compete for attention with snarling lions; both—in their natural state—are regarded as endangered species which must be preserved for the amusement and instruction of future generations. Animal and man blend into each other, actors in one and the same primeval spectacular. The much loved Karen Blixen consciously paired the native and the animal. In *Out of Africa*, the opening chapter is titled "Kamante and Lulu": Kamante is a brutalized Kikuyu herdboy she takes into her house; Lulu is a stray gazelle she befriends—and also takes into her house. She writes about the two with equal charm, and in exactly the same way. They are both what she calls "links with the wild."

Already I had met the German, a confirmed and passionate environmentalist, who had asserted that the preservation of Africa's wildlife was more important to him than the preservation of Africans. His was, of course, an extreme point of view. Yet his extremism was only a matter of degree. "Where then," asks the ecologically concerned author of an article in a magazine with some pretensions to respectability, "should conservationists look for hope in a world of darkening gloom?" They will, according to him, look in vain while humans—and he means *poor* humans, Third World humans—continue to breed at their present rate. "Man's influence" must be diminished. "Until the growth of human population is controlled . . . the eco-systems [will] remain in considerable danger."

The African, except where he remains primitive enough to fit without disturbance into the "eco-system"—and, hence, lends color to it while dying at a conveniently premature age—is a pest and a threat to other people's enjoyment. The new environmentalism is part of the privileged consumption pattern of the affluent and industrialized; those who can afford the air fares, the hotels, the Land-Rovers and the guides; those whose children don't draw water from wells and rarely get savaged by marauding hyenas.

"Look!"

"What?"

"A rhinoceros!"

"Where?"

"Over there!"

About half a mile away, a gray shape, rocklike in color and

immobility, was just visible. It turned and started to move away.

"Driver," Mrs. Mukerjee called, tapping the man's shoulder, "let us chase it. I would like to see how fast it runs."

"It will get angry if we do that," the driver said. "It will attack us."

We drove on.

"You have rhinoceros in India?" the driver asked.

"No," Mr. Mukerjee said. "But we have tigers."

"Ah—tigers." He looked sad. "We do not have tigers in Africa. What about giraffes? Do you have those?"

"No. We do not have those."

The driver looked happy again.

We caught up with the convoy, which had come to a halt near a grove of trees. There, in the shade, lay the tawny bodies of two lions, a male and a female. They did not stir.

"Are they dead?" Mrs. Mukerjee asked.

"They are asleep," the driver said.

"Blow the horn," she urged. "Wake them up."

"No," the driver said. "They must not be disturbed."

"They are so lazy. Why are they sleeping like that in the middle of the day?"

"Because their bellies are full. Because they have been hunting all night."

"But what is the good to see lions when they are sleeping? It is such a waste of time. Blow the horn."

The driver, however, would not oblige.

The elder Mukerjee boy took some photographs. He was ticking off in a notebook all the animals he had seen. Once "seen," once photographed, they appeared to lose all interest for him.

Our last stop was at a pool edged by tall water grasses. Here were gathered all the Land-Rovers from all the lodges that perch above the crater. Scores of tourists milled about, eating sandwiches, drinking beer and Coca-Cola and photographing the hippopotami who poked their blunt, glistening snouts out of the water. Thirsting animals would have to wait for us to depart before they could come to drink. The wind was cutting. I wandered away from the pool, climbing a low hill. In the distance were other hills, lilac-gray in color and smooth as hairless hide, their flanks thrown into sharp relief by patches of dense shadow. Their contours were harmonious and full of grace. But despite their clarity of outline, they seemed to lack solidity and to hover weightlessly—to be jointly produced by an etherealization of the earth and a condensation of the raining light. The crater invited movement across its lilting surface; it evoked deep-seated nomadic instincts. An antelope, standing stock-still, stared at me with a mixture of curiosity and alarm. Birds of prey circled overhead, shadows scudding swiftly across the withered grass. On the well-trodden path below me, tourists filed toward the latrines which were built on the summit of the neighboring rise.

CHAPTER 9

The Haven of Peace

I

COCONUT PALMS and mango trees signaled the nearness of the coast. The mud huts, the untidy bush, the humid heat reminded me of rural Trinidad. I had been traveling through the night in the cramped confines of a "luxury" bus, and now dawn was approaching. The bus halted. Driven by the compulsions of early morning, the passengers spread themselves at discreet intervals along the grassy verge. The sun rose quickly. Dar es Salaam began with a sprinkling of factories merging into dense suburbs of shanty-lined alleys. Overburdened buses of Rumanian origin swayed and jolted along the potholed highway. Crowds of men shuffled along the dusty roadside heading toward the city. An even greater number squatted idly in the thick roadside dust, arms limply hanging. Battered, indecipherable road signs adorned dilapidated traffic circles which looked like miniature dust bowls. Lines of washing hung from the balconies of moss-blackened tenements. Everywhere—dust, neglect, decay: the unpainted facades of the buildings, the potholes, the unswept and crumbling pavements told of a city that was falling to pieces.

I was already falling into that state of depression which

arrival in a strange place nearly always arouses in me. A new town meant new faces to become accustomed to; unknown "contacts"—strange names hastily scribbled down—to be contacted; the usual explanations of my presence to be offered. "So-and-so suggested that I try and get in touch with you while I was here . . . I'm visiting East Africa for a few months . . . yes—my first visit . . . no, no, not quite a holiday . . . well, I hope to write something about it . . . no, no, nothing political . . . not a novel either . . . well, if you could spare the time it certainly would be nice to meet, have a drink, a chat . . ." I was weary of it all, weary of the suspicion, the misunderstandings, the broken promises.

At the bus station I was besieged by taxi drivers.

"Tell me the name of a good hotel."

"Kilimanjaro . . ."

"New Africa . . ."

"Which is nearer?"

"New Africa . . ."

"Then take me to the New Africa." It was, I knew, an expensive choice (made even more so by the absurd official rate of exchange), but I yearned for coolness, comfort and sleep. I would pamper myself, if only for a day and a night.

On the umbrella-shaded terrace of the New Africa, people were having breakfast and reading newspapers. It looked promising. The reception clerk took a long time making up his mind as to whether or not he could offer me a room. I was surprised that the hotel was so full, being well aware that Tanzania's tourist trade was languishing. This was due partly to the fierce, efficiently organized competition from Kenya— so galling to the Tanzanians, whose lions slept in trees—and partly to Tanzanian ambivalence: tourists were regarded as a corrupting influence. The mystery was soon cleared up. It was not tourists who filled the New Africa, but aid workers and their families for whom the government could find no other suitable accommodation.

After thumbing through registers and scrutinizing charts, the clerk concluded that he could offer me a room. But I would, he warned, have to wait until the room was cleaned, an operation that could take one hour, two hours or even three hours.

I bought a newspaper and went out to the terrace. A waiter in a colorful smock dawdled toward me. I ordered breakfast— toast, fried eggs and coffee. The waiter dawdled away. A thickset dwarf, moustachioed and bearded, crossed the terrace and sat down at the table next to mine. He was, at most, four feet tall. From waist to head he was normally proportioned; it was the lower half of him which had been savagely compressed. He was smartly dressed in jacket and tie and long trousers. Our eyes met. I looked away, ashamed of my naked curiosity, and addressed myself to the newspaper. "Moon Beams," the astrologer of the *Daily News* (I had not expected to find astrologers in socialist Tanzania), was reassuring: "Your activities progress satisfactorily. More understanding in work environment. Clear ideas. Don't let anyone influence you."

"What does it say for Leo?"

The dwarf smiled genially at me.

"It says, 'Don't allow anyone to interfere in your private life. You could spend a pleasant day in the company of those you love. You feel self-confident.' "

The dwarf nodded and stroked his beard thoughtfully.

On the following page there was a photograph of laughing

Chinese peasants digging a ditch. I began to read an article on the National Lottery. "Make no mistake [ran the opening paragraph] Sportsmen and Culture Men are among the best ambassadors of our country. Filbert Bayi, that great metric miler of our time, Mwinga Mwanjala the diminutive sprinter who at the age of thirteen gave a tough time to experienced and well-groomed athletes even in Europe, and many others, have made a tremendous contribution towards putting Tanzania on the world map. So has the great though blind drummer, Morris Nyunyusa, who at the Expo 70 in Japan held the Japanese Emperor spellbound with the way he pounded ten drums at a go to produce music unheard of in that country. Mzee Nyunyusa's tom toms in Japan clearly sounded a warning to the world that Tanzania's cultural dynamite has not yet fully exploded . . ." The profits made by the national lottery, the article then went on to explain, had helped to make all this possible.

Half an hour went by and there was still no sign of my breakfast. My waiter was strolling nonchalantly among the tables. I called him over.

"What's happened to my breakfast?"

"It is coming."

"When?"

"It is coming."

He went away. Fifteen minutes later he returned. "It will soon be ready. The cook forgot."

The dwarf smiled sympathetically.

"They're very slow in Tanzania," he said. "They have no dynamism. Have you visited Nairobi?"

"Yes . . ."

"There people are much more dynamic. You must have noticed. Here it's as if they have no energy at all. For a businessman like myself it's very trying."

"You are from Kenya?"

"Can't you tell? I am a Kikuyu. Kikuyus are very dynamic."

I asked what his business was. He said he exported Makonde carvings.

"My real ambition, though," he said, "is to further my studies."

"What would you like to study?"

"I would like to take a degree in economics at the London School of Economics. I hear the teaching is very good there."

My breakfast arrived. I noticed there was no butter and asked for some.

"Butter you cannot have."

"Why not?"

"Because there is none."

The coffee I poured into my cup turned out to be tea.

"Is anything wrong, bwana?" The waiter looked at me worriedly.

"Everything's fine. Just fine."

"Since you are satisfied with my service, you will give me nice tip?"

"Tipping is illegal in Tanzania. Do you want me to break the law?"

He giggled.

"I think you are a capitalist roader. The Mwalimu will not like that."

"The Mwalimu will not know."

I handed him a hundred-shilling bill. "I want all my change back." I asked him to bring me a box of matches. Fifteen minutes later he returned, the bill intact.

"Change you cannot have."

"Is that possible?"

"The cashier has not yet been to the bank."

"What am I supposed to do about that?"

"Maybe you can ask one of these people sitting here. Maybe one of them will have change."

"Maybe *you* can ask."

"I have got some change," the dwarf said.

He hopped off his chair and came over to my table. His wallet was stuffed with bills of all denominations.

"What about the matches?"

"Matches you cannot have."

The check (including a small tip) having been settled, I went to see if my room was ready. It was not.

"How much longer do I have to wait?"

"That is difficult to say," the clerk replied. The cleaners, he said, were attending a meeting. "They are making big protest about the racist Rhodesian fascists."

I returned to the terrace. The dynamic dwarf had vanished. I sat and waited, watching the Rumanian buses jolting from pothole to pothole. After about an hour, I was summoned by the clerk.

"A little problem has arisen," he said.

I said nothing.

"The cleaners cannot get into your room to clean it." He smiled affably at me.

I remained calm. "Why is that?"

"The keys have been lost."

"Oh, well . . ."

"It is a great mystery. I cannot understand it. They have searched everywhere. I myself have searched."

"So I take it you cannot give me a room after all." My calmness intensified.

He laughed heartily. "Not at all. I also have some good news—I have discovered there is another room we can give you."

"But I have to wait until it is cleaned . . ."

His laughter swelled. "No. It has already been cleaned. You can move in straightaway."

A bellboy relieved me of my luggage. Not daring to trust myself to the elevator, I climbed the stairs to the third floor. The bellboy, after a vain and violent struggle with the door, realized he had brought the wrong key, looked amazed and disappeared. He returned with the right key. Depression turned to anger at the sight of the unmade bed. The bellboy once more looked amazed and disappeared. I felt that this time he would not return. Anger turned to despair when I discovered that the hot-water faucets did not work and that the towels were damp and smelled of recent use. I sat down on the bed and collected myself before calling the reception desk.

"What kind of hotel is this?"

"This is Five Star *hoteli*."

"The bed in my room was unmade."

"I'll send somebody to make it for you."

"The towels weren't clean."

"I'll send somebody with clean ones."

"The hot water doesn't work."

A short silence at the other end. Then: "Nobody has complained about the hot water before."

"Well, I am."

"You mean the hot water is not hot?" He spoke slowly, emphasizing each word.

"No," I said, "the hot water is not hot. The hot water is cold."

"I do not know what to say, bwana."

The cleaners came, bringing fresh towels and sheets. When they had gone, I turned the air conditioning on to its maximum setting and tried to sleep. After about an hour, I awoke with a start from disturbed, disjointed dreams in which the dwarf had figured prominently. My head was spinning; I was bathed in sweat.

Malaria!

The nightmarish thought panicked me. How could this happen after all the scrupulous care I had taken? I knew no one in Dar es Salaam. What was going to become of me in this godforsaken hole of a town? Rationality reasserted itself. I placed a hand against the grille of the air-conditioning unit. It was not working. I dressed, packed my clothes and went down to the lobby.

"You are leaving us so soon?" The clerk was flabbergasted. "Why?"

"Nothing works."

"That is a serious allegation, bwana." He became stern, dignified. "This is a Five Star *hoteli*. The best. Every modern convenience."

"I think something a little less modern might suit me better."

"You realize that I cannot give you back your foreign exchange?"

"I realize."

The smartly dressed lady at the Tourist Information Office

suggested that I might try one of the beach *hoteli*. "We have two run by the *governmenti*. Five Star."

"I do not want Five Star."

I went through the list she showed me. My eyes paused at the "Haven of Peace." It was relatively cheap, and its claims to comfort, though modest, were (I felt) sincere.

The lady did not approve of my choice. "That is not Five Star. Also, it is owned by a capitalist, not by the *governmenti*."

"Never mind. Will you telephone and see if they can have me?"

"I do not have to telephone. All beach hotels are very empty. You just go. Nothing more is necessary."

*

It was not easy finding a taxi prepared to take me to the Haven of Peace, which was some twelve miles out of town. Or rather, it was not easy finding a taxi prepared to take me for the officially prescribed fare—a board listing the official fares was nailed to the trunk of a coconut tree growing at the entrance to the forecourt. The drivers were demanding an extra thirty, forty, or, in one case, even fifty shillings.

"The road is very bad for our cars, bwana. It has many, many holes which make much mischief. It is not easy to get spare parts in Tanzania."

I complained to the lady at the Tourist Information Office.

"What they say is true," she said. "The road is not very good. You see, in Tanzania we are devoting all our efforts to developing the rural sector. That is *governmenti* policy. We are a nation of peasants and workers. Those are the people we are trying to lift."

"So what am I to do?"

She brightened. "But you need not take taxi! I was forgetting. For tourists we have special *hoteli* minibus which is very cheap. I will find out for you."

She ran across the road to the New Africa. She came back looking crestfallen.

"*Hoteli* minibus is not running. It has broken down." She stared at me gloomily. "I will see what I can do to help." She went outside and talked to one of the taxi drivers. She came back smiling. "I have found a driver who will take you if you pay extra twenty *shillingi*. That is not unreasonable."

The road out of town was in a truly terrible state, its existence often more notional than actual. We swerved crazily from verge to verge, dodging the potholes, some of which were the size of small craters. It was hard to believe that its condition could be traced back to the concentration on rural development. The road looked as if it had been pounded by murderous artillery. It was odd watching the oncoming traffic perform the suicidal ballet its negotiation required. The ocean appeared on our right, a restless sparkle of foam-flecked turquoise beyond the coconut groves. Near a small bridge spanning a sea-fed creek, a large sign strictly forbade the taking of photographs. Presumably, the bridge was considered a highly prized military objective. The tide was out, exposing a gray expanse of mud flats. An odor of sewage thickened the sultry air. At the water's edge women and children, squatting on their haunches, raked through the sand with their fingers. The sight brought back childhood memories of the Trinidad beach where I used to spend some of my school vacations. Similar groups used to forage in the sand at low tide in search of the edible shellfish we called chip-chip. Perhaps they were doing the same. We passed an army camp. Here also the taking of photographs was strictly forbidden. The buildings were neat; the roads within were bordered by whitewashed stones. Groups of citizens were standing around dismantled machine guns and being instructed in the arts of warfare. We turned down a sandy track leading toward the sea. A subsistence plot planted mainly with banana trees called itself the Ho Chi Minh Mixed Farm: in Tanzania it is impossible to escape the rhetoric of Revolution.

The arched gateway of the Haven of Peace came into sight.

II

Willi, the capitalist who owned and ran the Haven of Peace, was short, stockily built, growing bald, with skin bronzed and toughened by the sun. I took him to be in his middle sixties, but he may have been older than that. Willi (I never got to know his surname) was a bachelor. He lived with his dog in a small bungalow set a little apart from the main buildings of the hotel. A man of regular habits, he rose early and retired early. His manner, though somewhat abrupt and tinged with authoritarianism, was not unfriendly. An aura of mystery enveloped him. Like his surname, his personal history, apart from the few details he cared to volunteer, could only be guessed at. Willi had the air of someone burdened with secret knowledge, someone for whom life had long since ceased to hold any surprises—a man beyond the mundane pleasures and pains of day-to-day existence. But probably this aspect of him existed only in my own imagination. He might simply have been a reasonably content, reasonably happy individual who had succumbed to the indolence of the tropics.

"Originally I came here for the animals," Willi said, "and because in my youth I was a great romantic. When I was a boy growing up in Austria I used to read the books written about Africa by the German explorers and missionaries. Those books fired my imagination. They drew me here. Even now I keep with me many rare volumes to remind me of my youth. Someday, if you're interested, I will show you those books. They are very valuable, very rare."

He lit a cigarette, crossed his legs and gazed out at the sea. We were alone on the long veranda, furnished with cane chairs, which faced the sea. Willi's small, hairy dog lay at his feet, its tongue lolling out. From time to time he reached down to caress the animal's head.

"When I first came to Africa, I would go on safari for months at a time, out to the hills beyond the big lakes. Some of the tribesmen who lived there had never seen a white man before. I was the *first*." He had never, he said, met such honest people anywhere. "I would leave my things lying around. They never stole even a button or piece of thread from me." He wrinkled his broad, shining forehead. "That was only thirty years ago. Much has happened in thirty years." He flicked away his half-smoked cigarette. "Those people have lost their innocence. Today in those hills by the big lakes there are aid workers teaching the people how to read and write." He laughed.

"Do you regret that?"

"I regret nothing. It is nice to know girls when they are

still virgins. But a sensible man accepts that one day they will not be virgins any more. I am glad I had a chance to see something of the old virginal Africa."

"Will you ever leave?"

"Leave?" Willi's forehead wrinkled; he lit another cigarette. "Why should I leave? I am an old man now. I am happy here. All my interests are here. I go to Europe every couple of years for a few weeks. That is enough. More than enough. Most of my memories are here now. I think that where a man's memories are, that is where he belongs. That place is his home. No—I shall never leave."

His hotel, a complex of barracks-like buildings built of brick and roofed with corrugated iron, was a rambling relic of a place. Beyond the veranda where we sat, round wooden tables, embedded in the sand and shaded by umbrellas of thatched palm leaves, lined the entire length of the hotel's sea frontage. Behind the veranda was the dark and spacious dining hall, whose walls were studded with shells. The dining tables occupied bamboo-paneled alcoves roofed, as were the tables on the seafront, with palm thatch. In the middle of the room was a circular wooden dance floor. At the far end was a stage. On that stage, in happier and more prosperous times, a band would play on Saturday evenings. Several years had passed since a band had last played there, and it seemed unlikely that one would ever do so again. The rooms, housed in a separate building, were built around a quadrangle open to the sea. Gnawed, whitening bones, brought there by the stray dogs who patrolled the beach, were strewn amid the weeds that had long ago overwhelmed the lawn which had flourished on the spot.

"Back in the old days," Willi said, "you would have had to book months in advance to get a room here at the height of the season. This place was famous, the only beach hotel worth the name. People would come not only from Dar but from up-country as well. On some nights there would be two bands playing, one in the dining room and the other out here in the open. People used to dance all night under the stars."

His gaze swept along the line of untenanted wooden tables whose thatch rustled dryly in the breeze. He pointed out the concrete square, now almost buried under the drifting sand, where the band had played and his guests had danced away the night under the stars.

"Oh, no," he said, "in those days you couldn't turn up and expect to get a room."

The Haven of Peace took on the melancholy aspect of an archaeological site. However, Willi spoke unemotionally. He was giving information, making polite conversation. This neutrality was part of his mystery. Nowadays, at best half the rooms would be filled during the height of the holiday season. Mostly, though, only ten percent of the rooms would be occupied. Occasionally, there was no one at all. In fact, the hotel ran at a substantial loss. If tomorrow a buyer came along he would sell it. But where was a buyer to be found? In Tanzania buyers were as rare as gold dust. No one wanted to be branded an exploiting capitalist.

"So it continues to hang like the albatross round my neck." Willi pulled down the corners of his mouth, wide and fish-shaped.

Why did he not shut up the place and cut his losses?

He could not do that, he said. It was too risky. If the government saw it lying idle, they might take it away from him. "That would be an even greater loss for me."

Nowadays, Willi, leaving the hotel to run itself, devoted more and more of his time to his other interests. These were the export of exotic aquarium fish and shell collecting. The first was proving itself to be a highly profitable business enterprise, making up for the albatross that was hanging around his neck: the West seemed to have an appetite for exotic aquarium fish. His shell collecting fell into an entirely different category. What had started off as a hobby had over the years metamorphosed into a passion. Willi was obsessed with shells; they were his *raison d'être*.

"My collection is world-famous. All the books quote me now. If you see a book on East African shells that doesn't quote me, it's not worth reading."

Late one afternoon, as we sat together on the veranda talking about his shells, Willi rose abruptly. "Follow me!"

I trailed after him across the sand to his bungalow. The shells were everywhere, stored in chests of drawers, in boxes and in glass cases affixed to the walls of his sitting room. They were set out like jewels—each carefully packed around with cotton; each neatly labeled with its name, its date of acquisition, its provenance. Some of them, he informed me, were extremely rare, worth hundreds of dollars. He had scoured lakes, rivers, the sea to obtain them. Neither effort nor expense had been spared.

As I examined the collection, Willi sat in a rocking chair, watching me intently, a cigarette jammed between his lips, his feet resting on the gaping head of a lion skin that was laid out across the middle of the room. He flicked the burning stub of his cigarette onto the red-painted concrete floor. It lay there, the smoke coiling up unheeded. The room was crowded with objects—strangely colored and veined lumps of rock; antique Zanzibari chests intricately carved and inlaid and studded with brass; Makonde sculptures; Pokomo mats; an enormous, yellowing elephant's tusk.

"My biggest worry is what will happen to my shells when I die. About the rest—even about myself—I do not care. But I do not want my life's work to be broken up and scattered." He had made approaches to the museum in Dar es Salaam, since it seemed their most fitting final resting place. "You would think that they would have jumped at the offer, wouldn't you?"

"They didn't?"

Willi pulled down the corners of his mouth. He looked more fishlike than ever. "They were not interested. They did not even understand what I was offering. *Shells?* Why is this crazy old man offering us his *shells?* What is he making such a fuss about? The beaches of Tanzania are full of *shells.*"

He found comfort in the reflection that their ignorant response might well have been a blessing in disguise. They would not know how to care properly for the collection. Even worse, specimens might be stolen. So the ultimate fate of his life's work remained unresolved. Willi fell silent. I made farewell noises. He waved vaguely, not looking at me. I went out. It was a warm, windless night. Down on the beach, the surf crashed and hissed invisibly. The yellow lights of a stationary flotilla of fishing craft twinkled far out on the water. Mosquitoes whirred as I made my way across the bone-littered quadrangle to my room. A child was being beaten in the staff quarters. It wailed loudly, dramatizing its misery.

III

Banks of gray cloud massed in the sky. A dhow, going north, skimmed across the pallid gray water. One of the hotel "boys" was sweeping the veranda. He worked slowly, lethargically, leaving swaths of sand in his wake. Willi's dog slept in the shade of the eaves. Willi himself had gone into town earlier that morning to order supplies and collect his mail, and the place seemed even more abandoned than usual. I went down to the beach. The tide was out, laying bare a hard-packed plain of rippling sand, dotted with pools of clear water reflecting the sky. I walked the mile or so to one of the government-owned beach *hoteli*, built to look like a Moorish palace. Its emptiness was off-putting, and I did not go in. Nearby was a marine research station. An English biologist who worked there (he was spending a few months in Tanzania doing research on sea slugs) had told me that complicated equipment imported at great expense was slowly rusting away from lack of proper care and maintenance. There were supposed to be some ruins in the vicinity (ruins, that is, other than the marine research station), but my desultory wanderings did not locate them. On my way back to the hotel, I was overtaken by a straggling, heavy-breathing horde of men, dressed in khaki shorts and red shirts, under the command of an officer who kept shouting encouragement and blowing a whistle.

"Hup . . . hup . . . one, two, three . . . hup . . . hup . . . one, two, three . . ."

The Tanzanian Army was doing its keep-fit exercises. I watched them until they disappeared round a curve of the beach. It started to drizzle.

The Haven of Peace was busiest on Sunday mornings.

Then the staffs of the East European embassies arrived. Pale-skinned Poles and Czechs and Hungarians sat out under the thatched umbrellas lining the seafront, drinking beer and *konyagi*. As the morning wore on and the drink began to take effect, they would sing and dance. By about one o'clock, how-ever, only the most senior officials remained behind, their status exempting them from the ban on driving that came into effect at two on Sunday afternoons and lasted until six on Monday mornings. Very few people cared to run the gauntlet of the bands of zealous TANU Youth who patrolled the roads, ensuring that the ban was not evaded.

Sometimes there were campers, parties of half a dozen to a dozen, who were either on their way north to Kenya (com-ing from "South") or on their way "South" via Zambia, Bot-swana and Rhodesia. Tanzania, apparently, had no objection to this transit traffic. Willi complained that he made nothing out of these campers, asking, as he did, only a nominal charge for the privilege of pitching their tents on his property and making use of his washing and toilet facilities. He complained, but he never turned them away. I think he enjoyed—and was grateful for—their presence: they gave the hotel an air of occupation, of use. These campers—English people, Australi-ans, New Zealanders and Americans for the most part—were generally young, just out of high school or college; they were spending a year or two slumming their way around the world. They were a curiously impersonal and apathetic crowd, so alike as to be interchangeable.

There were occasional strays—chiefly aid workers of one kind or another from up-country, who periodically came down to the coast to recuperate from the strain of their phil-anthropic labors. One of the stranger specimens was a lone

American girl, dowdy in appearance and earnest in manner, who said she had come to Africa in search of "a relevant ethnic experience." I told Willi this.

"What she means," he said, "is that she wants to be fucked by black men."

But strangest of all was the Dutchwoman who turned up one evening on foot, covered with dust, her dress torn in several places, her skin purpled with bruises. Accompanying her were two crying children.

After dinner, when I was sitting out on the veranda writing in my notebook, she came and sat down next to me. She begged me for a cigarette—and a drink.

"I am sorry to ask you such favors," she said. "I will pay you back. Mr. Willi has been very kind. He has let me and my children have food and shelter. If he had not been so kind, I would have had to sleep on the beach with my children. The last two days have been very tragic for us." She had spruced herself up a little since her arrival, but the scars of the last two "tragic" days could not be hidden—the swollen lips, the lacerations on her shoulders and arms, the dark-circled eyes flitting restlessly. I imagined her to be in her late thirties.

I gave her a cigarette and bought her a drink.

"I will pay you back. You have my word of honor."

"You don't have to pay me back."

"But I will. I insist. I have no desire to owe you anything. Once you owe a man something, he begins to feel he can make demands."

"As you wish." I gestured irritably and went on with my writing, uncomfortably aware of being under her close scrutiny.

"You are a Hindu, aren't you?"

The question took me completely by surprise.

"How did you guess?"

"I can always tell if somebody is a Hindu."

"How clever of you. What gives the game away?"

"It's just a feeling . . . I can't explain. But I always *know*."
She massaged her arms. "Can I ask you a personal question?"

"Go right ahead."

"Are you dominated by your mother?"

"I don't think so."

"Then you can't be a Hindu. Or if you are, you are lying.
All Hindus are dominated by their mothers. That is why I
despise them."

"You seem to know a lot about Hindus."

"So I should. My lover was a Hindu." She pursed up her
mouth, passing her tongue over her lips.

"I take it that your lover was dominated by his mother?"

"No bastard could be more dominated by his mother than
he was. It was she who made him desert me and go back to
his wife and children. It was she who took him away from
me. And to think I left my husband for that bastard." She
spoke with what sounded like passion.

I expressed my regret on behalf of Hindus the world over.

"You are speaking to a *femme fatale*," she said.

"I can well believe it."

"Have you been to Moshi?"

"I passed through it."

"Then you must have heard of me." Having drained her
konyagi, she stared at the empty glass.

"I'm afraid I didn't."

"Then you can't have been to Moshi. Nobody can have

visited Moshi and not have heard about me. I'm the talk of the town."

"I only spent a few minutes at the bus station. Maybe that explains it."

She thrust her empty glass toward me. "Will you give me another cigarette and buy me another drink?"

I did as I was asked. She drank the *konyagi* greedily.

"It was two days ago that my lover abandoned me, that his mother came and took him away. The bastard didn't even put up a fight. He went without a word. Like a child. So I took my two children, put them in the car and just drove away . . ."

"What happened to the car?"

"It ran out of petrol. So I left it by the roadside and began walking. I had no idea where I was going. I just kept walking and thinking of that Hindu man and what he had done to me. Then an African truck driver who gave me a lift tried to rape me . . . that's how I got all these scratches and bruises . . ."

"How terrible!"

She blew a perfect smoke ring. It floated away, elongating itself, breaking up into uncoordinated wisps. She waited until it had disappeared before she spoke again.

"It was not the first time something like that has happened to me. I'm accustomed to that sort of thing."

"Are you?"

"Africans are always trying to rape me."

"Oh."

"My houseboy tried once. He came after me with a kitchen knife. Many people in Moshi heard my screams."

She rose from her chair, yawning. How much of a fantasist was she? Could anything she said be believed? Her bizarre arrival at the hotel was real enough; her scratches and bruises were real enough; the two weeping children were real enough —and her obsession with Hindus had seemed real enough. *Something* had happened to her; *something* was tormenting her. Possibly she herself was no longer able to distinguish between fact and fantasy. She walked slowly away from the veranda.

"Do not follow me," she said.

"Where are you going?"

"I am going for a walk on the beach."

"The beach is not supposed to be safe at night." I hesitated. "Especially for lone European women. There have been 'incidents.' "

She did not answer, moving out beyond the reach of the electric light into the shadows of the coconut trees.

In the morning, she—and her two children—had vanished, leaving no trace.

"They must have cleared out before dawn," Willi said.

"On foot?"

"I do not see how else they could have left."

"Did she tell you anything about herself?"

"She told me she had been robbed, that the robbers had taken her car. She said her husband, who was working in Moshi, had run off with an Asian girl . . ."

"A Hindu Asian girl?"

"I do not remember. I have to listen to many stories from people who cannot pay their bills."

It was a genuine African mystery.

CHAPTER 10

Words, Words, Words

I

A NAME hastily scribbled weeks ago on a sheet of notepaper . . . I could barely decipher my own handwriting. The receptionist watched me impatiently.

"Mr. Malillah?"

"You wish to see *Ndugu* Malillah?" *Ndugu* is the Tanzanian equivalent of "Comrade." The receptionist was the first person I had actually heard use it.

"Yes."

"Have you an appointment with him?"

"Well actually, no . . ."

She raised her eyebrows. "Is it business you wish to transact with Ndugu Malillah?"

"No . . ."

She studied me with intense suspicion. "If you have no business to transact with Ndugu Malillah and you are not a friend of his, why, then, do you wish to see him?"

Her logic could not be faulted. I tried my best to explain: I had been given Ndugu Malillah's name by a friend of his I met in Nairobi . . .

"What is the name of this 'friend' you met in Nairobi?"

I gave the name.

"I have not heard of such a person."

It was my turn to become impatient. I tried as best I could to explain why I wanted to meet Ndugu Malillah, who was reputed to be one of the leading lights in the world of Tanzanian publishing. She listened interestedly.

"I understand," she said. "But Ndugu Malillah is not here."

"Do you expect him back this afternoon? Perhaps I could leave you a note . . ."

"Ndugu Malillah will not be back this afternoon. Ndugu Malillah has gone to China. He will not be back for several weeks."

I exploded. "Why couldn't you tell me that before? Why go through all the rigmarole of asking me those absurd questions?"

She did not lose her composure, continuing to look at me levelly. "Would you like to see Ndugu Mussa instead?"

"Who is Ndugu Mussa?"

"Ndugu Mussa is in charge while Ndugu Malillah is away in China."

I agreed to see Ndugu Mussa.

"Then wait here. I will go and see if Ndugu Mussa is available." She disappeared down a corridor.

The publications of the house were neatly arrayed on the shelves lining the walls of the room. *Class Struggles in Tanzania* by Issa Shivji promised to discuss ". . . the emergence of contradictions between workers and peasants and the bureaucratic bourgeoisie, and the decline of the Asian dominated commercial bourgeoisie . . . including several famous cases of manager lockouts and factory takeovers." Ndugu Shivji also surfaced in another publication, *The Silent Class Strug-*

gle, a collection of essays by "well-known progressive social scientists." Shivji, however, was absent from *Resolutions and Selected Speeches from the Sixth Pan African Congress*, which "encompasses a redefinition of Pan Africanism for our revolutionary times." But Shivji was back again (this time as editor) in *Tourism and Social Development*, in which is examined the ". . . restructuring of the social behaviour and attitudes of a hitherto oppressed, dominated people." Seeking relief, I picked up a novel. Hamza Sokko's *The Gathering Storm*—a first novel—is set in a village. "Pitted against each other are Asian traders who have first monopoly on the village, the new African businessman who succeeds them, and the peasants who gradually realize that their struggle against exploitation must know no color." *Blood on Our Land*—another first novel—by Ismael Mbise "aims to try and expose the feelings of the oppressed. The resistance of Tanzanian peasants to colonial land policies is dramatically, but realistically, depicted." Regrettably, no one, so far as I was able to see, had written about the resistance of the Tanzanian peasants to the *ujamaa* program of collectivization.

The girl returned. Ndugu Mussa had agreed to see me.

She led the way down the dark corridor cluttered with cardboard packing cases. We ascended some stairs. Ndugu Mussa's office was on the first floor. He was sitting at a desk piled high with books and files. There were three other desks in the room, also piled high with books and files, but their occupants were absent. The walls were decorated with blown-up photographs of Mao (a face as smooth and lifeless as a waxwork—sculptures of the Buddha have more life), Che Guevara and Fidel Castro.

Ndugu Mussa dismissed the girl and rose to greet me. He

was a sparely built, ascetic-looking man. A floral-patterned tunic was buttoned up to his neck. He wore sandals. We shook hands formally. Having offered me a chair, Ndugu Mussa retreated to his seat. Chin propped on hands, he gazed sardonically at me from behind the files and books. I repeated my story. He listened without comment or change of expression.

"As you can see," he said, when I had finished, "I am a very busy man. There is much work to be done."

I nodded appreciatively and said it was not my intention to take up too much of his valuable time. But would it be possible, one day after work, for us to meet, have a drink together, a casual chat . . . maybe at the New Africa, which was close by.

"I am a very busy man," Ndugu Mussa said. "Extremely busy. My colleagues and I are extremely busy people. Only through hard work can we reconstruct our society. In any case, I do not drink."

"We can have tea or coffee . . . it doesn't have to be alcohol." His stubbornness roused my own. Our interview had become a battle of wills.

"I do not care for places like the New Africa," Ndugu Mussa said. "I never go there. I leave it to the tourists and our homegrown bourgeoisie."

"It doesn't have to be the New Africa. We can go somewhere else. Somewhere of your own choice."

"I am a very busy man," Ndugu Mussa said.

We looked at each other. Deadlock. I prepared to depart. Ndugu Mussa suddenly relented as I reached the door.

"One minute . . ." He leafed through his diary. "Can you come back here in three days' time? Then I can arrange a meeting for you with my colleagues. If you wish it, we can have a dialogue."

"Are you sure? I wouldn't want to disturb . . ."

"A dialogue is not a disturbance." Coming from Ndugu Mussa, the statement sounded aphoristic: a revolutionary dictum. "I am sure my colleagues will be very interested to meet you, to hear what you have to say."

That, I reflected, was not the idea. I wanted to hear what *they* had to say. However, I did not cavil. A "dialogue" was better than nothing, and it had been generous of Ndugu Mussa to make the concession. I said I would return in three days' time.

I decided, for want of anything else better to do, to visit the National Museum. The day was overwarm and noisy; the dazzling light hurt my eyes. There was a deafening clatter of road-working machinery; workmen were resurfacing the pitted street. The pungent, suffocating smell of boiling pitch soured the dust-laden air. I walked along slowly, sweat laving my body, seeking the shade. Beer drinkers crowded the terrace of the New Africa. I paused, debating with myself. In the end, I resisted the temptation to go in. I continued down Independence Avenue, going past the carpeted, air-conditioned interiors of the airline offices (a smiling lion beckoned me to Maputo, formerly Lourenco Marques), past the boys selling cigarettes and matches and peanuts. Old men lay sleeping under the arcades. To date, I had not encountered a single beggar in Dar es Salaam; nor had I seen many prostitutes. After Nairobi, these omissions from the city scene were startling. What had happened to the beggars and the prostitutes? Had they been reformed, converted to the joys of productive labor? Or had they simply been removed, put away out of sight? I had not been able to find out. Photographs of Jimmy Carter and Gerald Ford adorned the glassy facade of the United States Information Service. The grandiose Zambian Embassy had an abandoned look; the British Consulate, accommodated in whitewashed colonial elegance, radiated discretion.

The museum did not have an admission charge. Instead, visitors were invited to make a donation. I was more than happy to contribute ten shillings—but I had nothing smaller than a twenty-shilling note. The staff had no change. Mindful of my dwindling resources, I hesitated.

"Go on! Go on!" They waved me through the barrier.

The museum was a disappointment. The protohuman skulls dug up in the Olduvai Gorge were not anywhere near as exciting as I had imagined they would be. Dead things deadly exhibited in glass cases. Upstairs there was even less to look at—pieces of antique Chinese porcelain, photographs of the German period, photographs of coastal ruins, the usual tribal artifacts. Willi's shells might, just conceivably, have injected a touch of excitement and passion. I was the only person present.

On my way back, I entered, on impulse, the United States Information Service. The man I was instructed to see treated me cautiously.

"We try and keep a fairly low profile," he said. "Over here, China makes all the running." He seemed depressed, to be at a bit of a loose end. "The trouble is," he confessed, "that I am a capitalist. I just can't bring myself to believe in socialism." He drummed on the desk with his fingers. "It's like trying to teach an old dog new tricks. Just can't be done no matter how hard you try. Just can't be done." His dithering

legs sent out shock waves across the desk top. I felt sorry for
him. Professionally, a posting to Tanzania must be a rung on
the ladder to nowhere. "This is what I call a hoe culture.
What can you do with a hoe culture?"

As I was leaving, he handed me a copy of a document entitled "Foreign Economic Trends and their Implications for
the United States." "Read that. It tells you everything you
need to know. You'll find it most instructive."

Despite its diplomatic tone, the section on Tanzania was a
gloomy piece of work. "Tanzania's socialist framework," it
said, "and concern to prevent domination by foreign business and finance act to limit and define the role for potential
U.S. investment . . . The State controls all aspects of the
modern economy. It depends upon concessionary foreign
aid and domestic borrowing rather than private investment
. . . to exploit its resources. The country's depressed economy, infrastructural deficiencies, inefficient transport system
. . . further inhibit potential private investment and markets." It was all very sad.

I dropped in at the New Africa to see if the *hoteli* minibus
was, by any chance, back in operation. I was advised not to
depend on its reappearance in the near future. "That road,"
I was told, "is very bad for it."

*

Another name scribbled on a sheet of paper . . . but Abdallah's face was wreathed in smiles—a pleasant change from
Ndugu Mussa. Abdallah, an archaeologist, was loosely connected with the museum. He was in his early thirties, much
younger than I had been led to expect.

"Come," he said. "I have a Land-Rover with me. Let me take you for a drive."

Abdallah explained that the Land-Rover belonged not to him but to the museum. He did not have possession of it all the time and, when he did, clearly enjoyed making maximum use of it. We drove along the harbor, crowded with shipping. Russian and Chinese flags were much in evidence.

"You will observe the sort of things the imperialists do," Abdallah said.

"What sort of things?"

"They fill up the harbor with their ships."

"But I see quite a number of Russian and Chinese ships."

"They are different. It is the imperialists who try and block our harbor."

"What do they have to gain from doing that?"

Abdallah could not refrain from smiling at my simplicity. "They want to make fools of us, to show that we cannot take the load. The imperialists have many tricks. When the Great Uhuru Railway was opened, they sent all their ships to Dar to prove that we didn't have adequate facilities. I thought that was a very cheap thing for them to do."

"Indeed."

"Still," Abdallah said, "despite the machinations of the imperialists, we have made a great deal of progress in Tanzania. Before Uhuru we had few tall buildings in Dar. Now, as you will observe, we have several. In time, we will have many more."

I looked at him. Was he being ironic? Abdallah, however, betrayed none of the usual symptoms of irony. I could only conclude that he too was not familiar with either the Arusha Declaration or the paper on Socialism and Rural Development.

Abdallah pointed out the National Stadium. "A very historic place for us," he said, "built to mark our independence from the colonialists."

We drove past a compound filled with scores of Chinese trucks used during the building of the Great Uhuru Railway. This railroad, built by the Chinese, links the Zambian copper belt with the port of Dar es Salaam. "Other people would sell their trucks," Abdallah remarked; "they would take what money they could and clear out. But not the Chinese. They are not selfish like the imperialists. They take everything back home, repaint, repair and use it somewhere else. The Chinese are our best friends."

I suggested that the trucks, which had been lying idle for many months, might be more gainfully employed in helping to ease the grain-distribution crisis. Grain was rotting in the south of the country because of inadequate storage and transport facilities; elsewhere, people were on the verge of starvation. "Surely the Chinese wouldn't object to that?"

"The grain crisis cannot be blamed on the Chinese," Abdallah replied. "It is the capitalist contractors who sabotage the distribution of grain. It is they who create scarcity because they wish to push up prices and exploit the masses. We are yet to rid our society of all reactionary elements."

The pat words, the pat phrases, unleavened by thought, came pouring out of Abdallah's mouth. In this society he would qualify as an "intellectual." Did Abdallah—*could* Abdallah—really believe the nonsense he spouted with such ease? But no—it was not even a matter of belief. Did Abdallah really *understand* the nonsense he spouted? Did Abdallah actually know what he was saying? It was not his "ideology" that disturbed me: socialism provides, after all, one of the more sophisticated ways of interpreting, of looking at the world around us. Nor was it his naiveté—the equation of tall buildings with "progress." No. It was something else.

" 'Good night, sir. Save all sinners.'

" 'Good heavens! Where did you learn that?'

" 'Good morning, sir. God save the King!'

" 'A mission boy!' cried Hereward.

" 'Yes, bwana. I can read a book, I can write a letter . . .' "

Here, in another avatar, was the Mission Boy whom Elspeth Huxley had met in the Kenya Highlands sixty years before.

We drove out along the new highway linking the city and the airport: a multi-laned, buckling belt of asphalt, not quite finished, which must have cost a tidy sum to build.

"How does this fit in with *ujamaa* and the emphasis on rural development?" I asked. "I thought . . ."

I did not finish the sentence. What did I think? That words must be taken at their face value? That they have meanings which should be taken seriously? Had I not learned, after all this time, that nothing in Africa had meaning? That nothing could be taken seriously?

Dusk was approaching. The amber light was hazed with dust; the sun gilded every surface. The leaves of the coconut palms shone with a hard sparkle: drooping fronds of burnished metal. I invited Abdallah to have a drink. He accepted readily enough—despite his socialist fervor, he was free of Ndugu Mussa's revolutionary asceticism.

We went to one of the Five Star beach hotels, not far from the Haven of Peace. The hotel, built by Israelis, was done in African style—a counterpart to the other, farther down the beach, done in Moorish style. A vaulting thatched roof soared over the lounge. The lights were dimmed down to save electricity. Canned music drifted dismally through the emptiness. We sat out on the wind-cooled terrace overlooking the sea. The lights of the fishing boats were just beginning to show on the horizon. Below us, set about with tables, was the landscaped garden, crisscrossed by stone-flagged, meandering paths. Beyond it lay the swimming pool. We could hear the sound of waves breaking on the beach. The place was like a mausoleum, the haunted pleasure garden of a long-dead king. Abdallah shivered.

"Mwalimu has said that these *hotelis* are not meant for us." Abdallah stared about him guiltily. "He is afraid that we shall become enslaved by tourism."

"There seems little danger of that happening."

Abdallah, still shivering, laughed softly. A waiter loomed out of the obscurity. We ordered *konyagi*.

"I hope they have change."

Abdallah did not answer. He suddenly revealed that he had just been reelected to a second five-year term as leader of his ten-house cell.

"You must be a popular man."

He wagged his head modestly. "I cannot be sure about that. The fact is there are few who like being cell leaders. The work is too much and there is no pay for doing it."

"Why do you do it?"

Abdallah gazed at the darkening sea. "I try to be an idealist. Mwalimu wants all of us to be idealists."

"But not many are . . ."

"That is the trouble," Abdallah said. "Human nature—it is a terrible thing. Many pretend to be idealists but few are."

The waiter brought our drinks.

Abdallah's pessimistic view of human nature brought to

mind the story I had been told by a wealthy Nairobi businessman with Tanzanian connections. It concerned a Tanzanian government official ("a very big man over there"), a good friend of his—the official always stayed with him whenever he happened to be in Nairobi. This man ("A *bon viveur* if ever there was one," my informant said. "He drinks nothing cheaper than Chivas Regal"), on his frequent aid-seeking expeditions abroad, would invariably find an excuse for stopping over in London, where he would buy himself expensively tailored suits and other luxury goods. These he stowed away in the businessman's Nairobi house. When it was time for him to return home, he would readopt the humble garb of smock, baggy trousers and sandals. "Now," he was reported as saying, "I must go home and preach socialism and simple living to our starving, underdeveloped people." I cannot vouch for the truth of this story. Nevertheless, the businessman's wife, who was present during its telling, did not dispute any of it. In fact, she added her own portion to the scandalous tale. On one occasion, she said, the official had given her five hundred pounds. "What is this for?" she had asked. "To have a good time with," he was alleged to have replied. I believe the gift was gratefully accepted.

I asked Abdallah to tell me something about his work as a cell leader.

He began by saying that he was not typical because he did not have a great deal of work to do. He lived in a "middle-class" area of the city, and the middle classes seemed, on the whole, to prefer to keep their problems to themselves. The Asians were particularly bad, hardly ever approaching their cell leaders. Cell leaders in "working-class" areas had a much greater burden of work. Not only did they have many more people to contend with; they were also expected to organize such things as literacy classes—not always an easy task, since many of the working-class cell leaders were themselves illiterate. Abdallah, at my request, narrated two "cases" with which he had had to deal. They provided a glimpse behind the scenes.

The first was about a soldier who had got himself entangled with two women, both of whom became pregnant and both of whom announced that he was the father-to-be.

"For convenience," Abdallah said, "I will call one woman 'A' and the other 'B.' "

Apparently, the soldier's true love was A; with B he had merely been having a casual fling. The soldier did not deny that he was the father of A's child, but he had serious doubts about the paternity of B's child. "She was a wild girl," Abdallah said. Unfortunately for the soldier, the brother of B was his superior officer. He was so terrified of the punishments which the latter might be able to inflict that he deserted A and went to live with B. A presented herself to Abdallah, demanding reparation.

"What was I to do?" Abdallah asked.

"I can't think."

"I ordered him to pay half his salary to A."

"So the poor man was supporting both the women?"

"It could not be helped," Abdallah said. "He was going crazy. But the fault was his." Abdallah laughed. "One day he disappeared. Vanished just like that and was never seen again. The funniest bit is to come, though. Can you guess?"

"No."

"It turned out that neither of the babies was his. He was being deceived by both of them. Women can be real devils."

Abdallah's laughter rolled across the terrace. "There was no need for him to run away at all."

His next tale also involved star-crossed lovers. One day a man, returning home early from work, disturbed his pregnant wife and her lover. The lover jumped out a window and ran away. However, in his haste, he had left his shirt behind. "Whose shirt is this?" the cuckold asked his wife, "I do not own such a shirt. I have seen our neighbor wearing a shirt like this. What is our neighbor's shirt doing in my bedroom?" His wife pretended to be no less puzzled by the bizarre circumstance. The cuckold stormed over to his neighbor's house, taking the displaced garment with him. "Do you recognize this shirt?" he asked his neighbor's wife. "That shirt belongs to my husband," the woman replied. "If that is so," the man said, "what was it doing in my bedroom?" "If you found it in your bedroom," the woman replied with cruel logic, "it can mean only one thing—that my husband has been with your wife." The man went home and beat his wife. She complained to Abdallah. Abdallah told the man that he must "desist" from any further beatings. He promised that he would but, all the same, went on beating her. The woman complained a second time to Abdallah. Abdallah summoned the man once more. He warned that if the beatings continued, criminal charges would be filed against him. "I cannot control myself," the man said. "That child she is carrying cannot be mine. I wish only to kill her." Abdallah gave the woman asylum in his house and kept her with him until the baby was safely born.

"And was the baby his?"

"It was."

Husband and wife were reconciled; the adulterer's wife

took up with another man; the adulterer left the district. On the day the child was christened, the man ceremonially burned the shirt.

"These things happen," Abdallah said, "when women get to know they are pregnant. Then they get up to all kinds of wickedness. A pregnant woman has to be watched." He articulated the peasant wisdom of the ages with profound feeling. That wisdom lay deeper than, and transcended, his "socialism." As he spoke, militant, goose-stepping Tanzania faded out of focus, giving way to the images produced by an older, simpler society driven by older, simpler compulsions and obsessions.

In theory, the cell leader—"an agent of democratic socialism"—is an extremely important individual. No one with a grievance may go directly to the police or courts. He must first consult his cell leader and see if he can settle the matter. "The cell leader," writes a Political Education Officer, "can be called upon to reconcile people even at midnight and, as a true TANU leader, he must wake up and listen to the complaints and take the necessary steps to settle the matter. Quarrels or fights between husbands and wives, between drunken cell members, and between house-owners and their tenants, are by far the commonest cases. Often, a cell leader encounters some rough and uncompromising characters . . ."

But the agent of democratic socialism is also the agent of the totalitarian One Party State. "The cell leader," writes the same Political Education Officer, "has to keep a close watch so as to detect any new faces in his ten houses. When he sees a stranger, he must make enquiries and find out who he is, where he came from, where he is going, how long he will remain in the area and so on. Usually, the host reports to the cell leader about his guests and gives all the necessary infor- mation. If the leader doubts the stories of these strangers, he must report the matter to the branch officials or to the police." A cell leader can impound anyone suspected of being a *run- away*—a fine, old-fashioned term usually associated with slave societies. Who are the runaways? What are they running away from? Clause D of the TANU Creed recognizes "that every citizen has the right to freedom of expression, of *move- ment*, of religious belief . . ." The citizens of Iramba District (to take only one example) would not agree. They were com- pelled by a bylaw to grow a specified amount of cotton (to generate that foreign exchange, that money, on which the Arusha Declaration pours such pious scorn) and were for- bidden, on pain of punishment, to leave their farms and seek work elsewhere. Some peasants defied the order. The cell leaders of the locality ordered a "roundup"—that was the expression used—of the miscreants. Ndugu Shaila, the official who described this incident, waxes lyrical about the role of the cell leaders, whom he calls "multipurpose lieutenants: *E serikali yeze kuyesula* [the government knows how to un- earth or excavate] is a remark often uttered by cell leaders to warn a member who is regarded as a shirker or parasite. This comment best shows the achievement of the cell system. There is no longer 'any place to hide.' The long arm of the government can now touch almost everyone in Iramba . . . the cell system has exposed every inch for political action. The cell leader has become a tool for excavation as well as for political education . . . Consensus and cooperation have reached encouraging proportions."

As always, the language employed is full of sound and fury. The cell leader is not only an agent of democratic socialism and a multipurpose lieutenant; he is "the spearhead of rural development," a "channel for two-way communication" between the Government of Peasants and Workers and the peasants and workers. He is a "cadre" whose function is to "explain the meaning of socialism to the people and to fight against feudal and capitalist tendencies." And so on. Problems do arise. Many of the illiterate cell leaders, Ndugu Mshangama reports, do not have a grasp of the simplest concepts—exploitation, for instance. He was present at a seminar designed to rectify such counterrevolutionary deficiences. "As for exploitation, the cell leaders, some of whom had houses for rent, had a hard time understanding how a farmer who hired labor was an exploiter and how the nation at large could be exploited by local people and foreigners." The teacher responded spiritedly to the challenge. "As for exploitation, he said to think of a lake as national income, rain as continued production and therefore additional wealth, and rivers as exploiters. He argued that no matter how much it rained, the level of a lake will not go up as long as there are streams taking away an ever-growing share of the increase in the volume of the lake. So it is with national income, production and exploiters."

What dark reflections must invade the mind of a Tanzanian when he gazes out upon his landscape.

The intellectual backwardness of the cell leaders is only one among many problems. Cell leaders battle endlessly for influence and the spoils of office with the *jumbes* (traditional village headmen), the multiplicity of government officials and the multiplicity of Party officials who overrun the countryside. "The *jumbes* argue that they are the representatives of the government at local level," the Political Officer already mentioned says, "and that they are more important than the cell leaders, who are neither paid nor chosen by the government. On the other hand, the cell leaders argue that they are the direct representatives of the local people and that they are officials of TANU, which is the ruling and only party in Tanzania. The cell leaders also assert that the fact that the TANU flag flies over their houses proves that they are more important than the *jumbes*. When such conflicts arise . . . the whole village will be full of gossip and suspicion, making development impossible."

Human nature, as Abdallah had said, is a terrible thing.

When we arrived back at the Haven of Peace, Willi was taking the air on the veranda; his dog, rolled into a ball, lay at his feet. I introduced Abdallah, who had accepted my invitation to dinner.

"You work for the museum, do you?" Willi drooped his lower lip. His tone was aggressive, and Abdallah quailed. "Some time back I made you an offer. A once-in-a-lifetime offer. But you weren't interested. You couldn't give a damn."

"I do not recall . . ." Abdallah giggled anxiously, rubbing his palms. "I have not been working there a long time. What did you offer us?"

"My shells."

"Your shells . . ."

"I have a world-famous collection of shells."

Abdallah stared vacantly.

"All the authorities quote me now. But that wasn't good enough for them. Nothing is good enough for them."

"I am sorry . . . I did not know . . . if I had known . . ." Abdallah rubbed his palms contritely.

"Come!" Willi flicked away his cigarette. He set off for his bungalow.

Abdallah followed obediently.

It occurred to me that I had made a serious blunder in bringing him back to the Haven of Peace.

Half an hour later, he was released; he looked dazed. "That *mzungu*," he said over dinner, "wants to fill the museum with his shells. I think he is a little crazy."

*

The receptionist led me down the corridor cluttered with packing cases and up the stairs to the office on the first floor. Ndugu Mussa greeted me at the door. This time the three other desks in the room were occupied. Ndugu Mussa solemnly carried out the introductions. Present were the Swahili editor, the children's books editor and the English editor—a black American girl. A chair was brought and placed in the center of the room. Ndugu Mussa handed me a bottle of Coca-Cola. Then he returned behind his desk.

I examined my inquisitors. The children's books editor, dressed in suit and tie, was perched on the edge of his desk, swinging his legs; the Swahili editor smiled in a friendly manner, as if trying to put me at my ease; the American girl, doodling on the cover of a notebook, looked bored. Mao's waxen countenance afforded little comfort. Ndugu Mussa launched into an awkward prefatory speech.

He said that I "claimed" to have been born in the West Indies, that I "claimed" to have written a couple of novels, that I "claimed" that my purpose in visiting Tanzania was to gather material for a book. But he could not say what kind of material I was gathering and what kind of book I intended to write. I watched the American girl doodle. Ndugu Mussa invited me to outline the themes of my "literary works." I did what I could.

Then the "dialogue" began.

"You seem," the children's books editor said, "to have written mainly about Asians. Why is that?"

"We don't use the word 'Asians' where I come from."

"How has it come about that there are so many *Asians* in Trinidad?"

I ignored the implied taunt. "They were brought over, like the African slaves before them, to work on the sugar plantations. Many of them still do."

"Why do you not write about life on the sugar plantations?"

"Because I know very little about it."

The American girl smiled faintly, but remained silent.

"You are a member of the urban bourgeoisie?"

"I wouldn't put it quite like that."

"Surely it is your duty as a writer to know what life on the sugar plantation is like? Or are you not interested in the struggles of the oppressed masses?"

"I think every writer has to define for himself what his 'duty' is. No one else ought to define it for him."

"You see everything through your individual psyche?"

"I suppose you can put it like that."

"Pessimism always descends on writers like yourself. Your bourgeois ego reduces social reality to chaotic individual relations. You do not see what underlies these relations. For you, the appearance is sufficient. Only authors representing the rising class, the proletariat, can see any future or meaning in life."

The children's books editor spoke with scientific detachment; Ndugu Mussa nodded approvingly.

"In Tanzania," Ndugu Mussa said, "we publish only progressive literature. Unlike the bourgeois countries, we do not dish out decadent sex literature for mass consumption. Our books are a weapon in our cultural and ideological struggle. We use culture as a tool of liberation. The imperialists, on the other hand, use culture to oppress and exploit."

I held up my hand. "Can I ask a question?"

Ndugu Mussa smiled charitably. "Ask any question. This is a dialogue we are having."

"What do you understand by 'development'? What is it exactly?"

"It is the elimination of exploitation and oppression, the building of a truly classless society where each will give according to his ability and receive according to his needs," the children's books editor replied. "Our wish is to ensure that every man, woman and child will have a bowl of rice."

"What about the intellectual development of the individuals who make up the society?"

"I do not understand what you mean by intellectual development," Ndugu Mussa said. "Is it another of your bourgeois notions?"

The American girl smirked. "He wants starving people to like opera and ballet and read Proust. That is what he means."

Ndugu Mussa and the American girl looked at each other. The Swahili editor studied me sorrowfully.

"Do you deny," the American girl asked, "that the masses are being oppressed in Trinidad, where you say you come from? Do you deny that they are being crushed underfoot by the ruling middle-class oligarchy in alliance with foreign capital?"

" I deny it." I laughed. No one else did.

"Lord help us!" The American girl rose. "I think I've

wasted enough time," she said. "I have work to do." She
walked out of the room.

II

Words, words, words . . . They can, when handled promis-
cuously, gradually begin to take the place of reality. They
can, in the course of time, become a complete substitute for it.

In Tanzania, where performance consistently negates intention, where every commodity—butter, meat, milk, cheese,
fish, chocolate, knives, forks, spoons, cups, saucers, baby
diapers—is in short supply, the socialist revolution is being
built with words. (You will be told that these shortages do
not matter, that the items listed are used only by the bourgeoisie.) "We are at war," the Minister for National Education declares. But at war with whom? With what? With
capitalist exploitation, of course. With imperialism. With
neo-imperialism. With fascism. (But not with Rhodesia:
the "liberation struggle" too is a war of words: to call yourself
a "front-line" state and be called by others a "front-line" state
is satisfaction enough.) A Party official looks at the beautiful
volcanic peak of Mount Meru—and what does he do? He
renames it Socialist Peak. That is *war*. The English-born
marine biologist displays the child to which his young American wife has recently given birth. You ask the name of the
tiny, wrinkled creature lying asleep on its mother's lap.
"Yenan," he says, the name derived from the caves where
Mao lurked during his guerrilla days. "I thought it would be
an appropriate way of commemorating Mao's death," he

adds solemnly. Yes, you reply, trying not to look too astonished. Highly appropriate.

What, in fact, is *ujamaa*? No one really seems to know.
One version stresses the collective and ethical aspects of the
program, the remodeling of Man and Society according to
Socialist precepts—what one might call the Nyererean gospel;
another stresses the simple "coming together" of a scattered
peasant population in villages, which makes possible the provision of elementary services like schools, health clinics, piped
water and so on. But someone will intervene to warn against
confusing the *ujamaa* with the "development" village. You
ask what a development village is, and you are told it is a sort
of halfway house, not quite *ujamaa*, not quite private enterprise, not quite cooperative, not quite anything, designed to
accommodate those not quite ready for the *ujamaa*—or any
other—ideal.

So, you say, let's try and get this clear. Tanzania is divided
into *ujamaa* and development villages . . . Well, not quite.
In some parts of the country traditional patterns of land
tenure have been retained (because the people in those areas
will not tolerate any other kind of arrangement), and these
cannot be classed in either category. And, to further compli-
cate the picture, there are the State Farms and the surviving
private estates. All right, you say. Nothing is pure in an im-
perfect world. But is it or is it not the policy eventually to
transform everything into *ujamaa*? Some say yes—it is the
policy to transform everything into *ujamaa*; some say no;
some say yes and no; some say nobody—not even Mwalimu
—knows. You ask next what proportion of the population
has been *ujamaa*-ized. The estimates vary from as little as
fifteen percent to as much as seventy-five percent. It all de-

pends on how *ujamaa* is defined. Once more the discussion trails away into semantic dispute. In Tanzania, words are not used to depict existing reality: they are used to confound it; to replace it.

"I am very confused," the secondary-school teacher confessed. "I believe everyone is very confused by the *governmenti* policy. For instance, the *governmenti* has borrowed money from the World Bank. Now, that, to my knowledge, is a capitalist institution. How, I ask myself, does that fit in with our declared policy of Socialism and Self-Reliance?"

Job security, he said, was another problem. Recent mass sackings from the Civil Service and other government-controlled organizations had aggravated the fears of the workers. "That policy does not agree with the Musoma Declaration."

"What is the Musoma Declaration?"

"In that Declaration, work was promised to everyone in Tanzania. It said that no one was going to be allowed to remain idle. We have the Musoma Declaration one day and mass sackings the next. It is all very puzzling to me."

The roads, the lady at the Tourist Information Office had said, had been neglected in order that the government might concentrate its efforts on rural development. Would the peasants of Kyela District have appreciated that? "May I point out," a resident of the area had written to the editor of the *Daily News*, "that the economic position of Kyela today is appalling? To start with there is general apathy among the people . . . basic necessities are nowhere to be found." Soap, sugar, sheets and blankets were unobtainable. "The four 'cooperative shops' are ill equipped and serve the people who matter rather than the common people." Those who had dared voice criticism had been "intimidated and, in fact, locked up in police cells." Socialism, the correspondent warned (having made clear the genuineness of his own socialist convictions) was in danger of being "misunderstood and abhorred" by the inhabitants of Kyela. Kyela's troubles had arisen from the edict that summarily ordered the closure of privately owned shops. The result was semi-starvation.

Printed in large type below the letter from Kyela was "Thought of the Week"—a quotation from Mao Tse-tung on the nature of "contradiction": "Before it explodes, a bomb is a single entity in which opposites co-exist in given conditions. The explosion takes place only when a new condition is present . . . Contradictions and struggle are absolute and universal but the methods of resolving contradictions differ according to the differences in the nature of contradictions."

Tanzania abounds in contradictions, though, perhaps, not of the type Mao had in mind when he wrote his glutinous meditation on the subject. Tanzanian contradiction is to be found in the newspaper which can publish the thoughts of Mao and the astrological predictions of "Moon Beams" side by side; in the policy which allows the roads of Dar es Salaam to disintegrate and then, in a frantic attempt to halt the alarming acceleration of a process which threatens to make travel impossible, brings in private contractors to repair the damage; in the expensive hotels to which no tourists come; in the fight against exploitation which brings hunger to a place like Kyela; in the newly built sawmill which had to be closed down because there were no tractors to haul the logs; in the *ujamaa* ideal of love and brotherhood which the nation promotes by firing the homes and crops of obstinate peasants who refuse to give up their ways and move to the new villages. Contradiction—intention and the negation of intention in practice—becomes a way of life. The time comes when intention alone suffices; when it is confused with the deed.

As befits so cerebral a revolution, the academic analyses, foreign and indigenous, pour off the presses. "Book production is part and parcel of the struggle by workers and peasants to construct a socialist society and to break away from the grip of world capitalism . . . let us produce books!" Abstraction is linked to mindless abstraction. The formal, faceless universe of socialist algebra takes shape on the messily printed pages of the *Daily News*: symbols symbolizing everything in general and nothing in particular. There are no classes, in the sophisticated Marxist sense, in Tanzania—only peasants, Party officials and aid workers. Class struggle, since it does not exist, has to be invented. Marxism, like Christianity before it, has been reduced to caricature in Africa.

Words, words, words . . . But words can sometimes have unpleasant consequences, as the following letter, taken from the *Daily News* (which, let it be said, now and again takes the liberty of publishing a "negative" item or two from its readers), will attest. "I have just witnessed a most disturbing event," the correspondent writes. The disturbing event occurred while she was on a shopping expedition in downtown Dar es Salaam. When she arrived, the street was lined with the stalls of fruit and flower sellers. She went into a store. "I came out a few minutes later only to see most of the fruits and vegetables gone and caught a glimpse of the sellers disappearing down the alley across the street. A few seconds later, a van of police pulled up and about five uniformed men jumped out and with much laughter began throwing all the remaining food into their van." Having completed their work, the police moved up the street. "There a young boy was selling peanuts and magazines. Upon spotting him, the police surged out of the van and started chasing the young boy." Meanwhile, two other policemen "with smirking faces" began throwing "all the vendor's cones of peanuts into the van, tore up his magazines and smashed his small table to pieces. I want to know why this happened . . . is it because these people are supposedly economic exploiters?"

Alas, yes. The Tanzanian dream must not be sabotaged, not even by little boys (think of them as rivulets of exploitation) selling peanuts and magazines to earn a few shillings. Saboteurs rear their ugly heads in the most unlikely places. There was, for instance, the controversy over beer. It was alleged that the State-owned breweries were unhygienic—cockroaches had been found floating in a number of bottles. (Fortunately, I was never served a bottle containing a cockroach. In my experience, Tanzanian beer was merely flat and stale.) The Junior Minister for Industries sprang to the attack. The allegations made against the breweries were, he said, "a war being waged by capitalists against socialists . . . to discredit industries in the developing world. The imperialists are not happy . . . because we have already been able to make a special beer brand for export."

The peanut vendor was guilty of waging capitalist war against socialist society. If he had been caught by the police who chased him, he would, in all probability, have been driven out of town back to a regenerating peasant life. While I was in Dar es Salaam, the police carried out swoops on the city's unemployed and carted them off to the countryside.

That, presumably, is what the Chinese would have done; and Tanzania, as everyone knows, cites the "Chinese experience" as the ultimate justification for revolutionary fervor.

But what works in China all too patently does *not* work in Tanzania. Why? Because the "Chinese experience" has no relevance to anyone but the Chinese and people of similar cultural background. The Chinese renaissance is a *national* renaissance. Its true springs lie not in Maoist ideology—which amounts to little more than a mind-crippling technique (ah!— but how fervently wished on all the underdeveloped by liberal Western commentators) of mass mobilization—but in the Chinese sense of history and national consciousness. It is a reassertion of a natural importance by a people of high civilization; a reassertion of preordained destiny. Chinese communism is a means and not an end in itself. When China sends out laborers and technicians to build a railroad in Africa, it is not "exporting" socialism; it is not trying to teach anyone anything. The Great Uhuru Railway was designed to proclaim to the world China's grandeur and technological accomplishments. Of all the misconceptions and delusions underlying the Tanzanian "socialist" revolution, this, perhaps, is the greatest: that the "Chinese experience" can be utilized by the Tanzanians. Nothing could be further from the truth.

China's peasantry, inured over millennia to disciplined labor and highly centralized state control, acutely aware of its cultural identity and its superiority to neighboring nomadic peoples, is far removed from a tribal confederacy of low technical and intellectual attainment, only now reluctantly learning the advantages of village life. The "individual psyche" of the Chinese peasant cannot but be radically different in structure from the "individual psyche" of an African tribes-

man whose sense of nationality can hardly be said to exist.
Maoism can be successfully superimposed on the one because
it feeds on a receptive personality; when its techniques are
applied willy-nilly to the other, it declines not only into
caricature but into tragic absurdity.

III

"You say you want to visit *ujamaa* village . . ."

I nodded.

"I see . . . I see . . . That is most . . . most interesting.
Regrettably, it is not easy . . . no, it is not easy at all . . .
that is the problem . . . I hope you appreciate that . . . no,
it is not easy . . . not easy at all."

Ndugu Kaiza, the Culture Ministry official, blinked sleepily.
His head swayed; his eyelids drooped. He seemed about to
fall asleep. The office was icy: air conditioning was one of
the privileges accorded to officials of Ndugu Kaiza's status,
and he was making full use of it. Next door, beyond the
wooden partition, his less exalted minions were sweltering in
equatorial heat. Ndugu Kaiza's every movement appeared to
cause him immense pain. His hand trembled with the effort
when he lifted a paperweight or even when he took up a
pen; his speech was labored and slurred; he had a somewhat
swollen look—as if a layer of some noxious, debilitating fluid
had collected under the surface of his skin. I was gazing
upon, I felt, a very sick man; a man caught in the clutches
of a fatal, energy-consuming malady. After a few minutes in
his office, I realized that my diagnosis was wrong. Ndugu
Kaiza was not gripped by a fatal, energy-consuming malady.

He was dazed, numbed, by cold. I feared that, at any moment, his teeth might begin to chatter uncontrollably and that he would seize up altogether and tumble to the floor, lifeless as a mummy.

"You really must spend at least one week, preferably two or three, in an *ujamaa* village to truly appreciate the wonderful collective spirit of the People," an English aid worker had advised me. (But the same aid worker had refused to let me accompany him on one of his field trips.) Now, after days of wasted effort, days spent waiting in anterooms and being shunted from one government department to another, I had at last been admitted to the presence of the only man who, if he wished, could be of help to me. Or so, at any rate, I had been assured. If Ndugu Kaiza failed me, hope would be at an end. One cannot simply turn up at an *ujamaa* village and expect, in accordance with Nyerere's doctrine of universal familyhood, to be welcomed and made to feel at home. An interloper like me who wandered off the beaten track was much more likely to be arrested on sight as a spy and a saboteur come to wreck the Revolution.

"It is not easy . . . not easy at all . . ." Ndugu Kaiza blinked his half-closed eyes; his head swayed.

"You mean you will not help me."

Ndugu Kaiza took a minute or two to answer. "No . . . I did not say that . . . I did not say that I will not help you . . . but it is not easy . . . not easy at all . . ." He drifted off into hibernatory torpor.

"Your air conditioning is extremely effective, Ndugu Kaiza."

He managed a smile. "It is a good unit. The best. It was installed not many weeks ago."

One of his minions came in, handed him a sheet of paper and went out. Ndugu Kaiza threw a bleary glance at me and pushed it aside. "So much work . . . so much work . . ." He switched his attention to me again. "I will tell you frankly— *ujamaa* is not very interesting."

I gazed at him in some astonishment. "*Ujamaa* is the foundation of the Tanzanian Revolution, Ndugu Kaiza. How can you say such a thing?"

"It is people planting. That is all. Why do you want to see people planting? If you want to find out about *ujamaa*, read the works of Mwalimu."

"I have."

"Then why bother to give yourself all this trouble?" Ndugu Kaiza, after a protracted struggle, succeeded in placing his hands on top of the desk. He blinked exhaustedly at me. "People planting . . . that is all."

"But what about the spirit of Socialism and Self-Reliance?"

Ndugu Kaiza stared fixedly at his pudgy hands. It was as if he had run out of ideas as to what else he could do with them. "The spirit of Socialism and Self-Reliance is there. But you cannot see it. All you will see is people planting . . ."

"You refuse to give me a letter of introduction . . ."

Ndugu Kaiza sighed. "I will give you a letter if you so wish." He raised his hands an inch or so off the desk. The effort was too much. They fell back lifelessly, pads of inert flesh. "If . . . if you will kindly go next door and ask my secretary to come in . . ."

I summoned the secretary. Ndugu Kaiza murmured to her in Swahili. She went out again.

"My secretary will type you a letter . . . It might help you if you are in trouble . . . more than that, I do not know . . .

there have been many imperialist spies trying to stir up un-
rest . . . it is not easy . . ."

We waited in silence. I listened to the typewriter clacking
away in the next room. On the wall behind Ndugu Kaiza's
desk was a printed slogan: HE WHO DOES NO WORK IS A
PARASITE; THE LOITERER IS AN EXPLOITER. The office was
as clean and as uncluttered as the cell of a monk whose life
was given up to penitence and prayer. Maybe Ndugu Kaiza's
days were given up to penitence and prayer: he appeared to
have little work on hand. I pictured him immured, day after
day, in this solitary, refrigerated splendor, his hands, as they
were now, resting flat and immobile on his desk, his eyes
dulled with misty vacancy, his brain inexorably running down
as he succumbed to a homelier version of the Second Law of
Thermodynamics. Would the minions in the outer office be
able to distinguish between Ndugu Kaiza alive and Ndugu
Kaiza dead? Would the sad event remain unremarked for
days on end?

After about a quarter of an hour, the secretary came in
with the letter, which she placed on the desk directly in front
of Ndugu Kaiza. (It was in Swahili, so I had no idea what it
said.) He lowered his head toward the sheet of paper. She
handed him a pen. Ndugu Kaiza's fingers curled uncertainly
around the barrel of the instrument. Would she steady and
guide the faltering hand? It was not necessary. Ndugu Kaiza
shook himself and somehow managed to scrawl his signature.
I thanked him.

"It is nothing . . . nothing . . ."

Outside, the blast of equatorial air made my head spin.
Sweat soaked my shirt. I made my way across to the offices
of the State Travel Service.

"I would like to book a first-class seat on the Dodoma train."

"When do you wish to go?"

"As soon as possible. Tomorrow . . ."

"Tomorrow you cannot go."

"When can I go?"

"All first-class seats are taken for the next six weeks."

"What about second class?"

"Second class is also booked up."

"For the next six weeks?"

"For the next eight weeks."

"What about third class?"

"We do not deal in third-class tickets. I would not recommend third class for such a long journey."

"Can I fly there?"

"All air tickets are fully booked. You will not get a flight for many weeks."

"What about a bus?"

"The bus is also fully booked."

"What do you suggest I do?"

"Do you have a friend with a car?"

"No."

"In that case there is nothing you can do."

That was that. I stood in the shade of the arcade, my ears assaulted by the deafening din of the road-working machines, breathing in the fumes of boiling pitch. Ndugu Kaiza's letter was addressed to the Dodoma authorities. I was in no mood to return it to him and request an alteration. Anyway, what would be the point in doing that? There was no hope, as far as I could see, of my getting out of Dar es Salaam and going anywhere in the near future. I was trapped by the infrastructural deficiencies of the transport system. Even if I did manage to get out, there was no guarantee that Ndugu Kaiza's letter would be of any use to me. And maybe he was right: maybe there was no compelling reason to visit an *ujamaa* village. What would it tell me that I did not already know or could not already guess? The spirit of Socialism and Self-Reliance flourished all around me. I had been living with it for over two months. I had seen enough. I had had enough. I wanted no more meaningless words. I was sick to death of them. In addition, time and money were running out on me.

I strolled over to the terrace of the New Africa. The dwarf was there. He waved and smiled at me. I waved and smiled at him. A waiter dawdled toward me. I ordered a beer. It came after half an hour.

"That was quick."

The waiter giggled.

The beer was flat and stale. Undrinkable. Yes . . . I had had enough. I went to the reception desk and made my routine inquiry about the *hoteli* minibus. It was still not running.

When I arrived back at the Haven of Peace, I found that a new party of campers had installed themselves on the premises. They were on their way South, to "Jo'burg." It was agreed that I would travel with them as far as Lusaka. We would leave the day after the great solar eclipse.

*

For days the newspaper and radio had been full of the impending eclipse of the sun. Learned articles appeared explaining its cause and its significance; leading scientists from all over the world were reported to be massing in Tanzania; again and again the peasants were assured that there was no need to panic. They should carry themselves with dignity and should be proud that such a world-shattering event was about to take place over their country. Indeed, the overriding message of all this advance publicity was that Tanzania's involvement in the cosmic drama was not fortuitous. One writer even suggested that it should be interpreted as a triumph for socialism. The fact that the sun was about to go out over Tanzania was a portent of supreme revolutionary significance. It was a warning that the oppressed and exploited could no longer be denied.

The Haven of Peace benefited from the furor: about a quarter of its rooms were occupied on the eve of the eclipse. At dawn on the day, Willi presented me with a square of sooted glass which he had prepared the night before. Then we sat out together on the veranda and waited. Shortly before seven o'clock, as though a cloud had passed over the face of the sun, the bright morning light suddenly dimmed. The shadows of the coconut trees grew watery, acquiring the eerie transparency of X-ray photographs. A grainy twilight deepened over the beach, sucking color out of the ocean. Looked at with the naked eye, the unshadowed portion of the sun glowed with the incandescent, flaring brilliance of a pressure lamp. The shadow advanced swiftly across its surface, consuming the incandescence. I looked away from the frightening spectacle. The colorless ocean was tranquil; the air seemed peculiarly still. For a minute or two, the sun hung like a burned-out cinder, only a crescented edge flaring white.

Willi's dog howled. It was like a signal. The shadow began to shrink; the twilight weakened. Gradually, color and life returned to the world. The tropical morning reasserted itself.

I glanced at Willi. He shook his head, distending the corners of his fishlike mouth.

"I was not impressed," he said.

CHAPTER 11

Into the Void

I

WE LEAVE the Haven of Peace shortly after dawn. Willi, who has come as far as the entrance archway, waves a casual, abstracted farewell, then turns abruptly and walks toward the tanks where he keeps his exotic aquarium fish. Only his shells ever arouse anything akin to emotion in him. I feel a pang of sadness as the truck bumps and jolts down the sandy track: I had begun to feel at home in the Haven of Peace and even to develop a sort of affection for Willi. We go past the Ho Chi Minh Mixed Farm. A flock of goats scuttles across the track and disappears into the grove of banana trees; somewhere a cock crows.

There are seven of us in the windswept back of the truck, which is roofed over with tarpaulin. We sit on benches facing each other, not yet fully awake. I do a swift inventory of my companions for the next twelve hundred miles. Stevie, wrapped in a brown blanket, his legs drawn up under him, is huddled in a corner. Blue-black stubble peppers his cheeks, emphasizing his ivory pallor. His face is gaunt; his eyes, dark and circled, are sunken in their sockets. He is convalescing from an attack of malaria, an attack he has deliberately

299

courted by refusing to take any of the usual prophylactics. "Now," he had said to me the night before, "I can tell the folks back in California that I've had malaria in Africa. That'll really blow their minds. Real *macho* stuff."

Pru, from Australia, plays the part of devoted nurse to Stevie, soothing his forehead with a damp cloth and pouring him cups of tea from a thermos. She is short, plump and smooth-skinned. Her skirt, riding up above her knees, leaves exposed fleshy tracts of thigh. She has been traveling the world for over a year and is now slowly making her way back home.

Next to her is Cheryl Anne. She is from New Zealand. Cheryl Anne is hoping to find work of some unspecified kind in "Jo'burg." She talks of Jo'burg incessantly, as though it were a kind of earthly paradise. Her eyes are rabbit-pink, her voice fluting and reedy, like a schoolgirl's. However, Cheryl Anne is not a schoolgirl. She has a degree in physical education—and (of all things) "world affairs." When I ask her what she thinks about the killings in Soweto, she shrugs. "I'm not really all that concerned about what goes on in the black townships," she says. Her arms and legs are blistered with suppurating mosquito bites; the big toe of her right foot is heavily bandaged. There is something peculiarly pulpy and characterless about her. I feel that if I strike her, my fist will embed itself in boneless jelly.

Augustus, blond, curly-haired, American, is ensconced at the far end of my bench reading *Newsweek*. His T-shirt molds itself to his muscular diaphragm. It bears the legend NEXT TO SEX I LOVE MY HONDA BEST. His good looks are of the Greek-god variety. Cheryl Anne is visibly enamored of him. Augustus and Stevie, both from the same Californian university, are "buddies."

Sharon and Tracy, also American (from New York City), occupy the space between Augustus and me. Sharon is reading a biography of Nyerere with rapt attention. Tracy is peeling oranges, tossing away the skins into the bush. "It's okay," she says, smiling at me: "orange peel is biodegradable." They are an unfortunate-looking pair—both fat, both dowdily dressed, both remarkably hirsute. Sharon does make one concession to fashion: she wears a golden nose ring. Tracy makes no concessions at all. They seem to coexist with rather than to belong to the group. They radiate neglect and have slightly aggrieved expressions. From time to time they exchange whispers. I suspect, not without a certain amount of trepidation, that they regard me as a potential ally in their cold war with the others. They are hedged about with an aura of failure, of futility: I could see them being flung into jail on trumped-up charges, being swindled, being raped, even being murdered . . . nothing will ever go quite right for them.

I am, as it happens, not far off the mark. Tracy tells me of the Customs Officer they had run into on arrival at Nairobi Airport. He had accused them of drug smuggling, and for one whole night they had been detained and interrogated by the police. Their luggage had been taken to pieces, while they themselves had been stripped and humiliatingly searched.

"Sharon and I thought that we must be going mad. We don't even know what marijuana *looks* like. Two summers we had worked to save for this trip. *Two* summers. And then to have it begin like that. I wanted to take the next plane home, but Sharon wouldn't let me. What happened next was even more incredible. The following day the detectives turned up at our hotel and asked us to make an evening of it with them."

"Did you go?"

"Sharon felt they would be insulted if we didn't. She didn't want them to think that we were racially prejudiced and that kind of thing."

Sharon looks up from her book, her nose ring glinting. "They told us they were sorry about what had happened. They said it was a case of mistaken identity."

"You believed them?"

"Sure."

"They wanted us to sleep with them," Tracy says.

"Did you?"

"We didn't," Sharon says, "but not out of racial prejudice."

"Of course not . . ."

"We told them," Tracy says, "that we weren't good-time girls."

"They behaved like real gentlemen in the end." Sharon plays with her nose ring. "They told us to look them up if we passed through Nairobi again."

"Will you?"

"Sure."

The sun has long since burned away the early-morning cool; the wind-lashed tarpaulin crackles ceaselessly. We are in typical bush country. Stevie sleeps. Augustus reads. Pru and Cheryl Anne stare blankly at the road falling away steadily behind us. Now and then we pass a village where old men and women recline in the shade of the mud huts. Toward noon, the country becomes more parklike. Elephants, giraffes, zebras stand still in the honey-colored grass and watch us. Pru and Cheryl Anne begin to prepare lunch. We eat. Noon fades into early afternoon. The engine roars; the tarpaulin crackles; Stevie sleeps. Africans walking along the roadside wave hopefully at us. We do not stop. They display neither disappointment nor resentment. Eventually, though, the engine whines into a lower gear, we slow down, we stop. A hitchhiker, equipped with rucksack, climbs on board. He is German. His rimless spectacles give him an uncanny resemblance to photographs I have seen of the young Trotsky. His arrival brings temporary reanimation. He tells us that he has been staying at a mission station nearby; that he is going as far as Iringa, where a friend of his lives; that he is a student of classical Greek. I ask him if he has been having a good time in Tanzania.

"I did not come to have a good time. I came to see for myself what is happening, to learn. As a German, I have a special interest in what is happening in Tanzania. You must know that this was once a territory of ours. *Deutsch-Ostafrika*." He takes off his glasses and cleans them. Without them, his resemblance to the young Trotsky is less striking.

"What have you learnt?"

He puts his glasses back on. He considers me.

"It is unfashionable, but I think they have had too little colonialism."

"You mean that it should still be *Deutsch-Ostafrika*?"

He smiles—but does not reply. However, a little later he says, "They have so much to learn. Such a long way to go. Not even a hundred years might be enough for them. They need lots and lots of time. I am not sure that they will get it. There are too many things buried under the ground for them to be left alone. That is why I am afraid for them." He gazes darkly at me.

We are traveling through a narrow, steep-sided valley, following the course of a river with many exposed sandbanks. The brown slopes are rocky. On either side of us, jagged

ridges and summits are sharply defined against the brilliant
blue sky. Only the hitchhiker and I are awake.

"Why do they sleep all the time?" he asks. "What is the
point of traveling?"

At about four o'clock, Jeff, our New Zealand driver, halts
for a rest. The sleepers awaken. Baboons lope across the road;
they swing through the trees. Cheryl Anne throws sticks and
stones at them.

"Careful," Jeff warns. "They can bite."

The warm air trembles with Cheryl Anne's twittering
laughter.

Below us, the river, greenish-white, flows noiselessly. I
walk down toward it. The ground is carpeted with autumnal
drifts of leaves. Overhead, breezes rustle through the sparse
green leafage. Sunlight and shadow make dizzying, restless
patterns. The hitchhiker joins me, offering me a sip from his
bottle of beer. We stand on the crumbling bank, staring at
the coiling currents of the stream. A bird of iridescent plum-
age swoops low across the water and vanishes into the gloom
of the vegetation on the far side. The jungle silence is op-
pressive. Jeff's hoarse shouts summon us back to the truck.
He wants to get to Iringa before sundown. The baboons dart
across the road and into the safety of the trees as the engine
roars into life.

We lose sight of the river. I too, with the sun full on my
face, become drowsy. From time to time I return to consciousness with a start—but only to see the endless rolling upland and the glare of blue sky. The engine changes its tune.
I open my eyes. We are climbing, the truck agonizingly inch-
ing its way up a ledge sliced out of a forested hillside. The
road (built by the Americans), winding and looping, is an

impressive sight. A chaos of wild hills sweeps away toward the horizon. We skirt a gorge, its bed strewn with rocks sculpted into weird totemic shapes. The mangled skeletons of buses, trucks, cars can be glimpsed in its depths. I am beginning to doubt that the truck can make it to the top when, suddenly, the road levels out and we are on the undulating, sunlit plateau. Straggling settlements, merging into one, cling close to the roadside: a near-continuous belt of population extending mile after mile. TANU flags flutter from roofs. The *ujamaa* policy must be responsible for this unexpected and unnatural concentration of humanity.

Just before dusk we begin to ascend the bluff on which Iringa is built. As we rise, I gaze out on the expanding panorama of the land below—a jigsaw of yellow fields, columns of blue smoke, a meandering stream fringed by trees. At the crest of the bluff Iringa comes into view: a wreckage of corrugated-iron roofs enclosed by bare, boulder-strewn hills. The dusty jacarandas are not at their best. They look tawdry and spent. We come to rest in the compound of a dilapidated caravanserai that calls itself a "tourist class" hotel. Here we will spend the night. The hitchhiker bids us all farewell and sets off in search of his friend.

"I'm glad to see the back of that bloody Kraut," Augustus says. "Could never stand Krauts somehow."

Cheryl Anne giggles. Stevie grins cadaverously.

The owner of the hotel—a handsome, sweet-smelling Asian with oiled hair and fingers ringed with gold—seems overwhelmed with joy to see us. He knows Jeff well: Jeff has brought many truckloads of travelers to his door, and he hopes he will bring many more. He lives off the safari trade from and to the South.

"It is always such a pleasure to see you—and the friends you bring with you." His brown eyes dance over the girls. He bustles about, he claps his hands, he shouts orders to his staff.

"Be on your guard with Iqbal," Jeff says to the girls. "He's got some very strange ideas about white chicks, and he thinks he's irresistible. Iqbal's a wily Oriental gentleman."

Cheryl Anne simpers.

After dinner, Iqbal plies us with *konyagi.* "Tonight you are all my guests. Drink to your heart's desire. It's all on the house." His even white teeth flash eloquently at Pru.

We drink, as he has suggested, to our heart's desire. Augustus becomes maudlin. He tells me that he has come out to Africa to sort out his "emotional problems." Apparently there is a girl back home in California about whom he cannot make up his mind. He shows me her photograph.

"She's no Greta Garbo," he admits, staring critically at the photograph. "Still, she's got some really admirable qualities."

"It seems a little extravagant to come all the way to Africa to sort out your emotional problems," I say. "Why didn't you go to Mexico? That's so much closer to California." Out of the corner of my eye, I watch Iqbal discreetly—but nevertheless, relentlessly—chasing Pru across the sofa they are sharing.

"I've been to Mexico. Boy! Was I culture-shocked!"

"If you suffered from culture shock in Mexico, it must be even worse for you here."

"It's not too bad, because I don't care one way or the other about Africans." He stifles a yawn. "I come to see the animals. I've got this thing about elephants. I really *care* about elephants." He gazes at me earnestly; he lowered his voice. "What do you think it *feels* like to be an African? I wonder about that a lot."

"You ought to ask an African."

"Yeah . . . I'll tell you something, though. I am damned glad I was born a white Anglo-Saxon Protestant American."

Pru flees from the sofa, going across the room to Stevie. Iqbal, laughing away the setback, offers more *konyagi*.

In the morning, there is bad news. I come upon Jeff, stripped down to his underclothes, coated in dust and grease, sprawled under the truck. The fuel tank has sprung a leak. A mechanic will have to be found. We will, he announces, have to stay another day and night in Iringa. Another day and night in Iringa! I stare at the corrugated-iron roofs spreading down the slope of the main street, the faded jacarandas, the stony, scorpion-colored hills rising above the town.

I spend part of the day in exploration. The number of Asian shops that survive astonishes me. Impassive brown faces loom out from dark and claustrophobic interiors. I enter one of these *dukas* to buy a cake of soap. The Gujerati who serves me rubs his belly complacently. His pregnant, sallow-faced wife peeps out at me from behind the bead curtains that divide the cluttered shop from the family's living quarters. The commercial instinct hangs over them like a curse. The unswept streets are strewn with rubbish. Passing through the market I run into Tracy and Sharon. They have bought themselves straw hats. I walk on quickly. Half-naked children play in the dust with homemade toys constructed out of bits of wire and wood. A detachment of the People's militia swaggers through the heat, rifles aslant on their shoulders, singing TANU songs at the tops of their voices, shaking their fists at invisible enemies. That evening, Iqbal appears in tails, stiff-collared white shirt and black bow tie. Initialed cuff links glitter on his wrists. He smells more sweetly than ever. I cannot take my eyes off him. Has Iqbal gone mad? The truth is simpler, less dramatic. Iqbal is off to the annual dinner dance of the Lions Club of Iringa.

Late that evening, I hear Jeff's voice raised in argument with the African messenger who has brought what he claims to be the bill for repair of the fuel leak.

"You cheating sonofabitch. You've made this bill up yourself."

The man growls obdurately.

"You lying sonofabitch. I want a proper receipt. In the handwriting of the boss. The *baas*. Understand?"

"I have given you proper receipt."

"You thieving sonofabitch. Why are all you people such thieving sonsofbitches?"

I move out of earshot. I do not know how the dispute is finally settled. Somewhere in this town, Iqbal, his tails elegantly unfurled, is dining and dancing.

. . . The engine roars; the tarpaulin crackles; Stevie sleeps. On our left are ranges of rocky hills, their slopes covered with leafless thorn scrub. The road rises and dips, rises and dips. The sky is overcast, and it is piercingly cold. My sweater is insufficient protection. Luckily, there is a spare sleeping bag. I wrap myself up in it. Everyone seems stunned, gazing blankly at the empty land, not talking, not even looking at each other. Gradually, the morning warms up, the sky clears and the sun blazes down out of a cloudless sky. I discard sleeping bag and sweater. Clouds of smoke rise from the deep-blue recesses of the bone-dry hills. Sharon and Tracy prepare lunch. No one eats very much. I borrow Augustus's copy of *Newsweek*, but the world it describes seems quite unreal. I put it aside. Cheryl Anne dreams aloud about the paradisal delights that Jo'burg holds in store. The sun is low in the sky as we drive through the ragged outskirts of Mbeya.

The African manager of the guesthouse is stretched out snoring on a sofa in the lounge when we arrive. We pitch our tents in the backyard; a fire is lit. The lodge, formerly a private house, is falling to pieces: tattered curtains slant awry across uncleaned windows; the ceiling is rotting; cockroaches scurry across the floor. Some decaying volumes in a glass-fronted bookcase, doubtless the property of the former European owner, survive as a reminder of the past. There are editions of Jane Austen, Rudyard Kipling and George Eliot and assorted memoirs of missionaries and Victorian travelers in Africa. I am stooping in front of the bookcase, examining the collection, when a hand thumps down on my shoulder. Startled, I jump up. Facing me is an image of Asian dereliction —a shrunken, elderly man with bloodshot eyes, dressed in a blue "Kaunda" suit, smeared with food and drink stains. His tunic is unbuttoned, his fly is gaping open and his breath smells of *konyagi*.

"I saw you come with those *mzungus*," he says. He clutches my arm. "We are blood brothers. I must speak to you. Will you refuse to listen to your blood brother? Will you turn your back on him? Same color, same skin . . ."

I am reminded of the Asian whore I met in Mombasa who had suddenly reached up and touched my hair.

"Who are you?"

"I am *nothing*, sir. I am like the dust you walk on. My life has been ruined." He slumps down on the sofa where, earlier, the manager had been snoring.

"Why has your life been ruined?"

"Once I used to be a man of property, sir. I was rich. I was respected. Now I am nothing but dust."

"What happened to your property?"

"It was taken away from me, sir. They said I was an exploiter and a parasite. Now I exploit nobody and I am dust." A strangled giggle escapes him.

"Do you get drunk every day?"

"Every day without exception. Are you not pleased with me, sir?"

"Not very."

"Why is that, sir? Is it because I am drunk?"

I do not answer.

"What else is there for me to do, sir?" He spreads his arms wide.

"You could try and find some sort of job, some useful work."

"Do *you* have a job to give me, sir?" He leers at me, caressing his private parts. "I drink," he says after a while, "to stop the thoughts that go round and round and round in here." He slams the sides of his head with his fists.

"What kind of thoughts?"

"Bad dreams, nightmares . . . I have terrible dreams, sir. You cannot begin to imagine how terrible my dreams are. They are slowly driving me mad, sir."

His eyes, I suddenly realize, are the eyes of a tormented man; dark holes of upwelling anguish. I look away from them.

"I should have gone to Canada," he says. "If only I could have *pushed* myself to Canada." He propels himself forward on the sofa.

"What would you have done in Canada?"

"I have a cousin doing a little business over there. But the Canadians will not give me a visa. The Canadians will not even look at me. Shall I kill myself, sir?"

"No ... no ... I certainly wouldn't do that."

"Why not, sir?"

"Think of your family. Think of the grief you will cause them."

"I have no family. They have gone away and left me. The rats have deserted the sinking ship." Another strangled giggle. "My death will cause no one grief. I have no wife or children to weep for me. Can you give me, sir, one good reason why I should go on living? Just one good reason. That is all I ask." He holds up an index finger, staring cockeyed at it.

"Well ... you never know ... things might get better for you ... life might improve ... you never know ..." I look at him foolishly.

He explodes into loud, uncontrolled laughter, pounding the sofa. "That is good. That is very good. I like that very much. Things might get ..." He laughs so much that tears flood his eyes. After a minute or two, he recovers himself. "Are you *very* displeased with me, sir? Tell me frankly, blood brother."

I do not answer.

He pounds the sofa again—but this time he does so in anger. "If you have nothing more to say to me, then go back to your *mzungus*. Leave me alone. I do not like your face. Go! Go away from me!"

I start to walk away.

"Karim Lalji," he shouts after me, "that's me. That's my name. Write it down ... write it down. Remember it. Karim Lalji." He runs after me, he grabs my arm. "I live with Africans now. Wahehe. Have you heard of the Wahehe people? That is good. I would like you to know that they love me. When I go away from them, they cry like children. 'Don't go from us, Karim Lalji! What will we do without you, Karim Lalji?' That is what they say, because they love me. When I return, they dance and sing. 'Karim Lalji is back! Karim Lalji has come back to us!' I am a great man to them." He lets go of my arm and goes back to the sofa.

I could not help Karim Lalji. No one could. Africa had closed in over him.

In the morning, as the truck is backing out of the yard, Karim Lalji's face appears at a window. He shakes his fist at me. "Blood brother! Blood brother! Do not hide yourself from Karim Lalji, blood brother!"

. . . The engine roars; the tarpaulin crackles; Stevie sleeps. At midday we reach the border. "Welcome to Zambia. The Friendly Country." Jeff, armed with a bottle of Scotch and a bottle of vodka, departs to negotiate our entry.

That night we pitch our tents below an embankment of the Chinese railroad. After we have eaten, the men sit around the fire. Stevie asks Jeff, our acknowledged Africa expert, what Rhodesia is like.

"Fantastic," Jeff says. "Bloody fantastic. It's the *cleanest* country I've ever been in. Maybe Switzerland is just as clean. I can't say, because I've never been there. But Rhodesia . . ." Jeff gazes at the starless sky, words having failed him.

"Switzerland is pretty clean," Stevie says.

Jeff begins to describe the hygienic splendors of a public toilet he had once patronized in Bulawayo. So clean was it, he could see his face perfectly reflected in the brass fittings. "They employ two or three coons on a full-time basis to keep it that way. I tell you, man, I've never seen a toilet like that anywhere else, not even in bloody South Africa. It's so clean you feel it's a crime to use it."

Cheryl Anne creeps out of her tent and sits down next to Augustus.

Stevie stirs and pokes the fire with a stick. "You reckon the coons will ever take over there?"

"I figure they might," Jeff says. "But it will be the biggest bloody tragedy that's ever happened. What's more, the coons won't like it either." Jeff shakes his head. "Coons are strange," he observes philosophically. "The last time I was in Jo'burg I saw a coon bus leave the road and crash straight into a shop window. Bang! Flying glass everywhere. Blood everywhere. Coons rolling their eyes and screaming. Three coons dead. Five minutes afterwards, the other coons were behaving just as if nothing at all had happened. They were jumping up and down and laughing . . ."

"Perhaps they don't feel pain like we do," Augustus says. "That might be the reason coons make the best boxers and athletes."

"What always puzzles *me*," Cheryl Anne says, "is how coons can tell the difference between being clean and dirty. When they wash their hands, for instance. I mean, black always looks black to me, clean or dirty."

No one ventures an opinion: life, it has to be admitted, is full of insoluble riddles.

"What's South Africa like?" Augustus asks. "Is it as bad as some people make it out to be?"

"A weird and wonderful place," Jeff says. "I think I prefer Rhodesia though. The kaffirs might be as thick as glue. But some of those Afrikaaners take the cake. They have brains like breeze blocks."

"They say it's a beautiful country," Stevie says.

"The most beautiful country you'll see this side of heaven,"
Jeff says. "What a mind-bending place! I once saw a guy walk
up to another guy and stab him in the eye—just like that."

"What did he stab him with?" Stevie asks.

"One of those little ice picks," Jeff says.

"Wow!" Augustus shivers and hugs his knees.

"That must have been quite something," Stevie agrees. He
looks pale and haggard in the firelight. "Was one guy white
and the other black?"

"No," Jeff says. "Both were kaffirs. The fuzz didn't give a
damn. A weird and wonderful place is Jo'burg."

"Sounds a bit like America," Augustus says. "Do you
know that Washington, D.C., is almost eighty percent black?
Jeez! The capital of the United States of America! Can you
imagine that? Coons everywhere you look."

A train, its headlights sweeping the dark like searchlights,
rattles along the embankment. We have been four full days
on the road, and Lusaka is still some three hundred miles
away.

The Zambian landscape is one note endlessly repeated. At
the Tunduma frontier, the character of the land suddenly
changes. The rolling hills of south-central Tanzania fade
away and the table-flat upland of the Zambian plateau begins.
Open grassy country gives way to unending woodland, a
featureless wilderness of spindly trees twenty to thirty feet
in height. Mile after mile, hour after hour, it remains the same.
Occasionally, a low range of hills is glimpsed in the far distance, but their promise of release from the hypnotic monotony is deceptive. Their summits reveal nothing—nothing
but the woolly canopy of the wilderness stretching away on
all sides as far as the eye can see. Heat waves dance on the

mirrorlike asphalt. Now and then, in a clearing in the bush, there is the fleeting apparition of a village of mud huts. Women, squatting in the shade, look up expressionlessly from their labors; squads of naked children, shouting, arms flailing, come rushing over the beaten brown earth to wave at the truck. The wilderness closes in again. You doze, you wake up, you doze once more. Ahead, unwinding to a destination that seems increasingly unreal, the black ribbon of unswerving asphalt disappears over the crest of a rise in the middle distance, only to reappear on the summit of another, more remote acclivity. Nothing indicates that you have made any progress. You wait for some sort of resolution—the physical catharsis of a towering mountain, a rushing river, a blossoming of the unrelenting woodland into human cultivation. But there is no resolution, no release from the delirious sameness.

In some places the land is on fire, tongues of orange flame licking through the tinder-dry undergrowth. Banks of billowing smoke shroud the blackened skeletons of burned-out trees. Ash covers the ground like snow. Hordes of white butterflies whirl dizzily about the truck, immolating themselves on the radiator and windshield or being crushed under the wheels. At sunset, the land is a sullen, smoking desolation, the tepid air soured with the acrid odors of smoldering vegetation.

The Chinese railroad is a strange sight. With its neat stone and iron bridges, its tidily graveled embankments, it looks as dainty and as functionless as a child's toy. At intervals, there are "stations," brand-new pink-washed blockhouses with their names painted in large letters. These stations, opening onto untenanted bush, are no more than their names; seeds of unspecified hope scattered in the Zambian wastes. Zambia, with an area of nearly three hundred thousand square miles, contains fewer than five million people; the country is one of the most sparsely populated in the world. Lusaka is, in a sense, merely an upscaled version of those toy stations planted in the bush by the Chinese. There is, so far as it is possible to tell, no specially compelling reason for its being where it is. Suddenly, it looms up on the horizon, its skyscrapers silhouetted against the blank Central African sky.

II

From *The Times of Zambia*:

Five villagers—one man, two women and two boys—were convicted in Ndola High Court of the manslaughter of a man named as a "wizard who was responsible for the death of his niece."

Dennis Sankau, 21, Nyaluiji Sailunga, 57, Nancy Mangwela, 26, and the two boys, 16 and 15, admitted they killed Mr Kabanda Kazoka at Sandeleji's village, Solwezi District, on April 4.

Senior State advocate Mr Reuben Mwape, prosecuting, told Mr Justice Geoffrey Care that at the beginning of April, Mr Kazoka's niece, Wotela Mesala, died at Lwawo mission hospital in Mwinilunga.

After her burial, a decision was made to find by divination the person responsible for her death. Mr Kazoka, Sankau, Mrs Sailunga, Mrs Mangwela and the two boys travelled to a witch finder's village. Before they left, Mr Kazoka told a gathering that whoever was named as witch should be beaten. On April 11, at Sandeleji's village, relatives gathered to hear the outcome of the mission. Mr Kazoka announced he had been named as the wizard who had bewitched his niece.

Women began to wail. Sankau butted Mr Kazoka twice, blood oozed from his mouth and he fell to the ground. Sailunga Wotela's mother hit him twice with a bamboo stick on the head. The boys also beat him. But he got up and ran into the bush, hotly pursued by the quintet.

He fell down again, and was again beaten. Mrs Mangwela tore a piece of cloth from his shirt and gagged him, pulling hard at his penis. The boys beat and kicked him. He was stripped naked.

Mr Kazoka was taken to Lwawo mission hospital . . . he died on April 13 of head injuries.

"You are heading South?" Morgan, the half-caste Zambian businessman, seemed to regard it as the most natural thing in the world.

"I'm afraid not. Zambia is as far as I go."

"You should, you know. It's a really beautiful country."

"So I've been told. You go often?"

"Five or six times a year. Malachite is in terrific demand at the moment down there. You could make a three to four hundred percent profit."

For some reason, Morgan (he was one of those names scribbled on a bit of paper) had got it into his head that I was a businessman. I felt reluctant to disabuse him.

"Skins are another thing worth looking into," Morgan said. "They can't get enough. I've just done a neat little deal via Botswana. What's the skin market like in London these days?"

"I can't really say. Skins aren't my line of country."

"What's your line?"

"Mainly agricultural machinery and spare parts."

"Limited market for that here. How's business generally?"

"Not too bad. I've been hit a little by the recession . . ."

"Haven't we all!" Morgan laughed in comradely fashion. "I've been hit quite hard by this Rhodesian business. That used to be a lovely little market. What's going to happen if the blacks win out is anybody's guess. I'm keeping my fingers crossed. If it's Nkomo and his bunch, I don't think we have any need to worry."

Morgan went across to the padded bar at the far end of the room and brought out a bottle of South African "cane." Soul music poured forth from a complicated hi-fi set. The music followed wherever one went, relayed even into the garden by a network of speakers distributed through the shrubbery. We were in what Morgan called his "den." The red-painted walls were decorated with spears and tribal masks and stuffed animal heads. Copies of *Playboy* were scattered on a zebra-skin rug. Through the wide-open windows I could see a kidney-shaped swimming pool. The grass sprouting between the paving stones was being plucked by half a dozen near-naked boys, the offspring of Morgan's army of servants. A green sports car was parked on the curving graveled drive beyond the pool; a Mercedes-Benz was parked next to it. A blur of unreality—the result, possibly, of deep fatigue—overhung the scene. I half expected it all to suddenly disperse, like a mirage, and to hear once more the crackle of the tarpaulin and see all about me the featureless, fiery wilderness. In Zambia, I always felt myself to be teetering on the verge of hallucination.

"You really ought to go South," Morgan said. "I could give you some malachite . . ."

"I don't want any malachite, and I don't want to go South."
Morgan peered at me. "Don't tell me that you're hung up
about apartheid and all that shit!" He laughed. "What kind
of businessman are you?"

*

I had become alarmed—despite the bottle of Scotch and the
bottle of vodka—when Jeff had told the Immigration officials
at the Tunduma border post that we were in transit through
Zambia on our way to Rhodesia and South Africa. I was
amazed at his foolhardiness—surely not even a bottle of
Scotch and a bottle of vodka could compensate for sins
of such magnitude. After all, Zambia is among the foremost of
the "front-line" states supposedly locked in mortal combat
with the White Supremacist South. Kenneth Kaunda, one is
led to imagine, is made of sterner stuff than, say, Seretse
Khama of Botswana—another "front-line" president—who,
on falling ill, was immediately rushed off for treatment at a
"whites only" hospital in Johannesburg. Jeff, to make matters
worse, was a New Zealander: at that time New Zealand was
supposed to be in disfavor throughout Black Africa because
of its recent rugby tour of South Africa. My surprise was
great when, without comment, a smiling official stamped all
the passports presented to him.

I soon learned not to be surprised at this permissive attitude.
On the contrary: surprise was reserved for any display of its
opposite. Rhodesia and South Africa arouse more passion in
the West than they do among citizenry of the black "front-
line" states. The shelves of one Lusaka supermarket I went
into were laden with South African merchandise—meat,
toilet paper, detergents, canned goods of all kinds. In former
days, apparently, the source of supply used to be disguised.

Nowadays, no one bothers to take the trouble. As I strolled along the aisles of that Lusaka supermarket, I reflected rue-fully on the crises of conscience occasioned in the past by my consumption of South African oranges.

The Rhodesian question provokes irritation, not altruism. The irritation was rampant in the young clerk who com-plained to me about the steep rise that had occurred in the cost of living. He was, like all town-based Zambian males— and despite his declared poverty—flamboyantly attired: his shoes were platformed, his trousers flared, his red corduroy jacket exquisitely waisted, his tie exceedingly broad and color-ful. He did not attribute his poverty to the fall in the price of copper—which earns for Zambia the bulk of its foreign exchange—but laid the blame on the support the government was giving to the "liberation struggle." "The ministers are all right—they are rich men. The freedom fighters are all right—they get free food. But what about people like us who are not ministers and not freedom fighters?" He laughed. "How can a man on seventy-five kwacha a month [one kwacha is roughly equivalent to one dollar] support any-thing? My stomach comes first!"

I sympathized: Lusaka is one of the most expensive cities in the world. Zambia's finances are so bad that the salaries of civil servants are often in arrears; the university is unable to buy books to stock its libraries; cigarettes are in short supply because the manufacturers have no foreign exchange to pur-chase the necessary packaging materials. Zambia imports everything because it can make nothing. Most of the copper trinkets one sees for sale are processed abroad and reimported into the country. Foreign exchange is frittered away. In the copper-belt town of Kitwe, the shops are stocked with caviar and South African trout. (In Dar es Salaam I met a depressed official from the fisheries department. He had just come back from Lusaka, where he had been trying to persuade the Zambians to buy Tanzanian fish. "It is a hopeless task," he said. "They will not buy from us. They prefer to get their fish in boxes from U.K.") One of the most genuinely happy men I ever met was the expatriate representative of a major manufacturer of sewing machines. Machines costing between five and six hundred kwacha were being snapped up "like hot cakes." He could hardly contain his jubilation. Already half of a consignment of fifteen hundred machines had been spoken for before they had even arrived in the country. "They come to me," he said, "with their briefcases bulging with kwacha. I don't know where they get the stuff from."

When the copper markets sneeze, Zambia catches pneumonia. Many of the youthful unemployed and underemployed of Lusaka gaze with longing toward Rhodesia and South Africa. Several of those I spoke to said they would, if they could, go to those countries to seek work. Naturally, the Zambian government cannot allow that to happen. If it did, it would, of course, be behaving no differently from the government of another, avowedly Marxist, front-line state—Mozambique. The economy of Mozambique would probably collapse if it did not allow South African technicians to operate its ports and railroads and encourage substantial numbers of its citizens to work in the mines of the "enemy."

As is the case all over East and Central Africa, it is not the whites who arouse the greatest animosity, but the Asians. My stay coincided with a vigorous anti-Asian campaign in the Zambian press. Day after day, in *The Times of Zambia*,

lengthy articles and impassioned letters to the Editor were
devoted to this enthralling subject. Asian women were accused
of harboring feelings of superiority because they did not
sleep with or marry Zambian men. Photographs were published showing suitcases filled to the brim with paper money
seized from Asians attempting to smuggle currency out of the
country. Asian businessmen, predictably enough, were guilty
of monopolizing the distributive trades and exploiting innocent Zambians. Could Asians, one letter writer wanted to
know, ever become patriots? The climax came with the
front-page headline which read, ASIAN DOCTORS KILL THEIR
PATIENTS. It was an open secret, an Assemblywoman said,
that Indians could buy their medical degrees on the streets of
Bombay. They then came all the way to countries like Zambia
to practice their deadly art on unsuspecting black men. I do
not know precisely how many Asians there are in Zambia. My
guess would be that they do not exceed thirty thousand. In
other words, they form a tiny fraction of the population.
Tininess, however, provides no guarantee against demagogu-
ery. Hounding the Asian is a legitimate blood sport, a national
pastime. On another page of the same newspaper there was a
photograph of Indira Gandhi, who, a day or two previously,
had been in Lusaka preaching the gospel of Afro-Asian
solidarity. Afro-Asian solidarity aside, a man from Mars
would have had no trouble in deducing that Asians—not Rhodesians, not South Africans—were the overriding threat to
the security and well-being of the Zambian State and Zambian
people.

   Morgan was right: why get hung up about apartheid and
all that shit?

*

Expatriates staff the mines, the medical services, the factories, the technical colleges, the universities. Without them, the country would fall apart. Zambia makes nothing; Zambia creates nothing. The expatriate lecturer in English waved apologetically at the handful of books, perhaps half a dozen, on the library shelf.

"There," he said: "that's it. That's all the Zambian literature there is." For him, the paucity is a source of genuine embarassment. "I would dearly love to teach something Zambian to my students. But what can I do if there's nothing?"

(The dearth, though, does not necessarily breed humility: the same lecturer was attacked by one of his more militant students for teaching Shakespeare, on the ground that he was a "white writer.")

The man who writes a book in Zambia—usually a simple tale of tribal life—is immediately whisked away into the higher reaches of the administration. One of the writers represented on the shelf had become a member of the Central Committee of the Party; another had been put in charge of a large State-owned organization. But with the fruits of high office dangling so alluringly before them, Zambia is by no means short of would-be writers. I met one of them.

"The book I am writing," he said, "is highly symbolic. It's a story about maize, white ants and black ants."

I asked what the maize was supposed to symbolize.

"The maize symbolizes the people. I believe the white ants and black ants speak for themselves."

"What's the story line?"

"To begin with, I show how the white ants come and eat up the maize. Then I show how the black ants decide to form an army. They come along eventually and eat up the white ants."

"What happens after that?"

He seemed surprised by the question. "Nothing happens after that."

"That's the end of the story?"

"Of course."

"After eating up the white ants, aren't the black ants tempted to eat up the maize?"

"No, no, no." He laughed. "How can the black ants eat up the maize? They have come to *save* the maize." He became serious again. "After I finish that book, I intend to write another one."

"Will that be symbolic too?"

"Of course."

"What will the symbols be?"

"Mainly spiders."

"Spinning symbolic webs and so on?"

"Of course."

*

For some minutes I had been uncomfortably aware that one of the two well-dressed gentlemen sitting at the bar had had his eyes on me. Eventually, he beckoned me over. Without asking permission, he took from my hands the book I was reading: a biography of Kenneth Kaunda. He thumbed through the pages, pausing at the photographs—Kaunda as humble primary-school teacher; Kaunda as budding political agitator; Kaunda as unshaven political prisoner, haggard but undefeated; Kaunda as triumphant Liberator. When he was done, he passed on the book to his companion.

"You are from abroad?"

I said I was.

"It's good for people like you to read about our President. You will learn a lot from a study of his life. He's not only a great man but a great Humanist. We are Humanists too." He pointed in turn at his friend and himself. "Kenneth Kaunda is admired all over the world for Humanism. Is that not so?" He spoke challengingly.

I tried to imply that it was impossible for it to be otherwise, and to suggest that in my own country he was held in particularly high esteem. My reward was a bottle of beer. He swiveled himself around on his stool and looked me full in the face. "Would you believe me if I told you that tonight, this very night, I was with the President himself?"

I did my best to look flabbergasted.

"Do you see this hand?" He thrust his right hand under my nose. "Have a good look at it."

I did as I was bidden.

"Less than two hours ago this hand shook the President's hand."

"No!"

"Yes!" For some seconds, contemplation of the hand thus honored absorbed his entire attention. He seemed both saddened and exalted by the fact.

"How did you happen to be seeing the President this evening?"

He told me that he was a farmer growing wheat on an experimental basis. For the past two days he had been attending a conference organized by NAMBOARD—the National Agricultural Marketing Board. His companion was an official of that organization. (I studied his friend with greater interest: that very morning the newspaper had carried an article hinting that the conduct of certain NAMBOARD officials displayed, as Zambian jargon would express it, negative human inclinations.) The President had been kind enough to put in an appearance at the final session of the conference.

Had he actually talked to the President?

Indeed he had.

About what?

"It was like talking to my father." He seemed on the verge of weeping into his beer glass. "He wasn't pleased with me at all. It was just as if I was talking to my father."

"Why wasn't he pleased with you? He can't have anything against you for growing wheat on an experimental basis—can he?"

"It wasn't the wheat. He was very happy about that. It was my children."

"What about them?"

"He thought I had too many."

"How many children do you have?"

"You will be shocked if I tell you."

"Go on. Tell me."

"Fifteen."

"That does seem a little excessive."

"How can I help it?" His beer-reddened eyes were shining with anguish. "I am a polygamist."

"Then it's hardly surprising."

"I only have two wives. Some polygamists I know have three or four and *double* the number of children."

"Didn't you point that out to the President?"

"I did. But he said polygamy was not a truly Humanist way of doing things. I tell you . . . talking to him was like talking to my father all over again."

The barman began lowering the shutters.

The polygamist, panicking, ordered another two beers. "I wish I could be somewhere that served beer all night," he muttered. "I would drink right through to the morning."

His friend, hitherto silent and morose (what, I wondered, had the President been telling *him*?), roused himself. "But we *can* drink beer all night if we want to. You're forgetting we're staying in a hotel. We can order as much beer as we want."

The polygamist frowned petulantly. "You can see for yourself that the man is closing up the bar."

"True enough. But you are forgetting *room service*. When you stay in this class of hotel, you could ring through to room service all night. We can have as much beer as we like."

The polygamist's eyes widened with wonder.

*

Zambia practices neither *Harambee* (Pull Together) nor *ujamaa*. It has its own "philosophy," elaborated by the President. He calls it "Humanism."

"It means," a Lusaka police inspector told me, "that here in Zambia we put Man at the center of things. It is because of the policy of Humanism that the government has closed down all the orphanages in the country."

"What about the orphans?"

"Zambians have been ordered to adopt them. That is what we mean by Humanism."

I asked him to be a little more precise.

"Well," he said, after thinking hard for a while, "the color of your skin is not the same as the color of my skin. Do you agree?"

I agreed.

"That's it, you see! That's it!"

I looked at him perplexedly. My obtuseness obviously saddened him.

"You agreed that the color of my skin is different from the color of your skin. Would you also agree that we are friends?"

I said I would like to think that we were—even though we had met less than an hour before.

"That's it, you see! That's exactly it! Although my color is different from yours, it doesn't stop me being your friend because I look at you as a *human* being. And that is because I am a *Humanist*. Do you understand now?"

I said I understood a little better—but not fully. How, for instance, did Zambian Humanism differ from Tanzanian Socialism, which also claimed that it put Man at the center of things?

"Here in Zambia," he replied, "we are not so militant as they are in Tanzania. I would say we are about two-thirds socialistic. Here we have something like *ujamaa*, but we call it by a different name."

"What do you call it?"

"Village regrouping."

Zambia's Humanism is, if anything, even harder to pin down than Tanzania's rival state ideology. The Lusaka intelligentsia had been no more enlightening than my friend the police inspector. "Zambian Humanism," one of them had declared, as if reading from a prepared statement (he had, in fact, written a lengthy treatise on the subject), "aims at eradicating all evil tendencies in Man." Its ultimate goal was nothing less than "the attainment of Human Perfection," which the movement is to achieve by ridding society of "negative human inclinations such as selfishness, greed, hypocrisy, individualism, laziness, racism, tribalism, provincialism, nationalism, colonialism, neocolonialism, fascism, poverty, disease, ignorance and exploitation of man by man." He gazed at me breathlessly. When that comprehensive program of social renovation has been completed—and under the wise and inspired leadership of President Kaunda, it was already well under way in Zambia—the people would live by the dictates of Love and Goodness. Such things as prisons and police forces would become irrelevant.

I mentioned these hopes to the police inspector. "It looks," I said, "if all goes according to plan, as though you'll soon be out of a job."

He laughed. "I think it will be some time before *that* happens," he said, and happily poured himself—and me—yet another beer.

*

Beer is a major—some say *the* major—obsession of the Zambian people. Zambians, so the rumor runs, are second only to Australians in consumption of the beverage. Another rumored statistic, with which the first may not be unconnected, is that Zambia boasts the highest road-accident rate in the world—though the mesmerizing monotony of the wilderness must also be an important factor. However, it is the remarkable consumption of beer, not the mangled vehicles abandoned on the roadsides, that first impresses the visitor. Zambians, young and old, male and female, rich and poor, drink with a dedication I have rarely seen surpassed. When my friend the inspector ordered a round, it consisted of six bottles; and his round was followed by my "round." With certain individuals, dedication becomes naked worship. I have watched a woman, her eyes closed in ecstatic surrender, her head thrown back, sucking at the mouth of a bottle with all the world-oblivious

contentment of a baby at its mother's breast. I witnessed that
tableau not on the street but in the bar of the not-unrespecta-
ble hotel where I was staying. Some weeks earlier, a Zambian
delegation had been to West Germany on a goodwill tour. As
was only to be expected, the delegates paid particular attention to the German brewing industry. An account of the visit
was published in *The Times of Zambia*. "In Bavaria," the
writer, Stephan Mpofu, tells his readers, "traditional beer—
their version of our own *Kachasu*—is popular with drinkers
. . . it is made by monks from roots collected for them by
villagers from the bush . . ."

(The article as a whole is worthy of closer study. "Zambia," Mpofu goes on, "is one of the favourite places for European tourists . . . Take, for instance, our arts and crafts.
Everywhere we went people urged us to begin exporting
curios and other items like baskets . . . The Germans run some
of the most sophisticated, well-equipped youth centres and
kindergartens in an effort to conquer juvenile delinquency
. . . Mrs Joyce Mapoma—the wife of the Minister of Power,
Transport and Communications—who was in our group,
toured some of the centres in Hamburg and Munich and
quickly fell in love with the way they were run . . ." But
Hamburg nightlife gave Mr. Mpofu a bit of a shock. "A
black, beautiful girl said to be from 'Jamaica' had excelled
excellently in a traditional dance whose feats included swal-
lowing fire and spearing the void, African warrior-like . . .
But then she started 'rehearsing' the foreign culture she had
apparently gullibly adopted without modification to suit her
own background. She did this by demonstrating the stark
nakedness of a black beauty—and to most of us this meant
the girl was exhibiting to all those whites devouring her with
avid eyes just how every naked African woman looked like.

White girls had stripped before this one and we didn't seem to be worried very much because this was their culture anyway. But a black Eve in such a setting in this day and time! I observed a colleague or two next to me shoved their hands in their pockets and started fighting! I laughed . . .")

The State-run television service clamors for abstinence in between its canned British and American shows. How can Rhodesia be liberated if we Zambians spend so much of our time and money in taverns drinking beer? How can the Humanist society take shape? Beer, costing nearly ten shillings a bottle, is not cheap by Zambian or any other standards. Nevertheless, despite the complaints about the cost of living, despite the price, Zambians still seem able to find the money to buy it; just as they seem able to find the money with which to indulge their other great obsessions: clothes and sewing machines.

*

Late one evening I stopped for the night at a township in central Zambia. The manager of the single, shabby hotel greeted me with the sad news that there was no beer. My companion at dinner was a disgruntled captain of the Zambian Air Force, a unit of which was stationed in the area.

"They are fighting in the town over beer," he said. "The people are sad and miserable. This is not fair. The Minister should be told. It shouldn't be like this at all." He leveled his fork at me. "They said they were going to pay special attention to the rural areas. I know for a fact that in Lusaka there are over a hundred bars. In this town we have five. Five! I don't call that paying attention to the rural areas."

Our table—as was every other table in the room—was furnished with four bottles of Heinz Salad Dressing and three bottles of Heinz Ideal Sauce. These condiments were not manufactured under license in Zambia but imported from the United Kingdom. We were eating by candlelight—not because it was more romantic, but because there had been a power cut. I pictured the beerless townsfolk huddling disconsolately in their lightless hovels. The Captain sawed manfully at a tough slab of meat. Grotesque shadows played across the walls and ceilings.

"I wish I was in Lusaka," the Captain said.

"For the beer?"

"Not only for the beer. For the girls, too. I am a very gay bachelor. When I am in Lusaka I go to the Inter-Continental Hotel. There are many beautiful girls in the Inter-Continental. Already I have fathered four children by girls I have met there. I would like to father many more."

"The other day I met a man with fifteen children."

"Fifteen!" The Captain scrubbed his lips with a handkerchief. "That is nothing. I hope to have at least twice that number."

"The President won't be very pleased with you."

"He *will* be pleased. How can he not be pleased? I am bringing more humans into the world and that is a very Humanist thing to do. I am serving the nation. All my children will be Humanists."

"Could you support thirty children?"

The Captain shrugged. "A few may die. But people are born to die. I want to see lots of people in Zambia who look like me. It is in my blood to give girls a pregnancy. I *like* giving a pregnancy. And I pay."

"Pay?"

He explained that the families of the girls he seduced normally demanded compensation. A girl attending the university would fetch about nine hundred kwacha; a girl in the sixth form would fetch about seven hundred; a girl in the fifth form about five hundred; a form-two girl about ninety.

"I give a pregnancy mainly to form two. That is cheaper for me."

"Very sensible."

"If they make me a general one day, I will be able to pay more."

"Quite. Do you think you will be made a general one day?"

"It is my ambition."

"Then the university girls will have to watch out for you."

He laughed pleasantly.

A sad-faced youth who had been hovering nearby listening to our conversation started to clear the table.

"How many children would *you* like to have?" I asked. "The Captain here says he would like at least thirty."

"The Captain is a very fortunate man," he replied. "It is not possible for me to give a pregnancy."

"Why is that?"

"I . . ." He was overcome by confusion; he hung his head.

The Captain spoke to him in a local language. The boy murmured his replies.

The Captain looked grave. "He says . . . he says that he does not have a penis. There was an accident . . ."

I tendered my condolences.

"That's life," the boy said. He smiled resignedly. "That's *Zambian* life."

III

The dirt road, red, shadeless, seemed to stretch out forever before me. Far ahead, the pylons and wires of the Kapiri

Mposhi terminus of the Great Uhuru Railway shimmered in the late-afternoon sun. After twenty weeks of travel, all that remained was this final journey on the Chinese railroad. What had I learned? I could not say; nor, at that moment, did I care. A week before, in Kitwe, I had fallen ill and been confined to bed for a week; my South African "Coloured" doctor had diagnosed bronchitis and put me on a regimen of antibiotics. The Chinese, for reasons best known to themselves, had kept *their* railroad separate from the Zambian network. Neither bus nor taxi connected the two systems. Passengers had to haul themselves and their luggage a couple of miles to make the link. Now, at the end of it all, I could think only of the sun burning down on my aching head, the dragging weight of my suitcase, my thirst and the mile or so of red-dirt road that still separated me from shade and rest.

*

"I am learning to live like a civilized person again," she said.

The fat African in the pink shirt nodded enthusiastic assent. He had been nodding enthusiastic assent for the last fifteen minutes. Now and then he made some observation in an undertone. Then it was she who would nod enthusiastically and say, "Exactly! Exactly!"

I had first seen the English couple on the train that had brought me from Lusaka to Kapiri Mposhi. She looked a well-preserved forty. Long, straight, freshly washed hair fell to the small of her back. She wore carefully faded jeans, a striped cotton smock and rubber sandals. He, an inch or two shorter and spare of build, was graying and less ebullient; he was listening intently to her conversation with the African, but not taking part.

My attention had been drawn originally by the relentless smile she turned on for the benefit of every African who happened to catch her eye and by the exaggeratedly casual camaraderie with which she approached the staff in the dining car and bantered with the sullen and unforthcoming ticket inspector when he had appeared in our car. Out of nothing that smile would suddenly be produced, clamped down on her face like a mask, beaming out its message of charity, of hope, of goodwill, of universal brotherhood. If a smile could have changed the world, that smile would undoubtedly have done so.

The high-ceilinged hall was filling up with passengers. Pop music blared from loudspeakers. The functional Chinese architecture was dreary and depressing. Africans, surrounded by bulky, cloth-wrapped bundles, sprawled lethargically on the wooden benches and tiled floor. The railroad had been in operation for only a few months, but decay had already begun to set in. A row of brightly painted children's cots was arrayed on a platform that ran the length of one wall. A thoughtful touch—but not one of the cots was being used. Babies slept on sheets spread on the floor or crawled about in puddles of urine. I had been unable to slake my thirst: the drinking fountains were waterless; the handles of one or two were broken, reduced to jagged stumps of metal. The telephones were not working. The toilets were locked. The clock was wrong by hours. What must the Chinese think?

"Exactly!" the woman cried. "Exactly!"

I pricked up my ears.

The African murmured.

"Exactly! Exactly! We Europeans might have conquered the world, but we have lost our souls. We have lost our way."

The African nodded enthusiastically. His short, bullish neck, fleshy jowls and tiny eyes gave him an uncanny resemblance to Idi Amin.

"When two or three hundred years ago Europeans began to come out to Africa," the woman said, "they called it the lost continent, the dark continent . . ."

The African looked severe.

". . . now I believe that Europe itself is the lost continent, the dark continent . . ."

The African cheered up.

". . . there is so much we can learn from you, so much you can teach us. We have lost the art of living . . ."

"We in Africa have not lost the art of living," the African said.

"Exactly! Exactly!" She beamed at a filthy, urine-stained child who had strayed close to her feet. Her smile was like the noonday sun.

"The Europeans came here and said they 'discovered' Africa," the African said. "How do they mean 'discover'? We have always been here." He laughed away the silliness of it all.

"Exactly! Our arrogance has been simply breathtaking when you think about it."

Was the price of brotherhood self-calumny and self-abasement? "Perhaps this class-breaking business isn't so simple as it looked!" George Orwell wrote in *The Road to Wigan Pier*. "On the contrary, it is a wild ride into the darkness, and it may be that at the end of it the smile will be on the face of the tiger. With loving though slightly patronising smiles we set out to greet our proletarian brothers, and behold! our proletarian brothers . . . are not asking for our greetings, they are asking us to commit suicide."

Half an hour before departure we were permitted to board the train. The woman kissed the African on either cheek; her husband solemnly shook his hand. They gathered up their matching set of brand-new leather suitcases and hurried through the barrier. Groups of Chinese in gray overalls anxiously patrolled the platform. Music blared from the loudspeakers. There were five of us in my second-class compartment—an American, a Canadian and his Australian girl friend and a Tanzanian. On the dot of nine, whistles blew, doors slammed and the train, with a small jerk, began sliding out of the station. The Chinese on the platform glanced at their watches and looked relieved. Within seconds, we were swallowed up in the Zambian darkness. I went through to the dining car. The American soon joined me.

"Look," he said. He waved toward the shelves behind the bar.

They were lined with cans of South African meat.

We ordered beer and waited while the attendant searched in vain for an opener. The American seized the bottles and prised the caps off against the side of the table. Warm beer foamed everywhere.

"Folks call me Harry," he said. "What do they call you?"

Harry had been in Africa for a couple of years, working mainly in Kenya. He said he was a geologist. He had been trying to get into Rhodesia, but that country had refused to let him in because he did not have adequate funds. Now he was heading back to Nairobi. There he would find himself a job, save as much as he could and then tackle the Rhodesians again.

"That's keenness," I said.

"I want to experience White Supremacy at first hand. I figure there's a lot to be said for it. I've spoken to dozens and dozens of people. Not one has had a bad word to say about Rhodesia. It makes you think . . . When you've lived among kaffirs as long as I have, you begin to look at the world differently. I would say I'm a racist. Does that shock you?"

"Good Lord, no!"

"I've changed. I wasn't like this when I first came to Africa."

How many times had I heard that sentence?

Harry rambled on. His "racism," a recent discovery, seemed to excite him. Harassed-looking Chinese kept passing through the car. Harry put his feet up on the table. The attendant ordered him to remove them.

"Cheeky kaffir," Harry whispered. But he obeyed the command.

The train rattled rhythmically through the darkness. The Canadian arrived with his Australian girl friend. They sat down at our table. The Canadian—his name was Abraham—was also, as it happened, a geologist. Tessa, his girl friend, worked as a secretary. Abraham had been in Namibia ("South-West") prospecting for a uranium company. It was in South-West, among the Geiger counters, that he and Tessa had met and fallen in love.

"I'm going to live like a princess when we get to Europe," Tessa said. "I feel I deserve it." She gazed tenderly at Abraham.

"Did you have a good time down in South-West?" Harry asked.

"Fantastic," Tessa said.

"It's got this terrific desert scenery," Abraham said.

"And the people down there are really marvelous. Real pioneer stuff. The salt of the earth." Tessa tidied up her lipstick.

"What are the kaffirs like?" Harry asked.

"Primitive," Abraham said. "I learned to be patient. You have to be. You'd go insane otherwise."

"I bet," Harry said. "I'm something of a racist myself."

"I'm not a racist," Abraham said. "But let's face it. Those guys in South-West *are* primitive."

"When I first met Abe," Tessa said, "he used to lose his temper all the time with them. They couldn't understand the simplest things."

"Heard the one about the wheelbarrows?" Harry asked.

Thankfully, we all had.

"Ever used the *sjambok*?" Harry asked.

Abe shook his head.

"I fancy myself with a *sjambok*," Harry said. He twirled his wrist experimentally.

Grease-stained Chinese kept passing to and fro carrying wrenches and screwdrivers. The train rattled rhythmically. Abe yawned; it was time for bed.

The night was cold: I had not been able to get hold of any bedding—the key to the cupboard had been lost. I had a bad night. I awoke toward dawn, to the sound of violins. Was I hallucinating? I lay there listening, unable to believe my ears.

> *I'm dreaming of a White Christmas*
> *Just like the ones I used to know*
> *Where the tree tops glisten*
> *And children listen*
> *To hear sleigh-bells in the snow . . .*

The American voice flowed smoothly, serenely; the violins whined piteously. I raised my head. The compartment was lit by the subaqueous glow of the blue night-light. I saw the Tanzanian, dressed in striped pajamas, sitting on the edge of his bunk, staring dreamily at the reddening sky through the slats of the window blind. On his lap was a cassette recorder. What could have prompted so strange a choice of morning music? "Jingle Bells" followed "White Christmas." Outside, the derelict woodland was taking shape, featureless Zambian night turning into featureless Zambian day. I rose and went to wash.

The coffee and toast (eggs were unavailable) I ordered for breakfast were a long time coming.

"Can we share your table?"

My eyes traveled up the faded jeans and the striped cotton smock to the carefully preserved face, still with the sheen of sleep upon it. I, it appeared, did not qualify for the smile of charity, of goodwill, of universal brotherhood. Perhaps it was too early in the morning. While we waited to be served, *she* smoked Gauloises and read a paperback entitled *How Europe Underdeveloped Africa; he* stared at the unchanging woodland rolling past the window.

"They do take rather a long time," he said after a while.

"You're far too impatient." She looked up irritably from her book. She beamed across the car at the skulking attendant.

"I suppose this used to be proper forest at one time," he said after another interval of silence. "I suppose it's been cut down for charcoal and firewood and whatnot. It's tragic, all this deforestation."

Again she looked up irritably. "It's their land. It's none of our business what they do with it."

At last the attendant came. Food improved their tempers a little. They became more communicative. I learned that he was a doctor, that he had been given a three-year contract with the hospital in Kasama, that they had arrived in Africa only four days before.

"Can you tell us anything about Kasama?" she asked.

"Nothing at all, I'm afraid."

"I expect it will be all right." He spoke uncertainly, staring out at the woodland.

"Of course it will be all right. Why are you so tetchy about everything this morning?"

He did not answer.

"What are your first impressions of Africa?" I asked.

"I'm slowly coming to hate being white," she said.

"Are you? After only four days?"

She tapped the cover of the paperback she was reading. "It makes me boil inside when I read of the things the white man has done to Africa. I can even sympathize with Idi Amin."

"Can you?"

"When you think of the way white men have treated black men over the centuries, you can't blame them for wanting revenge. It's only natural. Amin's only reacting to all the dreadful things we whites have done to the blacks. I don't condemn him. Not for one minute."

"Come on, darling." *He* looked at her reprovingly. "You must admit Idi has done some unpleasant things."

"We have done much worse," she replied.

I felt a quarrel was brewing, and departed.

All morning the woodland rolled by; all morning, the batteries becoming progressively weaker, the Christmas music played. At one o'clock the batteries died altogether. An hour later, we entered the Kasama station. Chinese technicians drove up in Land-Rovers. The doctor and his companion appeared on the platform with their set of suitcases. They stared bemusedly about them; they moved away across the sunbaked platform. The wilderness bounded the horizon. Soon, they were lost from view among the crowd. What would they be like after three years? Would they emerge from the bush armed with the spurious expatriate wisdom to which the continent lent itself? Would they say, "We have changed; we weren't like this when we first came out to Africa"?

Orwell argues against "deliberate, conscious efforts at class-breaking." Not only are such efforts futile, they are often highly dangerous. "You have forced the pace and set up an uneasy, unnatural equality between class and class; the resultant friction brings to the surface all kinds of feelings that might otherwise have remained buried, perhaps for ever . . . the opinions of the sentimentalist change into their opposites at the first touch of reality."

*

The Immigration Officer (Tanzanian) poked a grinning face through the doorway of the compartment. He came in laden with forms, his stamp hanging loosely between his fingers. His navy-blue uniform was open at the neck, and he was sockless in unlaced running shoes. His casualness emphasized his menace. Border officialdom had begun.

"Passports." He held out a hand. His face was smooth and black and finely molded; his slitted, slanting eyes darted ominously.

He whistled as he flicked through the pages. The inspection was a thorough one, leaving nothing to chance: he looked from our photographs to our faces, scrutinized and compared signatures, read everything there was to be read. Throughout, he whistled and tapped his running shoes on the floor. One by one, the passports were stamped and returned. But he withheld Abraham's.

"This is a new passport. Can I see your old one?"

"I left it with the Canadian High Commission in Lusaka." The whistle changed to a hum.

"How long have you been traveling in Africa?"

"Six months."

"Which countries have you visited?"

"Zambia, Botswana, Lesotho . . ."

"Were you traveling on business or pleasure?"

"Pleasure."

The hum changed back to a whistle. "Did you visit South Africa?"

"No," Abraham said. "Only Zambia, Botswana, Lesotho . . ."

For the third time, he went through the passport page by page.

"Your old passport—are you perfectly sure you don't have it with you?"

"I told you. I left it with the Canadian High Commission in Lusaka."

The slitted eyes dwelt on him. "Maybe in your old passport there are some stamps you would not like me to see?"

Abraham said nothing. He was perched on the edge of the berth, his fingers intertwined. A film of sweat was beginning to form on his forehead.

"Now, if I searched your luggage and found your old passport there . . . if I found it, I would have to do unpleasant things to you. Very unpleasant things. Things even I wouldn't like to do." His running shoes tapped on the floor. Raising his head, he glanced up at the luggage on the racks.

Abraham was sweating badly now. His tormentor whistled.

"I do have my old passport. I lied to you. I am sorry."

"Show me, please." The officer held out his hand. Abraham gave him the old passport.

"You have been in South Africa . . ."

"Yes. I lied to you about that. I am sorry."

"*And* South-West Africa . . . Namibia . . ."

"Yes. I lied about that too. I am sorry."

"You have, I see, a permit for South-West Africa. Were you working in Namibia?"

"Yes. I was working. I lied to you about that too. I am sorry." Abraham had turned yellow with fear. "I am sorry. I lied . . . I lied . . . I should not have lied . . . I am sorry . . . very sorry . . ." He cringed. I feared he would collapse in supplication at the officer's feet.

"I always know when people are telling lies. I am no fool. I know." The officer was smiling now. "I have been doing this job for a long time. I know all the tricks people get up to . . ." He scribbled on both the passports. As he scribbled, he whistled.

"What are you going to do?" Abraham asked.

"I am going to send you back to Lusaka under police escort."

"No!" Abraham buried his head in his hands. "Please . . . please . . . I am sorry I lied to you. Very, very sorry . . ." He was crying.

The officer was not moved. "My job is to execute the immigration laws of Tanzania. Those laws forbid you entry to Tanzania."

"Oh, my God! Oh, my God!" Abraham sobbed. White was committing suicide before black.

Tessa started to argue. "Hundreds of people pass through Tanzania on their way up from South. Hundreds and hundreds. They do it all the time."

The officer stiffened. "You and your friend will return to Lusaka under police escort. That is final. Do not try to run away. That would be very foolish." He rose, bowed and went out.

Our Tanzanian companion giggled.

Now there were officials everywhere. The train was overrun with men in uniform wearing unlaced running shoes. My baggage was searched once, twice, three times; half a dozen times my passport was demanded; my books were examined; my traveler's checks were scrutinized; my loose change was counted and taken away; a bottle of *konyagi* was seized; I answered the same questions over and over again; I filled in and signed forms of all kinds. There seemed no end to the border nightmare. At Tunduma, Abraham and Tessa were taken off the train. I saw their persecutor, standing on the platform, chatting amiably with other uniformed friends, his stamp dangling from his fingers. He looked happy and fulfilled—he had every right to be. Rain poured out of a gray sky.

Out of this nightmarish chaos surfaced the Zambian official with gold braid on his shoulders.

"Passport . . ."

I handed it over automatically.

"Trinidad . . . but you are an Asian . . ."

I nodded.

"Are there many Asians in Trinidad?"

"Many."

He leafed through my passport; he put it in his pocket. "You will have to return to Lusaka."

My brain refused to function.

"But why? Why? What have I done?"

"You have overstayed your visa by two days. You'll leave the train at Mbeya. The police will be there."

On entry, I had stated that I would be in Zambia "approximately twelve to fourteen days." I had, I now discovered, been allowed the lower figure. Technically, the fault was mine.

"Why did you overstay your visa?"

"I fell ill."

"Have you a doctor's certificate?"

I did not. "But I do have the pills he gave me. Would you like to see those?" I brought out the box and showed him. It was one of those semicomic moments that frequently accompany despair.

"Pills are not good enough. You could get those anywhere. I want *documentation*."

There was nothing I could do. To traverse again that lunatic wilderness . . . I lay back in my berth and covered my face. I could not bear to look at the man.

"I want to know what you were up to in Zambia."

"I wasn't up to anything in Zambia."

"But you have no documentation to *prove* it. I believe in documentation."

Harry tendered his passport.

"You too have overstayed your visa," the man said. "Why?"

Harry spun an involved tale about missed connections.

The man stamped the passport.

"You believe him," I said. "Why don't you believe me?"

"Your case is different."

"Why?"

"The police will take you off the train at Mbeya," he said, and he left the compartment.

The Tanzanian leaned toward me. "I want to know something," he said. "How is that *you people* get everywhere?"

"I'll buy you a drink," Harry said.

In the corridor, we ran into a weeping Asian. "Why do they do such things?" he asked. "They have taken from me perfume I bought for my wife and some underclothes I bought for my children. Why do they do such things?"

I could offer no sympathy.

Harry said to me, "Give me one of your traveler's checks."

"What for?"

"Don't ask too many questions."

He vanished down the corridor.

I stared at the cans of South African meat stacked on the shelves behind the bar. Black and white deserved each other. Neither was worth the shedding of a single tear: both were rotten to the core. Each had been destroyed by contact with the other—though each had been destroyed in his own way. Black Africa, with its gimcrack tyrannies, its Field Marshals and Emperors, its false philosophies, its fabricated statehoods, returns to Europe its own features, but grotesquely caricatured—as they might be seen in one of those distorting funhouse mirrors. As for Western civilization, that had aborted almost from the beginning. Civilized man, it seems, can no more cope with prolonged exposure to the primitive than the primitive can cope with prolonged exposure to him. Everywhere, in the New World, in the South Seas, in Australia, his lusts, released from constraint, gained the upper hand. He too became a caricature of all that he claimed to represent. In European literature, the figure of Conrad's Kurtz stands as the supreme memorial to the civilized man's vulnerability to the call of the wild. Kurtz, who had written so eloquently and with such easy conviction of "Progress" ("By the simple exercise of our will we can exert a power for good practically unbounded") and of the White Man as Benevolent Deity, had given way, by the end, to the mad visions born of the craving for total power. ". . . the wilderness had found him out early, and had taken on him a terrible vengeance . . ." His degenerate suburban heirs, ruling to the South, still speak of Civilization and its Values. But their bullets defend only a system of servitude and plunder. Hopeless, doomed continent! Only lies flourished here. Africa was swaddled in lies—the lies of an aborted European civilization; the lies of liberation. Nothing but lies.

I returned to the compartment. Harry and the gold-braided Zambian official were talking. The Zambian held my passport open in his hand. His stamp was poised above it. He laughed when he saw me. For a few seconds, the stamp remained poised inches above the page. Then it descended.

*

At midday, the terrace of the New Stanley was packed. Nairobi seemed to be even more overrun by tourists than it had been when I had left it. Nowhere among the hats banded with fake leopard skin and the safari jackets could I find a space to sit. I stood for a while reading the messages on the notice board. "Europin required to adapt African child to give good home and education. Please apply . . ."

An American voice spoke close to my ear.

"Hey Stan! A friend! Look, I found a friend. I told you I got lots and lots of friends . . ."

The voice was familiar. I turned. I saw lank, shoulder-length hair, pale blue-gray eyes, wandering and unfocused. Behind him was a tall, sunburned man, his hair frizzed out into a dark, woolly halo.

I fled.

THE STORY OF AN AFRICAN FARM

Olive Schreiner

Since its publication in 1883, this novel has been acclaimed as one of the most astonishing and least expected fiction masterpieces of its time. It is a passionate story of two orphaned sisters growing up on a lonely farm in a Bible-dominated area of South Africa. Em is fat, sweet, and contented, a born housewife; Lyndall is clever, restless, beautiful . . . and doomed. Their childhood is disrupted by a pretentious Irishman, who claims blood ties with royalty and so gains uncanny influence over the girls' stepmother. As the story of Em and Lyndall's two careers—both, in their ways, tragic yet fulfilled—unfolds, we learn not only of colonial history but also of the whole human condition. Olive Schreiner, who wrote under the pseudonym of Ralph Iron, was an avid feminist and political activist.